The Basics of
Public Budgeting and
Financial Management

The Basics of Public Budgeting and Financial Management

A Handbook for Academics and Practitioners

Fourth Edition

Charles E. Menifield

HAMILTON BOOKS
Lanham • Boulder • New York • London

Published by Hamilton Books
An imprint of The Rowman & Littlefield Publishing Group, Inc.
4501 Forbes Boulevard, Suite 200, Lanham, Maryland 20706
www.rowman.com

6 Tinworth Street, London SE11 5AL, United Kingdom

British Library Cataloguing in Publication Information Available

Library of Congress Control Number: 2020943957

ISBN 978-0-7618-7211-5 (pbk. : alk. paper)
ISBN 978-0-7618-7212-2 (electronic)

Contents

List of Illustrations

List of Tables

List of Exhibits

Preface

The purpose of this textbook/workbook is to connect budgetary theory with practice and provide public budget and finance students with basic budgeting and financial management tools. From the perspective of a bureaucrat, students examine various concepts and then work through in-class and out-of-class exercises and problems to reinforce those concepts and ideas.

Chapter 1 begins with an overview of the basic budgeting concepts, types of budgets, and the various types of accounting techniques. Chapter 2 follows with a discussion of the budget cycle, budget calendars, and actors involved in the process. Chapters 3 and 4 examine personal services, operating, and capital budgets. Chapter 5 takes a close look at the various ways to fund public budgets. Chapter 6 examines budgeting techniques and analytical models, and shows students how these methods are useful in answering important policy questions. Chapter 7 discusses financial management issues that are important in the twenty-first century. This includes a discussion of cash management, risk management, procurement, debt management, incentivizing economic development, and cutback management strategies. Chapter 8 examines data sources, data quality and appropriateness; and the different ways to communicate budget data effectively using charts, graphs, and slides.

Each chapter provides the student with a list of important terms, phrases, and exercises that require the students to apply what they have learned in the chapter. These exercises assume that the students are proficient in a word processing program, Microsoft Excel and PowerPoint.

The fourth edition of the book provides in-class exercises for each chapter. These interactive exercises allow the students not only to compare their responses to their peers in small groups, but also to present those responses to the entire class with the goal of improving their presentation skills.

Charles E. Menifield Rutgers
University-Newark Newark NJ
January 2020

Acknowledgments

I am very thankful to the budget and finance students that I taught at the University of Memphis, Mississippi State University, Murray State University, Howard University, and the University of Missouri from 1996 to 2017. I am particularly thankful to Brenda Frantz, Vashun Coles, Yohance Duff, Yiesha Thompson, Tomeika Blackwell, Frank Robertson, Shayla Guy, Eric Raymond, Gerard Wellman, Kwame Antwi-Bosiako, and Xianting Li for their assistance in the first edition of the book. In addition, I would like to thank Rebecca Davis, a MPA student at the University of Memphis for all of her technical assistance and ideas on the second edition of the book. A very special thanks to Kendal Lowrey for all of her expert editing work on the third edition of the book and Kareem Willis for editing the book, Excel worksheets and PowerPoint slides in this fourth edition.

In addition, I would like to thank all of my colleagues, both past and present, at Murray State University, Mississippi State University, Howard University, University of Memphis, University of Missouri, and Rutgers University for their support. I would also like to thank the staff at Hamilton Books for supporting the fourth edition of the book. Especially the editorial work of Sam Brawand. There are no words that I can use to express my gratitude for your work and professionalism throughout this process.

Last, but certainly not least is my family. There is nothing more important than a good family and I am happy that I have one. Thanks to my wife Angela, my daughter Amber, and my grandchildren, DeAndre, Jamison, and Aiden; and my god children Christopher, Ethan, and Rosalind.

General Book and Class Guidelines, Suggestions, and Pointers

(1) There are several problems at the end of each chapter that require you to use a word processing program in addition to Microsoft Excel. Copies of partially completed Excel tables are located in the appendix of each chapter and electronic versions are available from the author (Charles. menifield@rutgers.edu). In addition, your instructor should have a copy of the ancillary materials.

(2) Always use Excel formulas to complete mathematical functions in the spreadsheets. Do *not* use a calculator and plug the numbers into the worksheets under any circumstances.

(3) Always round dollar amounts to the nearest cent unless you are told otherwise. For example, $34.5690 should be rounded up to $34.57 and $43.212 should be rounded down to $43.21. When using Excel, format dollar amounts using the Excel functions. Dollar amounts should look like a dollar amount rather than just a number. As a general rule, always follow the table formats used in the text.

(4) If meeting in person, always bring two hard copies of your work along with a flash drive to class. Be prepared to share you work on a computer with your class unless you are instructed to do otherwise.

(5) When you make changes in an Excel worksheet, make sure that you visually inspect the math to ensure that Excel is recalculating any changes that you make.

(6) Please note that Excel will round numbers differently when different formulas are used. That is, two different students can insert two correct formulas and get slightly different results. Normally, these differences are very minor.

(7) Each of the homework problems should be pasted into word processing program. It is not necessary to retype a long question on your homework assignment. However, it would be useful if you can capture the essence of a long question with a short phrase when completing an assignment in Excel. Then, paste the Excel worksheets (without the grid lines), graphs, charts, etc. directly into the word processing program. Your instructor may request a copy of the Excel file as well in order to verify that a formula was used to calculate the data.

Chapter 1

The Context of Public Sector Budgets

OVERVIEW

Taxing and spending is at the cornerstone of government. Conceptually, this appears to be an easy to understand phenomenon. However, it is not that simplistic. Budgeting is a two-fold process at the very least. First, someone has to decide how much money the government needs to operate/function at an optimal level. Second, someone has to determine the level of funding or allocation for each program/department. Since budgeting involves the allocation of scarce resources, it can be a difficult process. Although elected officials formally decide how to allocate funds, collecting revenue is an administrative function. Both procedures can be very complicated, sophisticated, and crucial to the very existence of governments.

The first chapter provides the reader with a general overview of budgets and the processes that go along with them. This includes, but is not limited to: the purpose of a budget, the different types of budgets, sources of revenue and expenditures, government accounting techniques, and audits.

WHAT IS A BUDGET AND PUBLIC BUDGETING?

A *budget* is a fiscal policy document that outlines the revenues and expenditures an organization needs to carry out specific functions during the course of a set period of time. With respect to the government, this period of time is called a *fiscal year* (FY), a twelve-month period where funds are collected and spent. For example, FY 2021 for most states begins on July 1, 2020 and ends on June 30, 2021. At the end of this period, the budget must be (legally) balanced and available for public scrutiny. The legal requirement for a balanced budget is the primary definitional difference between a public and private budget (Mou 2019). States and local governments should not carry *deficits* over to the next fiscal year. However, in many instances, particularly at the fund level, deficits are carried over on the budget basis. *Public budget-*

ing is the acquisition and use of resources by public organizations for the purpose of providing a public service or good (see Swain and Reed 2010).

Three roles emanate from budgets: allocation, distribution and economic development. First, governments have to decide what services will result from the allocation of funds. Second, they determine who will benefit from the distribution of these funds and who will pay for the services. Lastly, they determine what levels of income and job growth are required to maintain stability in the government (Musgrave 1959; Rubin 2020).

FUNCTIONS OF A BUDGET

The single most important function of a budget is *accountability*. It is one of many tools that can be used to determine if an organization has accomplished its objectives as laid out by legislative and executive institutions. Legislators and city councilmen alike use these documents when reviewing the activities of public agencies. A budget can also be used to *control* an agency. Council-members appropriate funds to an agency based on their strategic priorities. However, if they are dissatisfied with the agency, they have the legal right to withhold or *embargo* funds. A third function of a budget is to *plan*. By organizing costs around some function or activity, agencies have some estimate of what their tasks will cost and how to go about carrying out those tasks. It also forces the agency to meet deadlines and behave in an efficient and effective manner. In harmony with planning are good management skills. Agencies can organize and best utilize personnel by indicating performance standards and objectives. At the end of the fiscal year, an agency can review the year's activities in order to determine if goals and objectives were met. If resources were not spent in the best manner, changes can be made to remedy the problems (Bland and Rubin 1997; Howard 2002; Mikesell 2018; Musell 2009; Rubin 2020; Schick 1966; Solano 2004; Swain and Reed 2010). In the U.S. system of government, no expenditure can be made unless the governing authority-legislature, city council, Congress authorizes it. Rare exceptions include Executive orders, but even these do not completely negate the role of the legislative body.

BUDGET FORMATS

Generally speaking, budgets come in three formats: line item, program, and performance. However, there are also budgeting techniques that can be applied. One seldom used example is *zero-based budgeting* (Andrews 2011).[1] In this technique, each unit submitting a budget has to justify all of their budget requests from beginning to end without assuming a guaranteed allocation by defacto (see also chapter 7). An agency can also use an *incremental* approach to budgeting where they simply add or subtract from the previous year's spending. Although a state or local government may require an agency to submit a certain type of budget, they do have some discretion as to the type of budget that they prefer (Axelrod 1995; Gianakis and McCue 1999; Lynch, Sun, and Smith 2017; and Thurmaier and Willoughby 2001).

Among the typical budget formats, there is *a line item* or a *traditional budget.* This type of budget allocates funds to specific commodities or objects of cost. Emphasis is placed on personnel, supplies, equipment, utilities, contractual services, and capital expenditures. Each of these major categories can be broken down into individual items. For example, within personnel cost, there are: salaries, fringe benefits (pensions, social security, health care, etc.), retirement, and so on. Capital outlays are for higher costs items that have value for a number of years. This would include items such as: buildings, busses, highways, bridges, and equipment (see also chapter 4). Capital outlay equipment also falls into the high cost item category and therefore is not equivalent to equipment used as a major category. Equipment as a major category is for low cost items such as a single computer, a typewriter or a desk (see also chapter 3).

Line item budgets are probably the easiest of the three types to prepare because they are quick and simple. The major shortcoming of a line item budget is its inability to describe the activities that will be performed by the agency. This type of budget is used for control and accountability. Legislators determine salaries and benefits and can clearly delineate the differences between the various categories. Salaries and benefits constitute the greatest portion of a line item budget. Line item budgets are useful in that that they provide the exact cost of specific items. This is useful if a budget needs to be cut. Exhibit 1.1 provides a partial example of a line item budget for the Sanitation Department in Jefferson City.

Column one has each of the major categories of expenditures. Even though there is no category for equipment, it is possible to have this category as well. Whether or not a category is used depends on how the budget staff wants to categorize those items. Again, equipment that does not reach high levels of cost that reoccur over several fiscal years is not included in the capital category. The second column in exhibit 1.1 represents *actual spending* (act) for fiscal year 2020, while the third column has *estimated spending* (est) for the up-coming fiscal year (2021). In estimating cost, expenditures are rounded to the nearest dollar. However, rounding to the nearest dollar cannot be used when calculating actual costs. Every last penny must be accounted for when

Exhibit 1.1. Line Item Budget Sanitation Department, Jefferson City FY 2020 & FY 2021 Expenditures		
Personnel	*FY 2020 (act)*	*FY 2021 (est)*
Salaries	$165,459.78	$179,000
Fringe Benefits	22,410.56	25,000
Retirement	9,521.13	12,000
Insurance	6,510.87	7,000
Training	2,750.09	3,000
Subtotal	*$206,652.43*	*$226,000*
Supplies		
Disposable Trash Cans	$25,230.25	$29,000
Uniforms	6,298.69	7,530
Mechanical Brooms	10,498.91	12,300
Subtotal	*$42,027.85*	*$48,830*
Capital Outlay		
Equipment	$23,789.90	$28,987
Desks	2,987.32	0
Trucks- F 350	49,874.23	84,890
Subtotal	*$76,651.45*	*$113,877*
Total	$325,331.73	$388,707

Source: Created by the Author.

balancing a public budget. Given this detail, line item budgets should always be placed in a spreadsheet program to ensure fewer mathematical errors. This requirement does not necessarily hold for performance and program budgets due to the vast amount of dialogue that goes into the budget. In these cases, great care should be taken to ensure that there are no mathematical errors.

John L. Mikesell (2018) indicates that the policies of governments dictate using traditional budgets that do not develop long term profiles. This in effect makes it easier to control the agency, but it does not allow for good planning of activities that may be occurring over several years.

The second type of budget is a *program budget*. This budget allocates funds to programs or activities within an organization. A program budget lists items in categories by division, department or agency such as public works and public safety along with the cost of operating the agency. Program budgets are advantageous in that they allow programs of a similar nature to be combined rather than split into separate budgets.

Program budgets allow administrators and legislators to plan not only the current fiscal year, but also for future years. A good program budget lists the goals and objectives of an agency along with the funds that are allocated to achieving those objectives. These goals and objectives should be clear, concise and self-explanatory. This also serves the dual function of preventing redundancy among agencies as well as ensures that the annual review process will flow smoothly. Lastly, program budgets allow for the use of analytical tools to measure costs and benefits.[2]

Program budgets can be written using a variety of different formats. Exhibit 1.2 and 1.3 provide two basic examples for the Sanitation Department within Jefferson City. Let's take a look at exhibit 1.2 and note that the goal of the department is stated followed with objectives to accomplishing that goal.[3]

Exhibit 1.2. Program Budget One, Jefferson City FY 2020 Expenditures	
Sanitation Department	
The goal of this agency is to provide comprehensive sanitation services within the Jefferson City in the most effective and efficient manner as possible.	
Objectives: (a) Ensure that trash and debris is removed from the streets effectively. (b) Provide for the effective removal of recycled material. (c) Provide for street cleaning. (d) Provide for snow removal in an efficient and effective manner.	
TOTAL (actual):	$325,331.73

Source: Created by the Author.

In exhibit 1.3, notice how the budget directs attention towards the subject of the expenditure rather than the object of expenditure. In this example, there are three divisions within the department: trash collection, street cleaning, and snow removal and each division has a budget.

Although each division has a separate budget, their combined budgets make up the total budget for the Sanitation Department. If the budget director requests estimates or forecasts for future years, you can create a separate budget and modify your objectives and expenditures. If your objectives are the same, you can simply add another column next to the existing expenditure column with the appropriate fiscal year.

The last type of budget is a *performance budget*. A performance budget classifies funds based on some activity and the direct output created by that activity rather than the purchase of resources. This type of budget relies heavily on strategic planning, operational planning, and performance accountability. *Strategic planning* is a future oriented process of diagnosis and strategy

Exhibit 1.3. Program Budget Two, Jefferson City FY 2020 Expenditures	
Sanitation Department	
The goal of this agency is to provide comprehensive sanitation services within the Jefferson City in the most effective and efficient manner as possible.	
Objectives: (a) Ensure that trash and debris is removed from the streets effectively. (b) Provide for the effective removal of recycled material. (c) Provide for street cleaning. (d) Provide for snow removal in an efficient and effective manner.	
Divisions:	
Trash Collection	$200,375.00
Street Cleaning	85,456.73
Snow Removal	39,500.00
TOTAL (actual):	$325,331.73

Source: Created by the Author.

building. It closely monitors an agency's mission, capacity, and the environment in which it exists (Bryson 2010; Kelly and Rivenbark 2015; Poister 2010; Rubin and Willoughby 2011). *Operational planning* monitors the allocation of resources on a task-by-task basis in order to ensure that goals and objectives are met. Lastly, *performance accountability* measures progress by results. For example, measuring graduation rates, documenting the number of students in a classroom, or measuring the amount of snow removed from streets. The Governmental Accounting Standards Board (GASB) has a concept statement and provides examples and a framework that governments are encouraged to use when formulating accountability measures (see Dabbicco 2019; Joyce 2011; Lynch et al. 2017, 156).

An advantage to using a performance based budget is the direct correlation between spending and services provided (i.e., results). Performance budgets can be very useful for management because it provides accountability measures for both agency heads and legislators. This, however, is a double edged sword. On the one hand, agency heads must be very specific in detailing their operations. Legislators on the other hand must *appropriate funds* based on performance rather than the normal line item format (Gianakis and McCue 1999). In summary, this means greater effort on the part of legislators. Unless they have some level of expertise with that particular agency, they may find themselves ignorant of the details of spending and the long-term repercussions of their acts. The main benefit of a performance budget is that it allows for the outcomes of spending to be monitored every fiscal year. Hence, they are tied directly to performance reviews. Performance budgets date back to the early 1900s in New York City where attempts were made to bring greater accountability to agency heads and politicians (Lynch et al. 2017; Mendonsa 1983; U.S. General Accounting Office 1993).[4]

Exhibit 1.4 provides an example of a performance budget for Jefferson City. Note the exact functions that are to be carried out as a result of the expenditures. In addition, a performance budget can list the result of previous activities. For example, exhibit 1.4 shows that the number of neighborhoods served by the recycling program has increased. Also, note that the performance objectives are tied to the performance review.

Unfortunately, one of the problems with performance budgets is the inability to relate cause to effect. For example: Why are more people participating in the recycle program? Was it because more emphasis was placed on providing

Exhibit 1.4. Performance Budget, Jefferson City Sanitation Department FYs 2020–2022 Expenditures			
Program/Division: Trash Removal Description: Collection and removal of trash and recyclable material.			
Operating Expenses	*FY 2020 Actual*	*FY 2021 Recommended*	*FY 2022 Projected*
Personnel Services	$215,681.24	$235,050	$225,000
Supplies	35,500.00	39,000	45,000
Equipment	54,650.15	59,000	65,000
Printing	20,000.34	25,000	28,000
TOTAL	$325,331.73	$358,050	$363,000

Program Performance Objectives:

(1) Expand the recycle program to the southwest area of town.
(2) Provide multipurpose recycle containers to all of the existing customers.
(3) Provide feedback to the customers on the outcomes associated with recycling.
(4) Decrease the amount of recyclable material in the landfill.

Performance Review	*FY 2020 Actual*	*FY 2021 Estimated*	*FY 2022 Projected*
1. Neighborhoods Served	5	7	8
2. Recycle Containers Dispensed	920	1,045	1,200
3. Customer Recycle Newsletters	1,200	1,370	1,450
4. Materials Recycled	10 tons	15 tons	18 tons

Source: Created by the Author.

receptacles for the recycled material or because the newsletters highlighted the advantages to recycling? These problems are not necessarily limited to performance budgets. Similar problems exist with line item and program budgets.

One thing that the reader should recognize is presentation of the budget is very important. It is important that the user examines the budget and navigates through it with relative ease. If items are ambiguous and hard to find, it is a clear sign that the budget should be revised. If it is within their power, legislators and council members do not prefer to spend their days and nights working with budgets. As a result, your goal is to make the budget understandable to all users. In so doing, you can highlight important items by using the bold function, italics, underlining, and shading sections in your spreadsheet programs. In performance and program budgets, carefully placed words and explanations are also very useful (Lynch et al. 2017; Seckler-Hudson 2002; see also chapter 8).

READING A BUDGET

A good budget should be user friendly. The lay reader at the very least should be able to determine how much revenue the government intends to collect, how much the government plans to spend and on what (expenditures). As previously mentioned, there are three basic budget formats and they provide different types of information. However, there are several things that each of these budgets have in common.[5]

(1) *Budget Message/Budget Highlights/Executive Summary*: A good budget always has a message, usually in the form of a letter from the governor or mayor of the city directed to the state legislature, city council and/or the residents of the city or state. This message should indicate the law or statute that requires the submission of the budget and the time period that it covers. The message should also indicate the amount of revenue that is expected during the fiscal year and whether or not this is an increase or decrease from the previous fiscal year. If the legislative body governing the state or locality has recommended changes in budget allocations, those items should be indicated. If cuts were made, the reader should see what departments were cut in the message. If new programs were established or expanded, these should be highlighted. The letter should be followed with a table of contents outlining the remainder of the budget (see appendix 1A for an example of a Budget Letter).

(2) *Budget Summary*: The budget summary is normally a spreadsheet document indicating all of the revenue sources by type (property taxes, sales

taxes, user fees, etc.) and the expenditures by type (each agency or department should be listed). Small cities with limited revenue sources will frequently use this format. It is important that each fund is clearly labeled (see appendix 1B for an example).

(3) *Source of Revenue*: This section should detail to the reader exactly where all the revenue came from and the changes that occurred from previous fiscal years. Each source of revenue should be listed with, at a minimum, the actual budget for the previous fiscal year, budget estimates for the current year, and budget projections for the subsequent years. This page allows the reader to see the overall growth of the budget over the past years, as well as which revenue source is growing and which is decreasing (see appendix 1C for an example).

(4) *Source of Expenditures*: This section lists the major expense categories: personnel, operating, capital expenditures, and special appropriations for the entire government. You can also list the various departments by fiscal year along with the expenditures. A program or performance budget can follow the same format by listing the program or activity that is in use. Again, each of these categories show the comparisons between the current fiscal year and the previous two fiscal years with a column for the actual dollar amount change and the percent change from the previous fiscal year (see appendix 1D for an example).

(5) *Department/Agency Budget Information*: The bulk of the budget contains the individual budget requests for each department. There are several good ways to prepare this information in an efficient manner. The first way is to list the various line item expenditures of the department in the right hand column and then indicate the changes in the budget by fiscal years. On a second page, you should list the fund sources for that department and the changes that have occurred over the previous fiscal years. Again, the presentation of this information will vary with respect to the type of budget. To say the least, the reader should be able to determine exactly how much revenue is coming into the department and what it is used for. Since most agencies are balancing the budget from previous fiscal years, the spreadsheet should provide the reader with the amount of allocations from the previous two fiscal years along with the percent change in both dollar amount and percentage change (see appendix 1E for an example).

(6) *Supplemental Budgeting Information*: The budget document should provide the reader with any new laws, statutes, rules, or ordinances that affect the budget document. This is particularly true for capital improvement projects. Again, if necessary, a spreadsheet should be created for these projects in a format similar to the previous documents.

PUBLIC VERSUS PRIVATE BUDGETS

Although there are many common themes that exist in all budgets, public budgeting does differ from the private sector in many respects (see table 1.1). First, public budgeting often involves the interaction of many actors involved with a variety of different agendas. Private budgeting may involve one or a few personnel regardless to the size of the organization. Second, funds that are spent and collected in the public sector are collected from tax payers who may or may not want the monies to be collected and spent and may not receive any direct services as a result of paying the tax. On the other hand, monies collected in the private sector are not compulsory and services are directed accordingly. Third, public budgets are public documents and therefore are open to be scrutinized by citizens, while private budgets are not. Fourth, public budgets are well designed documents that are written to last an entire fiscal year (or two). Hence, they are not very flexible. When crisis or other unplanned events occur, it can be catastrophic to budget analysts as well as elected officials. Private budgets are very flexible and can be changed at a moments' notice in order to move with changes in the economy, budget shortfalls, etc. Fifth, the number of rules and actors involved in public budgeting far surpasses that in the private sector. For example, there may be rules affecting expenditures, tax collection, balancing the budgets, assessments, mandates, etc. While there may be rules applied in the private sector, the process does not tend to be overly bureaucratized (Rubin 2010). Last, appropriation acts and ordinances are legal documents that place limits on spending. Many governments have severe penalties for overspending appropriations, including jail time.

Table 1.1.   Comparing Public and Private Budgets
Public Budgets
<ul><li>Many decision makers</li><li>Revenue is collected from tax payers who may not benefit from the tax</li><li>The budget is open to the public</li><li>Covers an entire year and are not very flexible</li><li>Many rules affecting the collection of taxes (i.e. legally set tax rates)</li></ul>
Private Budgets
<ul><li>Few decision makers</li><li>Monies are collected and a service or product is provided</li><li>The budget is not publicly available</li><li>Budget is very flexible and can be modified to fit the circumstances</li><li>Fewer rules and regulations</li></ul>

Source: Created by the Author.

OVERVIEW OF REVENUES AND EXPENDITURES

State and local revenues come from a variety of sources.[6] *Revenues* are the monies collected by all levels of government to pay for the operation of government. *Expenditures* are financial obligations that flow from the operation of government. A major source of revenue for state and local governments is taxes. For some states, *income taxes* make up the greater proportion of taxes collected (in addition to sales taxes). Unlike state governments, some local governments have the option of collecting payroll taxes (income taxes) (see chapter 5).

Payroll taxes can be used for special purposes or serve as additional income for the local government. Income taxes are deducted directly from individual earnings and are compulsory. State income tax rates tend to be lower than federal income taxes and they are considered *progressive taxes*. That is, higher income individuals pay more taxes than lower income individuals. Although corporations pay income taxes, they tend to be a much lower percentage of all taxes collected. Individual income taxes make up about one-third of all taxes collected in a state. All states do not have state income taxes (Bland 2005; Johnson and Kriz 2019; Mikesell 2004).

A second major source of revenue in a state (and in some localities) comes from *sales and use taxes*. These are taxes placed on goods and services. Sales taxes are considered *regressive taxes* because citizens pay the same rate regardless of their income level. Each state sets its own sales tax rate. States and localities also have some discretion as to what items will be assessed sales taxes. For example, sales taxes are not applied to the sale of unprepared foods in Kentucky. Other sources of revenue for the state include: tobacco, alcohol, petroleum product taxes, inheritance taxes, automobile taxes, and public utility taxes. States can also allow local governments to create a *local option sales tax* which can be used to pay for a specific item of cost (Afonso 2018).

States also get a large amount of revenue from the federal government in the form of *grants*. Grants come in two major forms: categorical and block. *Categorical grants* make up the largest type of grants that a state receives. A categorical grant is used for a specific program and has very strict guidelines for the activities to be carried out within a specific time period. Categorical grants exploded during President Lyndon B. Johnson's Great Society programs in the 1960s. Formula and project grants fall within the umbrella of categorical grants. *Formula grants* use a distribution formula to determine the amount to be allocated to the state or locality. Population, geography, income and education are variables that are used in formula grants. A *block grant* is used for broad policy areas and can be used for a variety of programs and activities by state and local governments.

A major source of revenue for local governments is *property taxes*. These are taxes levied against real property, perhaps personal property and private utilities. Many local governments have the ability to impose sales taxes. The taxes are piggy-backed onto state sales taxes for collection efficiency. Many local governments have the ability to impose license fees on motor vehicles. Another source of revenue for local governments is licenses and permits, franchise fees and user charges. A *license fee* is a flat rate tax for business entities. The cost of the license fee differs by activity. For example, the cost of a hunting license is different from that of a license to operate a restaurant. Without a license, an individual or business is forbidden to engage in the activity legally. The owner of a license does not receive any specific government service by having the license. Under normal circumstances, everyone who applies for a license receives it (Bland 2005; Raphaelson 2004).

A *franchise fee* appears to be closely related to a license fee, but there are some subtle differences. Franchises are provided on a very limited basis. A franchise presupposes that the business will serve the entire community, operate with a certain quality and rate, and outlines the responsibility of the owner and the government.

A *user charge* is a fee charged to individuals who voluntarily use a publicly provided service. For example, large municipalities may implement a toll charge to pay for the construction of a new road. If you do not use the new road, then you do not pay the charge. The purpose of a user charge is to relieve the financial burden placed on the general revenue system. In most cases, user charges are geared toward the population that is benefiting from the public service. User charges are useless if they are not enforceable (Bierhanzl and Downing 2004).

Another source of revenue for local governments is the proceeds from *public utilities*. Public utilities are government owned business. These include but are not limited to water utilities, gas utilities, electric utilities, sewers, and inter-city transit. These government businesses have little or no competition (*monopoly*). One of the newest forms of revenues for states and local governments are the revenues collected from casinos, lotteries, and other forms of gambling. This revenue stream has grown tremendously over time and are frequently used for educational and public safety purposes.

Although *bonds* are not considered a source of revenue in most cities and states, they do serve as a major source of funds for the construction of public buildings, schools and other big ticket items. A bond is basically money that is borrowed from an individual with the assurance that the bond can be cashed in during a given period of time for a sum of money (principal and interest). State and local governments use bonds to finance projects that cannot be financed from the current revenue sources. The interest earned on bonds is not taxable by the United States government. There are two types of bonds: full faith and credit bonds (general obligation bonds) and non-guaranteed bonds. *General obligation bonds* are paid for out of the general revenue fund and are guaranteed by the state or local government that issued them. *Non-guaranteed bonds* have a limited backing, usually from a revenue source such as water and sewer revenue. The only backing is the revenue stream that is pledged to repay the debt. (Bland 2005; Han, Pagano, and Shin 2019; Lee, Johnson, and Joyce 2013; Vogt 2004).

Taxes and other sources of revenue are used to pay for government *expenditures*. An expenditure is the disbursement of revenue to cover the costs of a governmental unit's operation (Riley and Colby 1991). The majority of revenues collected by local governments are used toward the payment of salaries and fringe benefits to employees. In addition to personnel cost, supplies, equipment, contractual services and *capital outlays* make up the vast amount of the budget. Capital outlays are monies allocated for big ticket items that cannot be completed in a single fiscal year. Normally, personnel cost will range from 65 percent to 75 percent of a local budget. States typically have large expenditures for transfer payments to local governments or individuals, such as primary and secondary education allocations to school districts, payments to institutions of higher education, and Medicaid payments for low income individual. The operating expenditures for states typically make up only 35 percent to 45 percent of total spending. The percentage change would depend on the function of an agency. For example, police and fire departments frequently have higher equipment cost than an auditor's office.

Tables 1.2 and 1.3 provide examples of a revenue and expenditure summary for Jefferson City and the state of Alexander respectively. Table 1.2 shows that property taxes tend to make up the greater portion of all taxes collected by local governments, followed by sales taxes. In the expenditure column, the Executive and Highway and Streets departments have the largest budgets. A line item budget for each of these divisions would reveal that the majority of the budget is used for personnel services.

Table 1.3 shows that half of the revenue collected by the State of Alexander comes from taxes. It is also noteworthy to mention that expenditures are typically listed by department in a "line item" format. However, in a summary expenditure sheet, such as this one, there is no need to break down expenditures into sub-categories that detail personnel, equipment and capital outlays (Bahl 2004). That information would be provided in the individual agency line item budget sheets.

Table 1.2. Estimated Revenues and Expenditures, Jefferson City FY 2020	
Sources of Revenue	*Amount*
1. Property Tax	$361,250
2. Local Sales Tax	232,979
3. Beer Tax	59,752
4. State Sales Tax	153,000
5. State Petroleum Tax	59,500
6. Automobile Registration	15,725
7. Minimum Business Tax	21,482
8. Corporate Excise Tax	12,750
9. Solid Waste Fund	154,445
10. Debt Service Fund	65,025
11. Water and Sewer Fund	642,485
12. Other	120,210
TOTAL	$1,899,450
Sources of Expenditures	*Amount*
1. Executive Department	$282,455
2. City Recorder	133,790
3. Police	199,494
4. Fire	56,396
5. Highways and Streets	292,570
6. Playgrounds	64,770
7. Solid Waste	136,000
8. Water Utilities	218,926
9. Non-Operating Exp.	95,200
10. Bond Principal	60,106
11. Libraries	12,750
12. Other	346,993
TOTAL	$1,899,450

Source: Created by the Author.

Table 1.3. Estimated Revenues and Expenditures FY 2020 State of Alexander (in billions)			
Sources of Revenue	*Amount*	*Sources of Expenditures*	*Amount*
1. Tax Collections	$43.5	1. General Government	$2.1
2. Federal Funds	25.4	2. Health and Human Services	26.1
3. Licenses and Fees	7.4	3. Public Education	26.4
4. Lottery	4.4	4. Higher Education	11.9
5. Interest Income	3.9	5. Public Safety	7.0
6. Other Revenue Sources	2.7	6. Natural Resources	1.7
		7. Business and Economic Dev.	10.3
		8. Other	3.7
TOTAL	$87.3	TOTAL	$87.1

Source: Created by the Author.

GOVERNMENTAL ACCOUNTING

One of the most important functions of state and local governments is to maintain a meticulous accounting record. Unlike individuals who are paid a certain amount of dollars at some set period, governments receive various amounts of money throughout the course of a fiscal year. Hence, they must allocate and manage funds in order to cover all expenditures. State and local governments typically use a *fund accounting system*. The Governmental Accounting Standards Board (GASB) establishes accounting and reporting standards for state and local governments. This board created what is called Generally Accepted Accounting Principles (GAAP). Audits of state and local governments are performed based on GAAP and an opinion is rendered by an *auditor*. The federal government requires all governmental units receiving federal funds to adhere to the principles outlined in GAAP.[7] The GASB provides standards for reporting, but not budgeting. There are no standards for budgeting unless they are established by state law (Ball 2012; Lande and Rocher 2011).

Governmental accounting normally takes three forms: cash basis, modified accrual and full accrual. A *cash basis* system is very comparable to a personal checking account system. Budget officials basically add the revenue to an account when they literally receive the funds. On the expenditure side of the equation, funds are subtracted from an account as soon as they are spent. This technique will work for all sorts of accounts, but is not necessarily the best system for all accounts (see table 1.4).

Similar to a cash basis system, a *modified accrual* system records revenue when the funds are measurable and available. The terms measurable and available are mutually exclusive and are the result of donor contributions. They largely apply largely to the nonprofit sector. For accounting purposes, contributions must be recorded even though the funds may not be available immediately. The amount is known and available means that it is received during the fiscal year or soon enough after the end of the year so that obligations for that fiscal year can be paid. This period is typically sixty to one hundred and twenty days. However, expenditures are recorded when a fund liability is incurred. That is, an entity has agreed in principle to spend funds. A *full accrual* system records revenue as it is earned regardless to whether the revenue has been received. For example, property taxes are recorded when the bill is mailed (earned) rather than when the bill is paid (received). A full accrual system records expenses when a financial obligation is incurred. The accrual basis of accounting is used primarily for matching revenues to the cost of production. The basis of accounting for state and local governments is prescribed by the GASB based on the fund type that is involved.

Generally speaking, budgeting takes place on a prospective basis. That is, funds are deducted as soon as a commitment is made. For example, the Transportation Department gave a contract to Whitley's Construction Company to repair the city's streets. As a result, the dollar amount of the contract is immediately deducted from the department's budget even though the full payment has not been made. The accounting system will not record an obligation until services have been rendered.

Table 1.4.   Accounting Methods

Cash Basis System

(a) Revenue is recorded when the funds are received.
(b) Expenditures are recorded when the funds are spent.

Modified Accrual

(a) Revenue is recorded when the funds are measurable and available.
(b) Expenditures are recorded when a fund obligation is made.

Full Accrual

(a) Revenue is recorded when actually earned or when the government established a claim.
(b) Expenses are recorded when a financial obligation is made.

Source: Created by the Author.

Governments tend to be financially conservative when it comes to estimating or forecasting revenue. For example, local governments do not expect to collect 100 percent of the property tax, so they normally estimate anywhere from 90 to 95 percent based on the historical trend.

As a result, most governments use the cash basis method for budgeting taxes in general, although some use the modified accrual method. Some use a hybrid system—modified accrual for some sources and cash for others. The federal government uses the cash basis system except for interest and credit programs (*Analytical Perspectives: Budget of the U.S. Government*, 2004, 470). Private entities tend to use the accrual method since the objective is to match expenses to revenue (Laughlin 2012).

GOVERNMENT FUNDS

As revenue comes into the government, it is placed into separate *funds*. GAAP sets up three classes of funds—governmental, proprietary and fiduciary. *Governmental funds* are those that are used to carry out basic government services and are primarily supported through taxes and shared revenues. *Proprietary funds* are business-type in nature and are similar to those used in the private sector. *Fiduciary funds* are used to account for assets that are held by the government as an agent or trustee. Fiduciary funds are not used to carry out government activities. Within each class of funds, there are several types of funds. As a general rule, funds act as fiscal control agents. That is, they force governments to spend the money for the purpose that it was created.

The largest classes of funds are governmental funds. There are five types of funds within this class: General Fund, Special Revenue Funds, Debt Service Funds, Capital Project Funds, and Permanent Funds. With regard to the number of funds a government can have, the only limit involves the General Fund—there can only be one. GASB recommends that only the minimum number of funds needed for legal and operating requirements should be established. It is common for governments to have more funds for budgeting purposes than for external reporting purposes. For external reporting, governments tend to combine like funds, such as federal grant funds (Government Accounting Standards Series 1999).

- The *General Fund* includes all revenue not designated in another fund. It is the largest fund in terms of the dollars that transfer through it. An example of revenue that goes into this fund is property taxes, license fees, and income taxes.
- *Special Service Funds* are designed for earmarked revenue or revenues that are designated for special purposes. For example, taxes on petroleum

products would go into this fund. Governments frequently use grant funds in special revenue funds to ensure that monies are *allocated* for the designed purpose. A government is not limited to the total number of special revenue funds that it may have.

- *Debt Service Funds* are funds designed to collect revenue for the repayment of long term debt. Revenue in this fund frequently comes from transfers from the general fund. The purpose of the fund is to ensure that revenues are set aside for the repayment of debt. For example, general obligation bonds are included in this fund. There are no limits on the number of debt service funds.
- *Capital Project Funds* are designed to collect revenue for the purchase and construction of capital projects. For example, the proceeds from the issuance of bonds would go into this fund.
- *Permanent Funds* are used to report resources that are legally restricted to the extent that only earnings, and not principal, may be used for purposes that support the government's programs. For example, money may be donated to the government to maintain a cemetery and provides that only the earnings from investments can be used for that purpose.

PROPRIETARY FUNDS

Proprietary funds are for public service activities that resemble those of the private sector, proprietary or business like activities. This would include for example the use of a public gas company or a public golf course. There are two types of proprietary funds: enterprise funds and internal service funds.

- *Enterprise Funds* contain revenues collected from individuals external to the government. These are collected on a fee basis.
- *Internal Service Funds* contain revenue from agencies within the government for services rendered.

Enterprise funds operate much like that of a private sector business. They collect most of their revenue from user charges. For example, drivers pay a fee to cross the Bay Bridge from Oakland to San Francisco. Other examples would include public utility companies, public transportation, and government owned public radio and television stations. The purpose of this fund is to determine if the entity is collecting enough revenue to maintain its existence.

Unlike enterprise funds, internal service funds are used within the government and provide a service to other government agencies rather than the public at large. For example, Jefferson City has a central motor pool that provides transportation services for all of the cities agencies. When a car needs to be repaired, the city garage repairs it. Thus, revenues are shifted to this department from other departments when services are rendered. Since most agencies have funds dedicated for this service, they are likely to use it. There is no charge unless the service is used.[8]

The distinction between an enterprise fund and internal service fund is the primary customer. If the primary customer is outside the government, an enterprise fund is used. If it is within the government, an internal service fund is used.

FIDUCIARY FUNDS

There are also other types of funds that may be used by state and local governments. The first type is fiduciary funds. *Fiduciary funds* are essentially revenue held for other individuals or government organizations. There are four types of fiduciary funds: pension trust funds (and other employee benefit trust funds), investment trust funds, private-purpose trust funds and agency funds (Mikesell 2018).

- *Pension (and other Employee Benefit) Trust Funds* hold monies for government employee's pension plans, other post-employment benefits, or other employee benefit plans. This is usually the largest type of fiduciary fund.
- *Investment Trust Funds* are used to report the external portion of investment pools reported by the sponsoring government.
- *Private-purpose Trusts* are used to report trust arrangements under which the principal and interest benefit individuals, private corporations, or other governments.
- *Agency Funds* hold monies in a purely custodial capacity for individuals or other governments.

CONCLUSION

As the chapter shows, elected officials can use the budget as a tool to control the bureaucracy, as a plan of action, and to create accountability. The type of budget used plays a significant role in the information that is conveyed. Elected officials frequently do not have in depth knowledge of all the agencies that they ultimately govern and as a result, the type of budget used can serve several purposes. Similarly, the type of accounting methods used can affect how the monies can be spent and held. The next chapter will show the reader how elected officials close this information gap.

IMPORTANT TERMS AND PHRASES

Accrual Accounting

Agency Fund

Allocation

Audits

Appropriations

Balanced Budget

Block Grant

Bonds

Budget

Cash Basis Accounting

Capital Project Fund

Capital Outlay

Categorical Grant

Debt Service Fund

Deficit

Earmarked Fund

Economy and Efficiency Audit

Enterprise Fund

Expendable Trust Fund

Expenditures

Fiduciary Fund

Financial Audit

Fiscal Year

Franchise Fee

Formula Grant

Fund

Fund Accounting System

Gaming Fees

General Fund

General Obligation Bonds

Grant

Income Tax

Internal Service Fund

License Fee

Line Item Budget

Local Option Sales Tax

Modified Accrual Accounting

Monopoly

Non-Expendable Trust Fund

Outlay

Performance Accountability

Performance Budget

Program Audit

Program Budget

Progressive Tax

Proprietary Fund

Public Utilities

Regressive Tax

Revenue

Sales Tax

Set Asides

Single Audit

Special Revenue Fund

User Charge

Zero Based Budgeting

CHAPTER 1 HOMEWORK EXERCISES

Directions: Please read each question in its entirety prior to completing the assignment. Questions 1 and 5 should be typed in a word processing program. There are Excel worksheets for questions 2–4. All (text files and Excel sheets) of the responses to the questions should be pasted in a word processing document. Your instructor will provide directions on question 6.

(1) Describe/define the various types of budgets listed below. Your response should include things like: who proposes the budget, the period of time covered by the budget, and the overall benefits to using one type of budget over another type of budget. You will have to research these terms as they are not all defined in this textbook.

   (a) Estimated Budget
   (b) Projected Budget
   (c) Proposed Budget
   (d) Recommended Budget
   (e) Adopted Budget
   (f) Appropriated Budget
   (g) Actual Budget
   (h) Balanced Budget
   (i) Baseline Budget

(2) From the perspective of a bureaucrat, which government accounting method (Cash Basis, Modified Accrual or Full Accrual) is more feasible for each revenue source? Explain your response. The key to your response should be stability or volatility of the revenue source over time. Further, you should consider whether the revenue source can be broken down into components parts. For example, user fees collected from a street meter may differ in stability from user fees collected at a toll station. In addition, you should realize that the amount and percentage of revenues collected from each source can vary from year to year depending on any number of social, political and economic factors. In any event, be specific and justify your response. It may be useful to review the revenue information in Chapter 5, prior to responding to this question.

   (a) State Income Taxes
   (b) Public Utility Fees
   (c) Donations
   (d) Motor Fuel Taxes
   (e) Licenses and Fees
   (f) Sales Tax

    (g) Gaming Fees (casinos)
    (h) Block Grants
    (i) Property Taxes

(3) Mayor McClain has appointed you to head the newly created Recycle Department for the Jefferson City. Your first task is to prepare a series of budgets for your department. More specifically, the mayor has given you $500,000 in FY 2020 and $550,000 in FY 2021 to run the department. Using the Excel worksheet templates for chapter 1, prepare a budget estimate for FY 2020 and a budget projection for FY 2021 using a simple line item, program, and performance budget format allocating the fund that are listed above.

    (a) *Line Item Budget*: In your line item budget, use the categories (personnel, operating, and capital outlay) that are listed in the text. You are free to spend the funds any way that you see fit. However, remember that personnel costs usually consume the majority of a budget.

    (b) *Program Budget*: Consider the different types of activities (divisions) that a recycling department would be engaged in (recycling glass, paper, plastic, aluminum, etc.). Your goals and/or objectives should be slightly modified in the second year to show growth in one area and a decrease in another area.

    (c) *Performance Budget:* Set some specific goals that you can attain for either one of the divisions that you created in your performance budget (i.e., collect 6 tons of paper during the first year of operation).

    Suggestion: In addition to staff, a Recycling Department may need the following: recycling bins, aluminum compressors, trucks, marketing brochures, and trailers to hold the recyclable materials.

(4) Based on the information in the text and the goals and objectives that you have established for the Jefferson City Recycle Department in Question 3 respond to these questions.

    (a) Which one of these three budgets best describes what the Recycle Department does? Explain your answer.

    (b) Which one of these three budgets gives: the director of the department/agency; the mayor; and the legislative body, the most discretion/latitude in making budgetary decisions about the agency? Think about the roles of these persons prior to answering the question. The response for each entity should be explained separately.

(5) Using the internet, retrieve a copy of a local or state government budget. A list of states and cities is located in the appendices (F & G). Based on

the contents of the budget, decide whether or not the budget is "good" using the information in the section titled, "Reading the Budget" in the text. In addition, the Government Finance Officers Association (http://www.gfoa.org/) has a Distinguished Budgeting Awards program. These awards are presented to governments that have budgets that meet "best practices." Feel free to utilize their criteria as well. Justify your responses and attach a copy of pertinent sections of the budget to your homework assignment. Do not copy and turn in the entire budget. Pertinent sections should not exceed 7 pages.

Note: This question should be answered using the headings provided below along with any other items that you deem worthy from the GFOA web site.

Budget Evaluation

(a) State or City Budget Website Address
(b) Budget Message/Budget Highlights/Executive Summary
(c) Budget Summary
(d) Source of Revenue
(e) Source of Expenditures
(f) Department/Agency Budget Information
(g) Supplemental Budgeting Information

(6) Optional In-Class Assignment: Reconciling Accounting Methods and Revenue Sources (1- hour Exercise)

Step 1. Divide the class into groups (4–6 persons).

Step 2. Each group should discuss the responses to question 2. At the end of the discussion, the group should decide which accounting method is best and why that is the case. Do not spend more than five minutes discussing each item.

Step 3. Prepare a brief group justification for each item.

Step 4. Have one person from each group present and compare their responses with the other groups.

NOTES

1. With the exception of Georgia and the federal government during President Jimmy Carter's administration, no government has ever used zero-based budgeting.

2. See Gerasimos A. Gianakis and Clifford P. McCue (1999), *Local Government Budgeting: A Managerial Approach* (West Port, CT: Praeger); David Novick (2002), "What Program Budgeting Is and Is Not," in *Government Budgeting: Theory, Process, and Politics*, 3rd ed., ed. Albert C. Hyde (Toronto and London: Wadsworth),

52–68; John L. Mikesell (2004), "General Sales, Income, and Other Nonproperty Taxes," in *Management Policies in Local Government Finance*, 5th ed., ed. J. Richard Aronson and Eli Schwartz (Washington, DC: ICMA), 289–314; and Paul L. Solano (2004), "Budgeting," in *Management Policies in Local Government Finance*, 5th ed., ed. J. Richard Aronson and Eli Schwartz (Washington, DC: ICMA), 155–206, for additional information on program budgets.

3. In reality, the government would provide line item detail within the program. A legislator is not going to accept a single number without backup. The government would also present information by subprogram, such as street paving, striping, snow removal, etc.

4. See John L. Mikesell (2018), *Fiscal Administration: Analysis and Applications for the Public Sector*, 10th ed. (Belmont, CA: Wadsworth Cengage); and Thomas D. Lynch, Jinping Sun, and Robert W. Smith (2017), *Public Budgeting in America*, 6th ed. (Irvine, CA: Melvin & Leigh), for additional information on performance budgets.

5. See Susan L. Riley and Peter W. Colby (1991), *Practical Government Budgeting: A Workbook for Public Managers* (Albany: State University of New York Press); James D. Carney and Stanley Schoenfeld (1996), "How To Read a Budget," in *Budgeting: Formulation and Execution*, ed. Jack Rabin, W. Bartley Hildreth, and Gerald J. Miller (Athens, GA: Carl Vinson Institute of Government, University of Georgia), 140–53; and Lynch et al. (2017), *Public Budgeting in America*, for additional information regarding the common elements of a budget.

6. Chapter 5, "Funding the Budget," in this text, has a complete description of revenue sources for governmental entities along with the advantages and disadvantages of each source.

7. Review Riley and Colby (1991), *Practical Government Budgeting*; Robert L. Bland and Irene S. Rubin (1997), *Budgeting: A Guide for Local Governments* (Washington, DC: ICMA); Lynch et al. (2017), *Public Budgeting in America*; William Holder (2004), "Financial Accounting, Reporting, and Auditing," in *Management Policies in Local Government Finance*, 5th ed., ed. J. Richard Aronson and Eli Schwartz (Washington, DC: ICMA), 207–23; Solano (2004), "Budgeting," 155–206; and William P. Kittredge and Sarah M. Ouart (2005), *Budget Manual for Georgia Local Government* (Athens, GA: Vinson Institute, University of Georgia), for additional information on governmental accounting methods and fund accounting.

8. See Riley and Colby (1991), *Practical Government Budgeting*; Bland and Rubin (1997), *Budgeting*; Mikesell (2004), "General Sales, Income, and Other Nonproperty Taxes"; Lynch et al. (2017), *Public Budgeting in America*; and Solano (2004), "Budgeting," 155–206, for additional readings on enterprise and internal service funds.

Appendix 1A

Budget Letter

COMMONWEALTH OF ALEXANDER
OFFICE OF GOVERNOR
HARRISBURG

THE GOVERNOR

February 7, 2019

TO THE PEOPLE OF STATE X:

For too many years, politicians in Harrisburg have tried to do things the same way. We've taken a different approach by prioritizing important responsibilities like protecting our seniors, making sure children receive the quality education they need, working to reduce property taxes, joining with law enforcement and medical professionals to expand treatment to battle the opioid and heroin epidemic, and rebuilding Alexander's middle class by putting more people to work.

In this year's budget, I am again proposing significant changes to the way Harrisburg has done business. The proposed budget includes over $2 billion in cuts and savings and avoids any new taxes on Alexander families, while maintaining the investments we have made in our schools, protecting seniors, fighting the opioid epidemic and supporting Alexander's middle class.

This budget takes a hard look at state government and makes tough decisions. Just like when I was in business, this budget identifies savings and efficiencies, not just to reduce costs but also to better deliver services to the people of Alexander. By merging health-related agencies, we will reduce bureaucracy and redundancy. Our current fragmented approach to providing benefits often leads to confusion for program applicants and their families. Consolidation of these services into bureaus within one, combined department will drive better out- comes, improve customer service and reduce costs. As we approach this budget, we should not think about how we have done things before, but how we can better deliver services for the people of Alexander.

Through these savings and efficiencies, this budget protects our investments in our schools and our efforts to fight the opioid epidemic. Over the past two years, we have increased funding for Alexander's schools by nearly $640 million while implementing a fair funding formula. This is a good start toward reversing the devastating $1 billion in cuts made to schools during the previous administration, but there is still work to do. That's why I'm proposing additional investments in education at all levels.

Continuing to fight the opioid crisis will remain a top priority. The 2019–20 budget provided funding to implement 45 centers of excellence throughout the commonwealth that will treat nearly 11,000 people with substance use disorder. This budget builds on that effort by investing $10 million to expand access to naloxone for first responders, and expands drug courts and treatment funding to make sure those affected by opioids can get the help they need.

My budget presents a plan for rebuilding our middle class and making government more efficient so that we can protect education, job creation programs, and services for our seniors and most vulnerable. It's clear that we need to do things differently if we want to move Alexander forward.

I look forward to continuing to work with all members of the General Assembly to move our state forward.

Sincerely,
Tom Day

Appendix 1B

Jefferson City Budget Summary

Jefferson City Budget Summary FY 2020–2021				
	General Fund	*Central Garage*	*Water & Sewer*	*Sanitation*	*Grand Total*
Funding Sources				
Property Taxes	$1,483,000	$0	$0	$0	$1,483,000
Insurance Taxes	885,000	—	41,500	—	926,500
Vehicle Stickers	420,000	—	—	—	420,000
Business Licenses	350,000	—	—	—	350,000
User Charges		116,250	3,421,500	1,884,000	5,421,750
Special Assessments		—	195,000	$50,000	245,000
Other & Misc.	662,779	—	—	—	662,779
Fund Transfers	—	—	—	—	—
TOTAL Revenues	$3,800,779	$116,250	$3,658,000	$1,934,000	$9,509,029
Beginning Fund	$65,000	$0	$0	$50,600	$700,600
TOTAL Available Funds	$4,450,779	$116,250	$3,658,000	$1,984,600	$10,209,629
Expenditures				
General Government	$1,309,454	$0	$0	$0	$1,309,454
Public Safety	27,811,000	—	—	—	2,781,100
Public Works	360,225	—	—	—	360,225
Central Garage		116,250	—	—	116,250
Sanitation		—	—	1,984,600	1,984,600
Water & Sewer Operations		—	3,658,000	—	3,658,000
Cemetery Operations		—	—	—	—
Gas Systems Operations		—	—	—	—
Capital Expenditures		0	0	0	0
TOTAL Expenditures	$4,450,779	$116,250	$3,658,000	$1,984,600	$10,209,629

Source: Created by the Author.

Appendix 1C

San Pablo Revenue

San Pablo, Sources of Revenue FY 2020–2022					
	FY 2020 (act)	FY 2021 (est)	FY 2022 (proj)	Net Change	% Change
Balance Forward	$525,756.30	$174,868.50	$50,621.10		
Sales and Use Tax	$2,555,557.00	$2,715,000.00	$287,500.00	$160,500.00	5.91%
Income Tax-Ind.	2,095,499.10	2,299,760.00	2,472,728.00	172,968.00	7.52%
Income Tax-Corp.	496,023.90	512,000.00	512,000.00	0.00	0.00%
Other	708,760.60	657,882.90	674,568.80	16,685.90	2.54%
TOTAL Base Revenue	$6,381,596.90	$6,359,511.40	$6,585,417.90	$350,153.90	5.51%

Source: Created by the Author.

Appendix 1D

Source of Expenditures

Source of Expenditure, Nowhere Mississippi (amounts in millions)				
	FY 2020 (act)	*FY 2021 Request*	*Net Change*	*% Change*
General Government	$2,345	$2,498	$150	6.52%
Public Safety	7,129	7,893	764	10.72%
Health and Human Services	27,189	31,890	4,701	17.29%
Public Education	28,000	30,000	2,000	7.14%
Higher Education	13,685	14,589	904	6.61%
Judiciary	386	399	13	3.375
Natural Resources	1,693	1,785	92	5.43%
Business & Economic Dev.	10,456	11,000	544	5.20%
Regulatory	456	469	13	2.85%
Article IX	721	732	11	1.53%
Other	250	255	5	2.00%
Department TOTAL	$92,310	$101,510	$9,200	9.97%

Source: Created by the Author.

Appendix 1E

Jefferson City Fire Department

Jefferson City Fire Department FY 2020–2022					
	FY 2020 Actual	*FY 2021 Budget*	*FY 2022 Est*	*Net Change*	*% Change*
Salaries					
Education	150	500	500	0	0.00%
Life Insurance	1,268	2,150	1,500	–650	–30.23%
Medical Insurance	110,467	120,000	120,000	0	0.00%
Social Security	51,689	57,500	57,500	0	0.00%
State Incentive	70,054	72,500	72,500	0	0.00%
Workmen's Compensation	38,660	36,000	40,000	4,000	11.11%
Kentucky Retirement	126,853	137,000	145,000	8,000	5.84%
Subtotal	$1,058,080	$1,156,650	$1,202,000	$45,350	3.92%
Operating Expenses					
Station II Facility	$5,575	$3,500	$3,500	$0	0.00%
Fire Hydrants	23,414	23,500	24,250	750	3.19%
Water, Sewer, & Gas	3,344	3,500	3,500	0	0.00%
Electricity	1,641	2,000	2,000	0	0.00%
Office Supplies	1,581	1,500	1,500	0	0.00%
Gasoline	4,854	5,000	5,000	0	0.00%
Uniforms	15,554	12,000	12,000	0	0.00%
Training School & Supplies	703	2,500	2,500	0	0.00%
Vehicle Repair & Maint.	8,514	15,000	15,000	0	0.00%
Housekeeping Supplies	1,130	1,000	1,000	0	0.00%
Travel & Meetings	1,262	1,500	1,500	0	0.00%
Dues & Subscriptions	280	300	300	0	0.00%
Miscellaneous	5,014	5,000	5,000	0	0.00%
Fire Marshall Office	3,707	2,500	2,500	0	0.00%
Appropriations	1,223	1,500	1,500	0	0.00%
Subtotal	$77,796	$81,300	$82,050	$750	0.92%
Capital Expenditures					
Equipment	$8,209	$39,000	$10,000	–$29,000	–74.36%
Fire Truck Payment	24,369	24,500	24,500	0	0.00%
Subtotal	$32,578	$63,500	$34,500	–$29,000	–45.67%
TOTAL	$1,168,454	$1,301,450	$1,318,550	$17,100	1.31%

Source: Created by the Author.

Appendix 1F

U.S. State and Province Budget Offices

U.S. STATES

AL   http://www.budget.state.al.us/
AK   http://www.omb.alaska.gov/
AR   http://www.dfa.arkansas.gov
AZ   http://www.ospb.state.az.us
CA   http://www.dof.ca.gov/
CO   http://www.colorado.gov/dpa
CT   http://www.opm.state.ct.us/publicat.htm#Budget
DE   http://www.state.de.us/budget/
FL   http://www.dos.state.fl.us/office/admin-services/planning.aspx
GA   http://www.legis.state.ga.us/legis/budget/index.htm
HI   http://www.hawaii.gov/budget/
IA   http://www.dom.state.ia.us
ID   http://www2.state.id.us/dfm/index.html
IL   http://www.state.il.us/budget/
IN   http://www.in.gov/sba/
KS   http://www.budget.ks.gov
KY   http://www.osbd.ky.gov
LA   http://senate.legis.state.la.us/FiscalServices/Default.htm
MA   http://www.mass.gov/eoaf/
MD   http://www.dbm.maryland.gov/
ME   http://www.maine.gov/budget/
MI   http://www.michigan.gov/budget
MN   http://www.finance.state.mn.us/
MO   http://www.oa.mo.gov/bp/
MS   http://www.dfa.state.ms.us/Offices/OBFM/OBFM.htm
MT   http://www.budge.mt.gov/
NC   http://www.osbm.state.nc.us/osbm/index.html
ND   http://www.state.nd.us/fiscal/
NE   http://www.budget.state.ne.us/

NH   http://admin.state.nh.us/budget/
NJ   http://www.njleg.state.nj.us/legislativepub/budget.asp
NM   http://www.nmdfa.state.nm.us/
NV   http://www.budget.state.nv.us/
NY   http://www.budget.ny.gov
OH   http://www.obm.ohio.gov/
OK   http://www.ok.gov/OSF/
OR   http://www.bam.das.state.or.us/
PA   http://www.budget.state.pa.us/
RI   http://www.budget.ri.gov/
SC   http://www.budget.sc.gov/
SD   http://www.state.sd.us/bfm/
TN   http://www.state.tn.us/finance/bud/budget.html
TX   http://www.lbb.state.tx.us/
UT   http://www.governor.utah.gov/budget/
VA   http://www.dpb.state.va.us/
VT   http://www.state.vt.us/fin/
WA   http://www.ofm.wa.gov/
WI   http://www.doa.state.wi.us
WV   http://www.budget.wv.gov
WY   http://ai.state.wy.us/budget/index.asp

PROVINCES

DC   https://cfo.dc.gov/page/office-budget-and-planning
PR   http://www.agencias.pr.gov/agencias/FederalFunds/Pages/default.aspx
VI   https://dpp.vi.gov/agency/office-management-budget

Appendix 1G

U.S. City Finance/Budget Websites

Akron, OH. http://akronohio.gov/financ.html
Albany, NY. http://www.albanyny.org/Government/MayorsOffice/Budget.aspx
Alexandria, VA. http://alexandriava.gov/Budget
Anchorage, AK. http://www.muni.org/departments/budget/pages/default.aspx
Annapolis, MD. http://www.annapolis.gov/Government/Departments/Finance
 .aspx
Atlanta, GA. http://www.atlantaga.gov/government/finance/budget_091903
 .aspx
Auburn, AL. http://www.auburnalabama.org/budget/Default.aspx?PageID=53
Augusta, ME. http://www.augustamaine.gov/index.asp?Type=B_BASIC&
 SEC={FFE0E59F-5794- 4A67-89C8-D5D5E108464A}
Austin, TX. http://www.ci.austin.tx.us/budget/
Baltimore, MD. http://www.baltimorecity.gov/Government/AgenciesDepart
 ments/Finance.aspx
Baton Rouge, LA. http://brgov.com/dept/finance/default.asp
Biloxi, MS. http://www.dfa.state.ms.us/Offices/OBFM/OBFM.htm
Binghamton, NY. http://www.cityofbinghamton.com/department.asp?zone=
 dept-finance
Birmingham, AL. http://www.informationbirmingham.com/budget.aspx
Bismarck, ND. http://www.bismarck.org/index.aspx?nid=25
Boise, ID. http://www.cityofboise.org/Budget/
Boston, MA. http://www.cityofboston.gov/budget/
Bristol, VA. http://www.bristolva.org/
Brunswick, NJ. http://www.cityofnewbrunswick.org/09site/Government/
 Departments/Finance.html
Carbondale, IL. http://ci.carbondale.il.us/node/68
Carson City, NV. http://www.carson.org/Index.aspx?page=257
Charleston, SC. http://www.charleston-sc.gov/dept/content.aspx?nid=58
Charleston, WV. http://www.cityofcharleston.org/government/city
 -departments/finance
Cheyenne, WY. http://www.cheyennecity.org/index.aspx?NID=113

Chicago, IL. http://www.cityofchicago.org/city/en/depts/obm.html

Cleveland, OH. http://www.city.cleveland.oh.us/CityofCleveland/Home/
Government/CityAgencies/Finan ce/OBM

Colorado Springs, CO. http://www.springsgov.com/SectionIndex.aspx?Sec
tionID=64

Columbia, SC, http://www.columbiasc.net/budget

Columbia, MO, http://www.gocolumbiamo.com/Finance/admin.php

Columbus, OH. http://finance.columbus.gov/

Concord, NH. http://www.ci.concord.nh.us/Finance/OMB/concordv2.asp
?siteindx=H05,22,02

Dallas, TX. http://dallascityhall.com/financial_services/index.html

Denver, CO. http://www.denvergov.org/Default.aspx?alias=www.denvergov
.org/budget

Des Moines, IA. http://www.dmgov.org/Departments/Finance/Pages/default
.aspx

Detroit, MI. http://www.detroitmi.gov/DepartmentsandAgencies/BudgetDepart
ment.aspx

Dover, DE. http://www.cityofdover.com/City-Budget/

Fayetteville, NC. http://www.accessfayetteville.org/government/budget/index
.cfm

Flagstaff, AZ. http://www.flagstaff.az.gov/index.aspx?NID=15

Fort Lauderdale, FL. http://ci.ftlaud.fl.us/finance/rb_faq.htm

Frankfort, KY. http://www.frankfort.ky.gov/finance-department.html

Gary, IN. http://www.gary.in.us/finance/default.asp

Greensboro, NC. http://www.greensboro-nc.gov/index.aspx?page=182

Harrisburg, PA. http://harrisburgpa.gov/

Hartford, CT. http://managementandbudget.hartford.gov/default.aspx

Helena, MT. http://www.ci.helena.mt.us/departments/administrative-services
-finance/budget-studies.html

Honolulu, HA. http://www1.honolulu.gov/budget/

Houston, TX. http://www.houstontx.gov/finance/

Indianapolis, IN. http://www.indy.gov/eGov/City/OFM/Pages/home.aspx

Jackson, MS. http://www.jacksonms.gov/government/administration/budget

Jacksonville, FL. http://www.coj.net/Departments/Finance/Budget.aspx

Jefferson City, MO http://www.jeffcitymo.org/finance/finance.html

Jonesboro, AR. http://www.jonesboro.org/Finance/Finance.html

Juneau, AK. http://www.juneau.org/financeftp/budget.php

Kansas City, KS. http://www.kcmo.org/CKCMO/Depts/CityManagers
Office/Office%20of%20Managemen t% 20and%20Budget/index.htm

Lansing, MI. http://www.lansingmi.gov/finance/budget_office.jsp

Las Vegas, http://www.lasvegasnevada.gov/Government/finance.htm

Lawrence, http://lawrenceks.org/budget
Lexington, http://www.lexingtonky.gov/index.aspx?page=329
Lincoln, NE. http://lincoln.ne.gov/city/finance/budget/index.htm
Little Rock, AR. http://www.littlerock.org/CityDepartments/Finance/
Los Angeles, CA. http://mayor.lacity.org/Issues/BalancedBudget/index.htm
Louisville, KY. http://www.louisvilleky.gov/Finance/
Madison, WI. http://www.cityofmadison.com/finance/
Manhattan, KS. http://www.ci.manhattan.ks.us/index.aspx?NID=6
Memphis, TN. http://www.memphistn.gov/framework.aspx?page=20
Miami, FL. http://www.miamigov.com/budget/pages/index.asp
Milwaukee, WI. http://city.milwaukee.gov/budget
Montgomery, AL. http://www.montgomeryal.gov/index.aspx?page=1365
Montpelier, VT. http://www.montpelier-vt.org/department/80/Finance.html
Nashville, TN. http://www.nashville.gov/finance/omb/index.asp
New Orleans, LA. http://www.nola.gov/BUSINESSES/Department-of-Finance/
New York City, NY. http://www.nyc.gov/html/omb/html/home/home.shtml
Norman, OK. http://www.ci.norman.ok.us/finance/financial-services
Oklahoma City, OK. http://www.okc.gov/finance_tab/index.html
Olympia, WA. http://olympiawa.gov/city-government/budget.aspx
Omaha, NE. http://www.ci.omaha.ne.us/finance/
Philadelphia, PA. http://www.phila.gov/finance/
Phoenix, AZ. http://phoenix.gov/BUDGET/index.html
Pierre, SD. http://ci.pierre.sd.us/Department.aspx?id=3
Portland, ME. http://www.portlandmaine.gov/finance.htm
Providence, RI. http://www.providenceri.com/finance
Raleigh, NC. http://www.raleighnc.gov/home/content/AdminServBudget/Articles/BudgetAndManage mentDivisionPage.html
Reno, NV. http://reno.gov/Index.aspx?page=170
Richmond, VA. http://www.richmondgov.com/Budget/reports.aspx
Sacramento, CA. http://www.cityofsacramento.org/finance/budget/
Salem, OR. http://www.cityofsalem.net/Departments/Budget/Pages/BudgetCommitteeMeetingSchedu leRSS.aspx
Salt Lake City, UT. http://www.slcclassic.com/finance/2011budget/
San Antonio, TX. http://www.sanantonio.gov/budget/
San Diego, CA. http://www.sandicgo.gov/fm/
San Francisco, CA. http://www.sfcontroller.org/index.aspx?page=101
Santa Fe, NM. http://www.santafenm.gov/index.aspx?NID=300
Seattle, WA. http://www.seattle.gov/financedepartment/
Southaven, MS. http://www.southaven.org/index.aspx?nid=128
Springfield, IL. http://www.springfield.il.us/OBM/default.htm

St. Louis, MO. http://stlouis-mo.gov/government/departments/budget/index
.cfm

St. Paul, MN. http://www.stpaul.gov/index.aspx?NID=192

Syracuse, NY. http://www.syracuse.ny.us/Budget_Home_Page.aspx

Tallahassee, FL. http://www.talgov.com/gov/financials.cfm

Tampa, FL. http://www.tampagov.net/dept_Budget/index.asp

Topeka, KS. http://www.topeka.org/administrative/city_budget.shtml

Trenton, NJ. http://www.trentonnj.org/Cit-e-Access/webpage.cfm?TID=
55&TPID=5726

Tucson, AZ. http://cms3.tucsonaz.gov/budget/

Tuscaloosa, AL. http://www.ci.tuscaloosa.al.us/index.aspx?nid=26

Vicksburg, MS. http://www.vicksburg.org/departments/administrative/
accounting

If one of these cites does not function, go to the state's home page. The vast majority of state government internet home pages are: http://www.state.??.us. For
example, the home page for the state of Tennessee is: http://www.tn.us. If you
want to go to another state, just use the two-letter abbreviation for that state.

Chapter 2

Preparing a Budget Proposal

OVERVIEW

Chapter 2 of the book deviates somewhat from the basic budgeting terms, phrases, and practices that you learned in chapter one. In this chapter you will focus on preparing a budget proposal. Preparing a budget proposal and determining if a budget is efficient and effective. On the surface, this may seem to be an easy task. However, budgeting is not as simple as it appears. For instance, at any given time, a state or local government may be working on three separate budgets: the current year, previous year, and the upcoming fiscal year. This process requires the cooperation and efforts of a lot of individuals and agencies, including various groups and individuals that may have completely separate agendas.

The chapter begins by first examining the budget cycle and the various phases that it goes through. This section is followed with an analysis of the individuals involved in the budget process. The chapter ends with a discussion of determining agency needs and writing agency policy statements.

BUDGET CYCLES

Repetition of events essentially drives the *budget cycle*. A budget cycle is a period of time in which the budget has to be prepared and executed. This cycle or system ensures greater accountability for decisions. It also allows decision makers to modify the budget for greater *efficiency* and *effectiveness*. The budget cycle has three phases: executive preparation, legislative approval, and budget execution. However, there is also an audit/evaluation phase that occurs after the execution phase.

Phase 1. *Executive Preparation*: The chief executive of a state or local government is the one person who sets the tone for the policy issues that are addressed during the budget preparation phase. Guidelines are generally prepared by the chief budget/fiscal officer and given to agencies laying out key issues that will be addressed for the upcoming budget year, along with the timetable for submission of the budget. These include items such as policy priorities and proposed new legislation affecting the budget. A good budget should be very comprehensive in describing: anticipated revenues and proposed expenditures; provide accountability for spending; avoid *earmarking funds* which could hinder new priorities; and indicate the purpose for new spending and the desired results (Kittredge and Ouart 2005; Mikesell 2014; Musell 2009. Agencies in turn use this information when preparing their budget requests. In addition to preparing spending requests, agencies that have dedicated funding sources, such as federal grants, licenses and permits, and charges for services, provide estimates of revenue for the forthcoming budget year in their submission.

These requests are then forwarded to the chief executive's budget office to be reviewed and analyzed. Often, hearings will be held with the agency to clarify the budget request. The chief budget/fiscal office is responsible for the preparation of revenue estimates, particularly for the General Fund. In analyzing the requests, the revenue that will be available is a key factor during the internal budget deliberations. More often than not, the sum total of the budget requests for the General Fund exceeds the available revenue. As a result, decisions have to be made regarding the amount that will appear in the budget submission for each agency. It is not uncommon for department heads to be upset with the final recommendation. Some will try to get more money by lobbying the legislature/council, or will use special interest groups for that purpose.

Many state and local governments are legally bound to have a balanced budget pursuant to state law, local charter, or ordinance. The problem with most balanced-budget legislation is that it does not specify what "balanced" means. Usually, it is on the budget basis, which is most often cash. A cash budget can be manipulated by simply not paying bills at the end of the year. If the budget has to be balanced based on a modified accrual basis, then more discipline is added to the process since liabilities cannot simply be passed on into the future. Some balanced budget laws state that revenues have to equal expenditures (without stating the basis that is to be used). This means that available balances are not able to be used to fund a deficit.

Once the requests have been received and analyzed, they are assembled into a single document. The budget is then submitted to the legislative body and also released to the public. Some governments prepare a budget-in-brief, which is intended for the citizens. It contains summaries of the requests along with an explanation as to what will be accomplished during the upcoming year.

Phase 2. *Legislative Approval*: Similar to other legislation, a legislative body has to approve the budget. The chief executive forwards the budget to the legislative body and when it approves the document, it has the force of the law. This process seems very simple, but in reality it is not. Negotiations between the executive and members of the legislature or city council are very common. In some cases, these negotiations can be very stressful given partisan differences. Party politics plays a smaller role at the local level when compared to the federal and state governments (Lynch, Sun, and Smith 2017; Musell 2009).

For every state except Nebraska (which only has one house), the budget is submitted to the lower house, similar to the process used by the federal government. The Finance Committee is in charge overall. However, other committees are involved. For example, the Transportation Committee hears the request for the Department of Transportation. After they conclude the hearing, the recommendation is forwarded to the Finance Committee. During the course of the hearings, many parties comment on the request. The department head provides an overview of the request. Public interest groups offer their comments as well. Most states have legislative budget offices that provide projections independent of the executive, which are used by the legislature in formulating the appropriations. Once the lower house completes its hearing, they vote on the measure. It is then sent to the upper house (Senate), and the process starts all over again. Once the upper house completes its process, more often than not changes are made from the version passed by the lower house. As a result, a conference committee is formed with representatives from both houses. The responsibility of the conference committee is to come up with a single appropriation act that is acceptable to both houses. Although it is desirable to have the budget passed before the start of the next fiscal year, it often does not pass quickly because of political differences. In that case, a *continuing resolution* is passed, so that government can operate while the problems are worked out. Eventually, an appropriation act is passed and sent to the governor for signature. Many governors have the ability to use a line-item veto, by which specific appropriations can be vetoed. The legislative body has the ability to override the veto if it can muster the necessary votes.

The process is much simpler in local governments. The legislative body is the council, board, or commission. The executive branch still presents information regarding the request. The public and special interest groups still have the ability to testify and offer ideas. Eventually, an appropriation ordinance is passed and signed by the chief executive officer. Many local governments have charter or ordinance provisions that require the budget to be enacted before the start of the fiscal year.

Phase 3. *Budget Execution*: At the beginning of the fiscal year, agencies carry out or execute their approved budgets. Spending is monitored by the agencies and the executive budget office in order to ensure that appropriations are not overspent. This is usually done through the use of accounting software that is designed to ensure that spending is within the authorized amounts or allotments. This process helps to ensure that agencies do not spend all of their funds in the first month or quarter of the fiscal year (Musell 2009). Monthly, quarterly, and midyear budget reports are issued so that comparisons can be made between appropriations, actual revenue received, revenue projections, and actual expenditures (See appendix 2D for an example). If revenue projections are off the target, modifications should be made to ensure that the budget is balanced. Budget shortfalls can cause serious operating and personnel problems for agency heads (Lynch et al. 2017; Nice 2002). Many state and local governments have legislation that requires the chief executive officer to take action to reduce spending if revenue projections are not met.

Most states and large local governments use an allotment process to help control the budget. At the start of the year, each agency is required to allot the annual appropriation by quarter. This, in effect, means that agencies are managing quarterly budgets. Another budget control tool is the *encumbrance*. When an agency enters into a contract or purchase order, an encumbrance is established setting aside that amount so that when the goods and services are received, funds are available to pay the expenses.

Audit/Evaluation Phase: The purpose of this phase is to determine if the budget was executed and implemented by the bureaucracy in the manner that was set forth in the legislation (Mikesell 2014; Musell 2009; Nice 2002). That is, does the approved budget and actual budget match up? An audit occurs after the fiscal year has ended and can be done internally or externally. Individuals working within the agency conduct *internal audits*, and *external audits* are done by paid professionals outside of the organization. Audits vary according to the type of budget that is used by agencies. Generally speaking, there are two types: financial and performance. A *financial audit* checks to ensure that an agency's financial statements fall within the principles of Generally Accepted Accounting Principles (GAAP) and gauge whether an agency has followed the laws and statutes regulating its spending.

A *performance audit* concentrates its efforts on efficiency and effectiveness, by examining procurement, duplication, utilization of staff, legal compliance and measuring and reporting performance (Lee, Johnson, and Joyce 2013; Lynch et al. 2017; Solano 2004). Basically, what was accomplished with the funds that were spent? There are two types of performance audits: economy and efficiency, and program audits. *Economy and efficiency audits* determine whether the governmental unit is acquiring, protecting, and using its resources economically and efficiently and whether it has complied with laws and regulations on matters of economy and efficiency. *Program audits* determine the extent to which desired results are being achieved and whether there are related compliance issues. There are also *single audits* that concentrate more closely on the expenditure of grant resources than do other types of audits. A single audit is required by the federal government for all state and local governments that have $500,000 or more in federal grant awards and requires auditors to test to see if grant provisions are being followed.

David B. Pariser and Richard C. Brooks (1997) highlight some generally accepted government auditing standards that administrators should have in place as a follow up to determine the effectiveness of the audit. That is, were the recommendations followed and did they achieve desirable results? They suggest that the following bulleted items should be included in an audit recommendation follow up system (337).

• Firm policy basis for following up on audit recommendations.
• Organizational commitment to implementation.
• Evaluation of recommendations including budgetary and organizational impact.
• Clear assignment of follow up responsibilities.
• Preparation of corrective plans.
• Special attention to key recommendations.
• Periodic review to evaluate the adequacy of actions taken on recommendations.
• Preparation and distribution of periodic status reports.
• Use of status reports for oversight and management evaluations.

Further, management should be fully committed to implementing the suggestions from the audit and this should be evidenced by formal policies or a procedures manual that describes the details of the audit recommendation follow up system as well as securing individuals to be responsible for implementing the recommendations.[1]

THE BUDGET CALENDAR

Since state and local governments work around a fiscal year, budget approval has to occur prior to the beginning of the fiscal year. The beginning of the budget cycle differs for most states and cities. For forty-six states, the fiscal year begins on July 1st and ends on June 30th. Exhibit 2.1 provides a summary of the various budget periods.

Exhibit 2.1. Budget Fiscal Years	
Government	*Fiscal Year Beginning*
U.S. Federal Government	October 1–September 30
46 States	July 1–June 30
2 States	October 1–September 30
1 State	September 1–August 31
1 State	April 1–March 31
Local Governments	Variously January, July, September, October

Source: John L. Mikesell (2018), *Fiscal Administration: Analysis and Applications for the Public Sector*, 10th ed. (Boston: Wadsworth Cengage Learning).

Many local governments begin the fiscal year in January, July, September and October. The federal fiscal year is October 1st through September 30th.

Exhibit 2.2 shows the budget time frame for Jefferson City. Although the fiscal year (FY) 2021 begins on July 1, 2020 for the city, the process began officially on March 12, 2020. At this point, the city makes the final adjustments to close out the FY 20 budget while they are in the FY 21 budget season. So, they are in affect managing three budgets simultaneously. By establishing exact dates and times for forms and meetings, it brings a lot of order to the process. Unless something out of the ordinary occurs, agency personnel and elected officials tend to stick to the set times frames.

Exhibit 2.2.   Jefferson City Budget Timetable FY 2021
(1) March 12, 2020, Audit & Finance Committee meets to finalize time table with agencies and departments on budget request.
(2) March 13, 2020, Send out notices to agency heads that deadline to submit appropriation request will be Friday, March 31st.
(3) March 30, 2020, Deadline for Agencies, Boards and Commissions to submit budget proposals to CAO for copying for elected officials.
(4) April 9, 2020, A&F Committee Meeting. Preliminary revenue Projection and summary spreadsheets of requested expenses submitted to Mayor and Audit and Finance Committee from CAO and Financial Director.
(5) April 16–20, 2020, Agency and Department Appropriation Hearings before Audit and Finance Committee.
April 16th (Monday): Agencies-7:00 to 10:00 a.m. April 18th (Wednesday): Agencies-7:00 to 10:00 a.m. April 20th (Friday): Departments-6:00 to 10:00 p.m. Public Works-6:00 to 7:00 p.m. Police Dept.-7:00 to 8:00 p.m. Fire Dept.-8:00 to 9:00 p.m. Administration Dept.-9:00 to 10:00 p.m.

(6) April 23, 2020, A & F Committee Meeting. Final revenue Projections submitted to Mayor and Audit & Finance Committee. Mayor and Committee discuss budgetary emphasis and priorities, and agree on strategy to handle revenue shortfalls, request overruns, etc.

(7) May 7, 2020, MRA/LGEAF Budget Hearings held as required by state law.

(8) May 21, 2020, Mayor's Budget and Budget Message presented to Council. Mayor usually delivers his proposed budget at a special called meeting late in the month.

(9) June 4, 2020, First Reading of the FY 21 Budget Ordinance.

(10) June 18, 2020, Second Reading of FY 21 Budget Ordinance.

(11) June 20–30, 2020, Publication of FY 21 Budget Ordinance.

THE BUDGET GAME

Making budgeting decisions can be a very complicated process given the number of individuals involved and their ideas and goals. In an executive budgeting system, the chief executive plays the major role in the budgeting process. That is, he/she initiates the process. However, there are a number of others involved in the process as well, including the budget office, legislature, and agency directors. In addition, there are some non-governmental actors that can play a role in the process such as interests groups and individuals (Rubin 2010). All governments however do not use an executive budgeting system.

County governments tend to have administrators, auditors, or someone in the legislative branch prepare the budget. Some states have legislative budget offices that expend enormous amounts of energy and paperwork on the budget

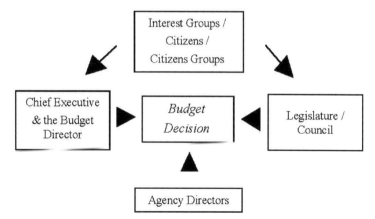

Figure 2.1. Actors and Budget Decisions

(Lee et al. 2013). Under normal circumstances, the word game and government would not go together. These two terms tend to go hand in hand at the state level and in very large cities when it comes to devising the budget.

Budgeting is a bit more bureaucratic in smaller governments. However, when one considers the entire decision making process, it does display some of the same characteristics of a game. Players/decision makers use strategy and sometime they win and sometime they do not. Policy makers render decisions that are good and bad for certain individuals and agencies. Figure 2.1 illustrates the four main actors involved in the process as well nongovernmental actors (Bland and Rubin 1997; Lynch et al. 2017; Mikesell 2018; Rubin 2006).

BUDGET ACTORS

(1) *Chief Executive.* The chief executive is the only person responsible for the entire institution of a particular governmental entity. As a result, executives try to ensure that spending is done as harmoniously as possible in order to satisfy the greatest number of individuals and agencies. The executive, via the *budget director*, initiates the budgeting process and is responsible for sending letters to the various agencies informing them of important dates and deadlines for information.[2] Although the chief executive may appoint agency heads, this relationship may not be as friendly as it appears. The executive has the option of saying no, and does so frequently. You must also consider the role of interests groups, citizens, and citizen groups. Mayors, governors as well as legislators and councilmen are frequently bombarded with requests that may impact budget decisions. Given the nature of their position, they cannot ignore the existences of these external groups and the potential impact that they could have on their electoral fortunes.

In sum, the chief executive works hand in hand with the budget director to put the initial budget together. Then, it is the responsibility of the legislative body to decide the final spending patterns and enact the appropriations. Last, the chief executive carries out the mandates of the legislative branch.

(2) *Budget Director.* The budget director runs the budget office for the chief executive. This office is the center for the city or state's budget processing. Budget requests are generally sent to the budget office rather than directly to the executive. Once this office receives all of the requests, it goes about balancing expenditures against expected revenues. This effort can be eased when the executive informs the agencies of expected increases or decreases in revenue prior to their submitting budget requests. However, budget projections are not finalized until the last possible moment. Given the constraints of limited revenues, the budget office must ensure that items

of high priority, as deemed by the chief executive and legislative body, be provided for. However, this process can cause a lot of friction between the budget office and the agency directors. Although there are many different reasons why an agency may be denied funding for some program, common reasons would include the following: (1) Items were not adequately justified; (2) The money is not available; (3) Items do not fit the goals and objectives of the agency; and (4) Items are not in harmony with the executive's priorities (Bland and Rubin 1997; Kittredge and Ouart 2005; Lynch et al. 2017; Mikesell 2018).

(3) *Legislators/Councilmembers.* This group of persons is responsible for approving the budget. They are always looking for an opportunity to bring in programs and projects that will benefit their constituents. Most legislators/councilmembers do not have a good grasp of the budget process from a micro perspective. This is not necessarily a bad thing given their role in the budget process. They are often given dense information with little time to react to it. As a result, they tend to center their efforts on their individual pet projects. Legislators on powerful committees and party leaders can use their influence to secure pet projects a lot easier than less senior legislators. Unlike the chief executive, the decisions made by legislators and councilmembers are more likely to be impacted by interest groups, citizens, and citizen groups.

(4) *Agency Directors.* Agency directors head the various departments within the *bureaucracy*. These departments provide the services that affect the well-being of the citizens. Since their efforts gravitate towards the individuals that they serve and the agency's goals and objectives, agency directors are constantly defending their budget requests from both a technical and political perspective. However, it is not clear as to whether all agency directors engage in a *budget maximizing strategy* (Lynch et al. 2017; Sigelman 1986; Wildavsky and Caiden 2004). That is, do they ask for the greatest increase in their budget as possible? However, it is clear that agency directors attempt to maintain the existence of their agency. They do this by maintaining a good relationship with legislators and the chief executive. Particularly, they need proponents in the legislature or the city council that will defend them in times of severe budget cuts. Irene S. Rubin (2006) points out, agency directors often engage in strategies to improve budget passage. First, they may instill a sense of urgency. That is, if the request is not funded then x, y, and z might occur. Second, they may indicate how the request may be cost efficient and effective and thus save money over time. Third, the agency head may ensure that the chief executive or key legislators/councilmen are getting their individual demands met in the request.

As an agency head making a request, it is very important that you articulate the needs of the agency in a manner that is clear and understandable to those who can control your budget. Therefore, you must connect the goal and objectives of your proposal to the needs of citizens and desires of politicians. These goals and objectives must also coincide with easy to understand performance measures that you must include in your proposal.

AGENCY ROLES EXPANDED

While requesting budget statements from an agency, the budget office project revenue collections for the upcoming year based on available data (previous tax collections, inflation, interest rates, population movement, etc.). This increase (or decrease) is compared with the *baseline* for agencies to continue at their current rate and the new demands brought on by new legislation and priorities that have been set by the chief executive. If there are gaps between expected revenues and expenditures, the chief executive (first line) and the legislative body (second line) have to decide where cuts should be made to compensate for the disparity.

In most cases, budget requests are denied rather than raise taxes. As a result, each agency has to essentially defend its budget in a formal hearing. In preparing for a hearing, each agency should submit to the budget office a narrative explaining the purpose, goals and objectives of the agency, a budget request, and a detailed explanation justifying new requests. This would include items such as a request for a new employee. It is much easier for an agency to defend spending new monies when they can show that it fits the goals of the agency, the mission of the chief executive, and the priorities set by new legislation. If an agency cannot elaborate in detail why it needs to expand a program or hire a new employee, it will be extremely difficult for that agency to receive new funding during a period of *budget constraint*. A request for spending is not limited to one occasion. An agency may request additional funding during the course of the fiscal year (Lynch et al. 2017; Mikesell 2018; Solano 2004).

JUSTIFYING AND DEFENDING THE BUDGET

Ideally, the best news for an agency is to find out that their entire budget was approved. Unfortunately, agencies frequently find that the chief executive and the legislative body demand more services with less money. Rarely is a budget completely funded without some changes. As a result, it is imperative that agency heads are completely prepared to justify their budgets. If they are not prepared, they may quickly find the agency on the short end of the revenue stream. Hence, agency heads must know how to sell their budget.

The phrases *political budget* and *technical budget* are two methods that characterize the process. Generally speaking, all budgets are political in nature given that government is political. However, some budget processes are more political than others. Likewise, all budgets should be technical in nature. That is, contain budgetary facts. However, the stance used to sell the budget can vary. A description of political and technical budgets is explained below.

POLITICAL BUDGETS

An agency director who uses a political budget strategy plays the political game. Rather than concentrate on the numbers, they use other slight-of-hand tricks in an effort to out-maneuver the politicians. Aaron Wildavsky (1979), Roy T. Meyers (1999), Jacqueline H. Rogers and Marita B. Brown (1999), and Wildavsky and Naomi Caiden (2004) offer several *budget maximizing strategies* that an agency director may employ. Using these methods are not sure fire methods to selling your budget. Policy makers are not ignorant of these "tricks."

- Cultivate a clientele in the legislative and executive branch.
- Serve a specific clientele and encourage them to contact their elected officials and sing your praises.
- Build confidence in your agency by not covering up bad deeds.
- Cut or eliminate programs that are popular with complete knowledge that they will be reinstated.
- Shift the blame of cutting the program onto the policy maker.
- Combine new programs with old programs so that they do not appear as new programs.
- Argue that new programs are modified old programs.
- Lower the budget levels for new programs with the assumption that you will get more funds later.
- Maintain your baseline and use the funds for other purposes.
- Argue that some of your expenditures are short term.
- Study the political scene and use crisis to expand or create new services.
- Show how expenditures will save money later.
- Show how a program will pay for itself in user charges.
- Use workload data to build up the budget base.

Again, there are no guarantees that these or any other strategies will work. Agency directors should assess the political environment and proceed from there. If revenues increase, it may be easier to use the technical strategies. In some cases, legislators and executives may take it upon themselves to cut or limit agency programs despite the efforts of the agency director. In some cases, they may simply cut a program. This is particularly true when resources are limited. In fact, legislators and council members may quickly find that their pet projects will disappear. It is a lot easier to cut a program that is utilized by one district rather than the entire jurisdiction (Meyers 1999; Mikesell 2018; Swain and Reed 2010).

TECHNICAL BUDGETS

A technical budget concentrates on the numbers or budgetary facts. Expenditures can be split into two categories: mandatory and discretionary spending. A baseline (Base) is a technique that can be used in both categories.

Mandatory expenditures are reflected in state and local law. That is, the agency is legally required to conduct the service. These expenditures include: salaries, Federal Insurance Contributors Act (FICA), pensions/retirement, unemployment compensation, and any other legal obligations. While there are always questions surrounding how many employees are actually needed to provide services, eliminating an employee or cutting the personnel budget is the last thing that a politician wants to do. Under normal circumstances, elected officials honor mandatory spending.

Discretionary spending constitutes the smallest part of the overall budget. These funds often only represent increases in the budget and are sought by everyone. While not necessary for the general operation of the agency, these funds will allow the agency to expand services and operate more efficiently and effectively. Due to limited funding, agency heads should put a lot of effort into justifying spending. Data indicating population shifts, economic up swings, legal requirements are all useful in justifying new positions and an expansion in services (see also Lee et al. 2013; LeLoup 1977).

Base expenditures are expenditures that an agency needs to maintain the same level of services from the current fiscal year. This includes operating expense items such as office supplies, printing, equipment, utilities, vehicles, tools, and other related items. Agency directors can justify these items using the previous year's budget, the current year's budget, ongoing projects, or projects for the upcoming year. In any case, the director should be able to justify the request given any change in the amount of the request. This would include an increase or decrease in any part of the budget. By highlighting productivity, a budget is much less likely to be cut.

KEY COMPONENTS OF THE BUDGET PROPOSAL

The budget proposal has several key components and the agency staff must be prepared to defend every portion of the budget. Below is a short description of the key parts of the budget proposal.

(a) *Project Title*: Believe it or not, a name does matter. One should spend a few minutes thinking about the label that captures the essence of their project. The title of the project should capture the interest of the reader as well as offer a very brief description of the project in five or fewer words. For example: Working Together to End Homelessness.

(b) *Description and Rationale*: This section of the budget is the beginning and the end to the success of your budget. It should describe what you are trying to accomplish and why it is needed in as few words as possible. For example, a rationale could be as simple as saying: We need a homeless shelter because the number of homeless people has increased by 50% since the electrical plant closed and the city wants to increase and expand employment opportunities.

(c) *Objective Justifying the Need*: Objectives emanate from the description and the rationale. Objectives related to the homeless theme could include:

- The city wants to improve tourism in the downtown area. Therefore, we must eliminate people sleeping on benches, in alley ways and in front of businesses.
- The city can provide educational and job training and/or retraining at the homeless shelter.
- Statistics show that a fair number of homeless people are engaged in illegal activity in the downtown area. Hence, we can reduce the crime rate as well as pan handling.

(d) *Budget and Budget Description*: The budget as a set of numbers is fairly straight forward, but the description, should be direct. That is, briefly describe who or what you need in order to accomplish your goals. For example, it is reasonable in the example above to expect that someone has to manage the homeless shelter, provide training and educational materials. Thus, you will need staff as well as computers, desks, printers, etc. to manage the facility. So, these persons and items should be highlighted in the description.

(e) *Measures of Success*: This is also a critical part of the budget proposal. The measures of success must be tied to the theme and objectives provided in the previous sections of the budget. For example, measurement for our homeless theme could be:

- We expect to lower the number of people sleeping on benches in the downtown area by 50 percent during the first year.
- We expect to train and find jobs for fifty people during the first year of operation.
- We will provide housing in a safe environment for one hundred men and women in the first year of operation.
- We will seek external funding to enhance our budget.

Councilmen and legislators are looking for a reason to deny your budget, particularly during periods of revenue shortfalls. So, you should make sure that your budget proposal is clear, concise, and answers more questions than it raises to the reader. See appendix 2A for an example of a budget proposal.

CONCLUSION

By now the reader should have concluded that preparing a budget is an arduous task as well as ensuring that it is defensible. While there are time frames established to make the process logistically more efficient and effective, any number of problems may come up along the way. In fact, establishing the time frames may be the easiest part of the process. Unfortunately, budget decisions are not always technical in nature. Budget games are real and are played throughout the fiscal year. If an agency wants to achieve the most for the organization, the wise decision is to be completely prepared to argue for the political or technical budget. In addition, one must be prepared to provide data indicating that programs and services are achieving their intended purpose.

IMPORTANT TERMS AND PHRASES

Audit
Baseline/Base Expenditures
Budget Calendar
Budget Cycle
Budget Director
Budget Execution
Budget Game
Budget Maximizing Strategy
Bureaucracy
Chief Executive
Discretionary Spending
Earmarking Funds
Economy and Efficiency Audits
Efficiency
Effectiveness

Encumbrance
Evaluation
Executive Preparation
External Audit
Financial Audit
Hearings
Internal Audit Budget
Legislative Approval
Mandatory Spending/Expenditure
Performance Audit
Political Budget
Program Audit
Single Audit
Stakeholders
Technical Budget

CHAPTER 2 HOMEWORK EXERCISE

(1) The legislative body of the city is preparing to discuss the budget for the
various departments. Below is a copy of the performance budget for the
Jefferson City Recycling Division in the Sanitation Department. Based
on the data in the budget, has the division been successful in achieving an
efficient and effective operation since its inception in FY 2018? Explain
your response.

Recycle Division Budget	
FY 2018	$1,500,000
FY 2019	$2,000,000
FY 2020 (est)	$2,200,000
FY 2021 (proj)	$2,200,000
FY 2022 (proj)	$2,500,000

Recycle Division Performance Measures (in tons)					
	FY 2018	*FY 2019*	*FY 2020*	*FY 2021*	*FY 2022*
Plastic	2	4	5	5	4
Cardboard	5	7	8	9	8
Glass	7	8	7	4	3
Metal	10	11	13	15	20

(2) Directions: Please read the entire assignment prior to beginning the assignment. You will need an electronic copy of the Original Agency Budget Proposal Request Form in order to complete this assignment. Should
your instructor choose to use the assignment in class, you will also need
a Revised Agency Budget Proposal Request Form and several sheets
from a city or state budget, and the Evaluation in order to complete this
assignment. You are free to expand the length of your proposal, but it
should not be longer than three pages. See appendix 2A for an example
of a budget proposal.

Step One: Outside of Class Homework

First, each student should obtain a line item or a program budget for an
agency/department, within a city, using the internet or by going to a local city
and requesting a hard copy of the budget (see appendix 1F and 1 G in chapter

1). After you locate the budget, select an agency/department that you feel comfortable writing a budget proposal for a new activity or function. Make a copy of the first two pages of the agency/department budget and turn it in with the rest of your assignment.

Second, using the *Original Budget Proposal Request Form*, in appendix 2B, which follows the same format as the example in appendix 2A, determine how you (the Agency Director) can improve that agency/department by adding a new activity or function to the agency. For example, you could create a new Child Care Program within the Department of Human Services for the City of Jonesboro.

After you decide whether to add a new program or function to the agency/department, you should type your responses on the *Original Budget Proposal Request Form* using a word processing program. Remember, your job is to convince others that you have a good idea. So, sell the idea. You are limited to a maximum of $400,000 in your initial request.

Should your instructor decide to use the assignment in class, you will need to make additional copies of your proposal for use in class. In addition, you will need a blank copy of your proposal, which will be used to make changes to the original document.

Provide your instructor with a copy of the pertinent sections from the city or state budget that you retrieved, a copy of your Original Proposal Budget Request Form and your Revised Budget Proposal Request Form from the in-class portion of the assignment.

Again, if you are not completing the in-class portion of the assignment, you only need the Original Budget Proposal Request Form and the sections from the budget that you are adding to.

Step Two: In Class Games

As pointed out earlier, there are four main individuals/groups involved in the budget process. Hence, the class should be split into groups of four or five. If someone is left out, he or she can be assigned the role of a council member and added to any particular group. Each person in the group will defend his or her budget request from the role of agency head while the remaining group members will assume the other roles. Given what has been stated about each one of these actors in the text book, decide whether to approve each budget request.

The blank *Revised Budget Proposal Request Form* should be used to make notes of any changes requested by your group members (See appendix 2B). The original unmarked and revised budget request form should be turned in to the instructor at the close of class. Each agency director has a maximum of ten minutes to defend his or her budget request to the group and ten minutes to answer questions after the other actors have reviewed the budget request. When the time limit has expired, the three or four members in your group will vote yea or nay to approving the budget based on the quality of the budget and the quality of the responses to the questions. Your grade is not determined by whether or not your budget is approved by your group, but by the quality of your work.[3]

Step Three: Selection of the Best Proposal

Each group should choose one budget that was "the best." This budget should be briefly presented to the entire class. If time allows, one or more budgets can be discussed.

Step Four: In Class Evaluation

When you have finished discussing each of the budgets in your group, complete the *evaluation form* (See appendix 2C).

Step Five: Completed Assignment

Give your instructor the following items:

(1) Original Budget Proposal Request Form (Do not write corrections on this form).
(2) Revised Budget Proposal Request Form (Only include the items that you changed).
(3) Evaluation (Completed).
(4) The Budget sheets that you used to create your new program.

NOTES

1. See Robert L. Bland and Irene S. Rubin (1997), *Budgeting: A Guide for Local Governments* (Washington, DC: ICMA); Thomas D. Lynch, Jinping Sun, and Robert W. Smith (2017), *Public Budgeting in America*, 6th ed. (Irvine, CA: Melvin & Leigh); Jacqueline H. Rogers and Marita B. Brown (1999), "Preparing Agency Budgets," in *Handbook of Government Budgeting*, ed. Roy T. Meyers (San Francisco: Jossey Bass), 441–501; and Paul L. Solano (2004), "Budgeting," in *Management Policies in Local Government Finance*, 5th ed., ed. J. Richard Aronson and Eli Schwartz (Washington, DC: ICMA), 155–206, for additional information on budget cycles.

2. The director (and staff) issues the guidelines, reviews requests, formulates revenue projections, and provides written analysis to the chief executive. The budget director attends the budget hearings.

3. Note: All of the parties are not necessarily involved at the same time. The first thing the agency head has to do is sell the chief executive on the budget via the budget director. If you are unsuccessful at that stage, your idea is not likely to succeed. The agency head could *back door* the request by lobbying the legislator, but that might get the agency head fired. The legislator is not involved until the budget gets to him/her. That is, when the outside parties are also involved.

Appendix 2A

Budget Proposal

Agency Name: Jefferson City Sanitation Department
Proposal Name: Recycling Program
Submitted By: Kendal Lowrey
Date: June 7, 2019

Year	Total	General Fund	Federal Funds	State Funds	Recycling Funds
FY 2020	$850,000	$500,000	$100,000	$50,000	$200,000
FY 2021	$355,000	$0	$0	$0	$355,000
FY 2022	$262,000	$0	$0	$0	$262,000
FY 2023	$267,000	$0	$0	$0	$267,000

Introductory Summary: The Sanitation Department will start a new recycling program that will service the entire city beginning in August, 2018.

Statement of Need: The state passed a law in 2019 requiring all cities to institute a recycling program no later than fiscal year 2021. They also provided a one-time allotment of $50,000 to begin the process. In addition, we can apply for $100,000 in federal funds for our start-up costs. The city would need to allocate $500,000 towards the project. Jefferson City has 100,000 residents that generate tons of recyclable materials each month. Much of this material has value in the business sector. More specifically, our pilot study indicates that we generate four tons of glass, two tons of plastic, six tons of cardboard, and ten tons of aluminum and other metals each month. We estimated that we would be able to extend the life of the landfill by ten years if we recycled each of the aforementioned items. In ten years, we estimate that the recycle department will be able to fund its operation from the sale of the recycled materials.

Program Description: The program will use existing trash trucks to pick up the recycled materials in the designated trash bags that the city will provide.

In addition, the Sanitation Department will need to purchase equipment that cost $600k to compress the metal and the recycle the glass. The pickup schedule will run concurrently with the trash days. Since, we are creating less waste for the landfill, we will only need to hire two more staff to manage this new program. Other staff will be moved from landfill operations.

Benefits: The city will benefit as well as the environment. Ultimately the city will save money in the long run because we will extend the life of the current landfill. In addition, the division will be in the black during the first year given the sale of the recycled material. In addition, we will contribute less waste to our environment and essentially promote a healthy environment for all of the residents of Jefferson City. Last, the city will be in compliance with state law.

Performance Measures: The program will reduce the amount of paper, glass, aluminum and plastic in our environment. The program will extend the life of the landfill. The program will save money over time and operate more efficiently and effectively.

Recycled Material	FY 2020	FY 2021	FY 2022	FY 2023
Paper	30 tons	32.5 tons	40.5 tons	45 tons
Plastic	20 tons	25 tons	32.5 tons	35 tons
Aluminum	15 tons	17.5 tons	20 tons	22.5 tons
Glass	20 tons	21 tons	23.5 tons	24 tons

Costs: The total cost for the program is $850,000 in year one with a $150,000 allocation from the state and federal government. In the first fiscal year (20) we will purchase a machine to compress the metal and glass. In FY 2021, we will purchase a machine that wraps the cardboard and plastic and compresses it. The remaining increases in the budget will cover the cost of increased wear and tear on the equipment.

Staffing Impact: We will use $225,000 of the budget to fund two full time employees and their benefits. We will use existing employees for the other services.

Equipment: In fiscal years 2020 and 2021, we will purchase trash compactors to compress the recycled material. No other equipment is needed for the foreseeable future.

Options: We do not have the option to not create a recycling program as it is a state requirement. However, we can institute the program by recycling one of the items in the first fiscal year and add a new item each fiscal year thereafter.

Budget Allocations:

	FY 2020	FY 2021	FY 2022	FY 2023
New Personnel	$225,000	$230,000	$237,000	$242,000
Equipment	600,000	100,000		
Supplies	25,000	25,000	25,000	25,000
Capital Outlay	0	0	0	0
TOTAL	$850,000	$355,000	$262,000	$267,000

Accompanying Legislation: State Mandate, HB 4239.

Appendix 2B
Original Budget Proposal Request Form

Agency Name:

Proposal Name:

Submitted By:

Date:

Budget:

Introductory Summary:

Statement of Need:

Program Description:

Benefits:

Performance Measures:

Costs:

Staffing Impact:

Equipment:

Options:

Budget Allocations:

Accompanying Legislation:

Appendix 2C

Evaluation of the Role Playing Assignment

Name:

Date:

(1) After playing the role(s) of various budgeting officials on several proposals, do you feel that government priorities were maintained while approving the agency requests? Briefly explain your opinion.

(2) Are you satisfied with the outcome of your proposal? Why? Why not? What could you have done to improve the success of your proposal?

(3) Which of the four actors appear to play the greatest role in determining the outcome of a budget proposal in your opinion? Why?

Appendix 2D

Jefferson City Budget, FY 2020–2021

Jefferson City				
FY 2020–2021	Estimated Revenue	Year to Date Actual Revenue	Uncollected Balance	Uncollected Percent
GENERAL FUND				
Tax Revenue-City Portion	$1,780,000	$1,649,781.71	$130,218.29	7.32%
Auto Property Tax	225,000	161,377.07	63,622.93	28.28%
Prop. Tax Int & Penalty	10,000	13,171.73	<3171.73>	–31.72%
Prop. Tax Int/ Penalty Prior	90,000	7,831.06	82,168.94	91.30%
Auto Tax (State)	—	3,576.97	<3576.97>	
Prop Tax Delinq 96 Prior	—	36,560.21	<36560.21>	
Prop Tax Delinquency 97	—	238,490.52	<238490.52>	
Property Taxes (State)	35,000	35,920.50	<920.5>	–2.63%
Payment in Lieu of Taxes	68,000	28,589.12	39,410.88	57.96%
Bank Deposits Tax	90,000	100,863.58	<10863.58>	–12.07%
Tobacco Tax	—	6.02	<6.02>	
Payroll Tax	6,225,000	4,693,517.87	1,531,482.13	24.60%
Payroll Tax Penalty	6,000	11,631.66	<5631.66>	–93.86%
Business Licenses	600,000	43,612.99	556,387.01	92.73%

(continued)

Appendix 2D

FY 2020–2021	Estimated Revenue	Year to Date Actual Revenue	Uncollected Balance	Uncollected Percent
Business Lic. Penalty& Int	—	3,711.08	<3711.08>	
INS Premium License Tax	1,575,000	1,186,939.63	388,060.37	24.64%
Liquor and Beer Licenses	19,000	1,693.75	17,306.25	91.09%
Cable TV Franchise	150,000	95,538.35	54,461.65	36.31%
Franchise Tax	65,000	103.24	64,896.76	99.84%
Court Revenue	125,000	93,696.78	31,303.22	25.04%
Severance Tax	25,000	24,374.24	625.76	2.50%
Insurance Payroll DED	—	—	—	
Investment Interest	325,000	250,744.95	74,255.05	22.85%
Rent Income	3,000	2,250.00	750.00	25.00%
Misc Inc Used Veh/Equip Sale	15,000	17,950.66	<2950.66>	–19.67%
Misc-Income Police CT Sale	—	—	—	
Building Permit Fees	60,000	59,960.02	—	0.07%
FEMA Flood Reimbursement	—	12,690.00	<12690>	
Miscellaneous Income	25,000	20,091.96	4,908.04	19.63%
DARE Program Reimbursement	17,000	21,026.30	<4026.30>	–23.68%
HWY Safety Program Reimbur.	35,000.00	14,743.25	20,256.75	57.88%
Building Demo Reimbursement	10,000	—	10,000.00	100.00%
Housing Authority Grant	33,000	24,099.02	8,900.98	26.97%
Stadium Prop Sale	9,000	—	9,000.00	100.00%

FY 2020–2021	Estimated Revenue	Year to Date Actual Revenue	Uncollected Balance	Uncollected Percent
Circuit Court Clerk Fees	4,000	3,890.00	110.00	2.75%
Police Department	8,000	5,679.20	2,320.80	29.01%
Animal Control License Fee	20,000	—	20,000.00	100.00%
Parking Meters	—	—	—	
SUBTOTAL General Fund Net	$11,652,000	$8,864,113.44	$3,110,445.81	
SUBTOTAL GENERAL Fund Prior YR	$820,179	$—	$820,179.00	
TOTAL General Revenue Fund	$12,472,179	$8,864,113.44	$3,930,624.81	

Source: Created by the Author.

Chapter 3

Personnel Services and Operating Budgets

OVERVIEW

Typically, a budget has three main components: personnel services, operating and capital outlay expenditures. The purpose of this chapter is to introduce the reader to the components of a standard personnel services and operating budget. Specifically, the chapter provides information on: writing the budget, justifying new positions, position classifications, pay ranges, and calculating benefits for different types of employees. The chapter also discusses calculating Social Security contributions (Federal Insurance Contributors Act, also known as FICA), Medicare contributions, and pension benefits. Lastly, the chapter considers the different formats, advantages, and disadvantages of an operating budget. Capital outlays are discussed in chapter 4.[1]

WRITING A PERSONNEL SERVICES BUDGET

The personnel services budget is normally funded out of the general fund. Personnel services include salaries and *fringe benefits* for employees and can be managed in a step by step process.[2] A *salary* is simply the wages paid for services rendered over a given period of time. Salaries can be calculated very easily using a spreadsheet. However, many governments have software that automate the calculation of salaries and associated benefits. That is, it is very easy to increase or decrease salaries using a very simple formula. Fringe benefits are payments and services rendered by an agency in addition to normal wages to an employee. Fringe benefits can be based on a percentage of pay roll, such as *pensions*, *Social Security* (FICA) and *Medicare*. Social Security and Medicare are represented as a tax on your pay stub. Some argue that these two items are personnel costs rather than benefits. A second group of benefits represent a flat amount that can vary based on the employee's circumstances. These include: life and health insurance. Non-monetary benefits include: paid time off, such as holidays, vacations, sick leave and personal leave which are a component of the annual salary; take-home cars; free parking; employee incentive programs; and time off for educational purposes. Social Security is required for all government employees according to federal law unless the government has its own retirement system. Medicare is required for all government employees. It is not a legal requirement that an employer provide: health, life insurance, training supplements or any non-monetary benefits to all of its employees. There are a variety of circumstances that dictate who should receive benefits. One of the important factors is full-time versus part-time status.

Another important factor in the personnel services budget is overtime. This is particularly true for police and firefighters, since they typically have 24/7 schedules. Overtime is normally paid at the rate of one and one-half times the hourly rate of pay. Overtime can be a significant cost for many governments. Percentage-driven benefits, such as pensions and Medicare are also a component of overtime. Many governments prefer to pay overtime rather than add employees because it keeps the headcount down. Another advantage is that new employees have to learn the job while existing employees are familiar with the job requirements.

CALCULATING FICA AND MEDICARE

The federal government sets agency contributions to Medicare and Social Security annually. Currently, agencies match the 6.2 percent Social Security rate that employees have deducted directly from their paycheck. Hence, the employee and employer contribute a total of 12.4 percent. In 2019, the Social Security tax or FICA rate applied to earnings up to $132,900 (U.S. Social Security Administration N.d.). No taxes are due from the employee or employer beyond that amount. For example, if a public administration professor had a salary of $135,200 in 2019, she would have $8,239.80 subtracted directly from her salary and the university would also contribute $8,239.80 on her behalf for a total of $16,479.60 ($132,900 × 0.124 = $16,479.60) in Social Security taxes for the year. Note that the remaining $2,300 of her salary is not subject to Social Security taxes when calculating FICA during the current calendar year.

The rate for Medicare is 2.9 percent, and is split equally between the employer (1.45 percent) and the employee (1.45 percent). Contrary to Social Security, the Medicare rate applies to the full salary. Let's consider the professor used in the above example. Based on her annual salary of $135,200 in 2019, the Medicare tax is $3,920.80 ($135,200 × 0.029 = $3,920.80). Medicare is mandatory at the full amount for all employees regardless of age or employment status. If an employee is a part-time or a contract worker, he or she may not qualify for full fringe benefits. For example, if the agency does not pay their share of Social Security and Medicare benefits, the employee (full and part-time) has to pay the full amount to the federal government. Hence, the employer's contribution of half the Social Security and Medicare payment is considered a fringe benefit or an additional cost. So, it is important that you remember that you should only consider the government's portion of the payment when creating a budget rather than the total amount. Employee contributions to Social Security, Medicare, pensions, etc. is included in a separate budget document.[3] Again, when calculating Social Security and Medicare taxes in a personnel budget, you should only include the government's contribution.

PENSIONS

For the most part, nearly all full-time government employees participate in what is commonly called a pension plan. Some government pension plans are in lieu of Social Security while others may have both. Very small governments may only have Social Security. A *pension plan* provides financial benefits to an employee after he/she retires and/or has reached a certain age. Some plans allow an employee to retire after attaining a certain number of years of service, such as thirty, at any age. Others require both a particular age and a minimum number of years of service. Still others have only a strict age requirement. Both employee and the employer contribute funds to the pension plan (not necessarily at the same rate) and both receive benefits. The employee receives the monetary benefit and security of knowing that they will have funds upon retirement. The government benefits because they can serve their personnel management objectives. They want employees to make a career out of public service. The experience and training that is gained through the years contributes to a professional bureaucracy. So, in order to recruit the best people and keep them in the public sector, the government must provide a good retirement package (Hildreth and Miller 1996; Lynch, Sun, and Smith 2017). Pension rates can range from a low of 2 percent up to a high of 30 percent or more of an employee's salary. There may be an equal contribution or the greater burden may be on the employee (Stalebrink, Kriz, and Guo 2010).

A pension resembles and behaves like Social Security. However, unlike Social Security, pension funds are invested in accounts that belong to the employee. Social Security is a "pay-as-you-go" system, whereby current contributions are used to pay the cost of past retirees. As history would indicate, it is possible for pension fund balances to suffer or grow as the economy changes. When the economy or the investment portfolio takes a turn for the worse for an extended period of time, it is important that fund managers ensure that enough funds are set aside and the tax base is stable enough to make up for the difference in lost investments (Lynch et al. 2017). As a general rule, pension fund portfolio managers should ensure that they are making socially beneficial investments. This process is facilitated with a *pension board of directors*. Normally made up of member representatives along with outside appointments, they are responsible for implementing legal requirements (Hildreth and Miller 1996; Hildreth and Adams 1997).

Pension investments normally fall into two categories: fixed income securities and equity securities. *Fixed income securities* are obligations that provide a steady stream of interest payments barring any defaults, such as a corporate bond or corporate annuity. *Equity securities* (which are more risky) are investments in *stocks*, which may or may not pay *dividends* (Petersen 2004; see also Hildreth and Adams 1997).

As years have passed and budgets have tightened, public pension fund accounts have grown and have become more and more susceptible to fungibility issues. Again, it is important that the pension fund managers and the board of directors make sure that these funds are not transferred to other funds haphazardly (Nollenberger 2003; Petersen 2004).

Until the mid-1990s, virtually all government pension plans were defined benefit plans. When an employee began work, he/she was handed a book that stated exactly how much could be expected at retirement based on age, years of service, and final average salary. Pension fund managers have the liability for pensions calculated by *actuaries*. The actuaries determine how much the employer and employee have to contribute to fund the pensions. It is the responsibility of the managers to find investments that will yield the amounts necessary to cover all members in the system. When the economy has significant downturns, as happened in the late 2000s, investments are not able to keep pace with the required amounts. This means that the pension contributions should be increased. However, that is not easy to do. It requires legislation to raise contributions. Some pension plans have had to borrow to meet their obligations.[4] Others have had to supplement pension contributions with general fund subsidies.

Since the mid-1990s, a number of governments have established defined contribution plans. The government and employee each contribute a required amount for the pension. However, the employee is responsible for investing the funds. Employees are provided various investment options and select an option that is appropriate. *Defined contribution plans* are portable. That is, when the employee leaves government service, the pension stays with the employee. The advantage to the employer of a defined contribution plan is that there is no long term liability. In a *defined benefit plan*, the employee may not get back any of the contributions or may receive a refund of his/her contribution. Some governments, such as Orlando, Florida, have replaced a defined benefit plan with a defined contribution plan for all employees coming on board after October 1, 1998.

Calculating the Pension Benefit

While the years of service can vary, most state and local governments require that their employees reach an age between sixty-two to sixty-five years old and work at least five to ten years in order to receive a pension. However, there are a number of other factors that can take place to change that scenario. These would include things like disabilities.

There are two key factors involved in calculating the pension benefit—final average salary and the annual multiplier. The final average salary is based on the highest earning years of an employee and can vary from three, four or five years depending on the pension system. An annual multiplier is the percentage of final average salary that is applied to each year of service. For example, a pension plan provides for each year of service to be multiplied by two percent. An employee working thirty years would receive 60 percent of his/her final average salary. This comprises the total percentage value. An employee that works five years, the usual minimum vesting period, would receive 10 percent of their final average salary.

Exhibit 3.1 provides a model that can be used to calculate retirement benefits. In this example, Mrs. Deepthi Kollipara worked thirty years for the city and is 64 years of age. The last piece of data needed to calculate her retirement benefit is her five highest calendar year salaries. In order to calculate her benefit, you must:

- First, multiply her years of service times the percentage value per years of service.
- Second, her five highest years of service should be added up and divided by the years of service (5).
- Third, her average five-year salary should be multiplied by the total percentage value (TVPP).
- Based on the formula, Mrs. Kollipara would receive $46,722.85 per year and $3,893.57 per month for her thirty years of service. Note: When age and years of service are not on the same line, choose the factor that best benefits the employee.

Exhibit 3.1. Sample Calculations of Retirement Benefits						

Step 1: Creditable Services and Percentage Value

	% Value Per Years of Service		Total Years of Service		Total # Value Per Plan (TVPP)
Retirement up to Age 62 or 30 Years	1.60%	x		=	
Retirement at Age 63 or 31 Years	1.63%	x		=	
Retirement at Age 64 or 32 Years	1.65%	x	30	=	49.50%
Retirement at Age 65 or >32 Years	1.68%	x		=	

Step 2: Average Final Compensation (AFC)

Mrs. Kollipara worked for 30 years in the same system and retired at age 64. In this step, we add her five fiscal year salaries and divide the total by five (years).

$85,000
87,590
95,890
99,569
103,899
$471,948

AFC = $471,948.00 / 5 = $94,389.60

Step 3: Annual Benefit Calculation

AFC x TVPP = Annual Benefit $94,389.60 x .4950 = $46,722.85

Step 4: Monthly Benefit Calculation

Annual Benefit / 12 = Monthly Benefit $46,722.85 / 12 = $3,893.57

Source: Thomas D. Lynch, Jinping Sun, and Robert W. Smith (2017), *Public Budgeting in America*, 6th ed. (Irvine, CA: Melvin & Leigh).

Exhibit 3.2 is an Excel spreadsheet of the same person that is calculated in exhibit 3.1. This computer program expedites the process and provides the user an opportunity to examine various retirement scenarios.

There are some other issues that this model does not examine, but they are still important to the employee. This includes things such as vesting, portability systems, cost of living adjustments, early retirement, and disability/survivor protections. *Vesting* occurs when an employee works a certain number of years making them eligible to receive retirement benefits. The minimum number of years required for vesting can range from three to five, but really depends upon the system where you work. In some cases, you can move your vested status to another government job (portability). This is simple

Exhibit 3.2. Short Version for Calculating Retirement Benefits (in Excel)					
% Value Per Year of Service	*Total Years of Service*	*Total % Value PP*	*Average Final Compensation*	*Annual Benefit*	*Monthly Benefit*
1.65%	30	49.50%	$94,389.60	$46,722.85	$3,893.57
5 Highest Years					
$85,000.00					
87,590.00					
95,890.00					
99,569.00					
103,899.00					
$471,948.00					
$94,389.60 Ave AFC.					

Source: Created by the Author.

when you stay in the same system (work for the same municipality or state), but less likely to occur if you move to a different city or state. This is one of the drawbacks of the defined benefit plan and one of the advantages of the defined contribution plan.

There is an array of issues and questions related to disability status. For example, will you be able to receive pension benefits if you become disabled prior to becoming eligible for benefits? Will your children or spouse receive your pension if you die prior to receiving benefits? Will you qualify for benefits if you permanently injure yourself outside of work? The answers to these and many other questions will vary based on where you are working. It is important that a government address all of these questions with written policies (Hildreth and Miller 1996; Lynch et al. 2017).

POSITION CLASSIFICATIONS AND SALARY RANGES

Exhibit 3.3 shows a simple agency budget with each of three main categories along with classification codes. Classification codes are for administrative purposes and make it easier to locate a specific line in a budget. This particular budget represents a specific division within an agency. Because it is in a line item format, it essentially tells the reader the amount of funds necessary to run the division without any cost associated with a particular individual and their responsibilities. However, the budget does not tell the

Chapter 3

Exhibit 3.3. Simple Agency Budget		
Agency: Central Budget Office Division: Procurement		
Code	*Item*	*Adopted Budget*
1000	1. Personal Services	
1001	Salaries	$146,000
1002	FICA	18,104
1003	Insurance	6,000
1004	Retirement	19,578
	Subtotal	$189,682
2000	2. Operating Expenses	
2001	Contractual Services	$6,500
2002	Training	650
2003	Travel	505
2004	Utilities	3,000
2005	Printing	1,700
2006	Misc. Supplies	12,500
	Subtotal	$24,855
3000	3. Capital Outlay	
3001	Vehicles	$35,000
3002	Equipment	2,500
	Subtotal	$37,500
TOTAL Agency Budget		$252,037

Source: Created by the Author.

reader the number of persons who work in the Procurement Division, nor does it break down the fringe benefits by employee. Most budgets are typed into a computer spreadsheet. This expedites the budget process and reduces mathematical errors.

The most common employee classification is a *full-time equivalent* (FTE). Full-time positions are normally thirty-five to forty hours per week. A full-time employee (equivalent) is eligible to receive the full range of fringe benefits. *Part-time employees* (PTE) normally work fifteen to thirty-five hours per week and are not eligible for full fringe benefits. Some part-time employees may receive *prorated benefits*. A school bus driver would be an example of a part-time employee who works for the majority of the fiscal year and could be eligible for fringe benefits.

Temporary positions may also exist. These are employees who may work full-time, but are not permanent, such as summer employees for a park and recreation department or a secretary or janitor hired during peak season on a temporary basis. They may also be eligible for prorated fringe benefits as well (Riley and Colby 1991).

The classification FTE is used by the government in calculating the number of hours associated with a position. For example, a full-time employee who works for the entire fiscal year would be the equivalent to 1.0 FTE. Four janitors, each working six months out of the year, would equal 2.0 FTE's (0.5 for each person). By using this system, the government views personnel cost in terms of the number of positions and costs needed to complete a job rather than the number of people.

State and local governments frequently use pay plans for employees. These plans normally apply to full-time employees. The plan lists each position class along with the salary range for that position. It is very difficult to justify paying a particular employee a salary out of the range without raising the bar for all other employees in that classification. The *Salary Range Plan* includes the title of the position, administrative code associated with the position, and annual salary range. Exhibit 3.4 contains an example of a salary range classification.

Exhibit 3.4. Salary Range Classification			
Position Code	Class Title	Min. Salary	Max. Salary
1100	Accountant	$65,000	$79,000
1101	Administrative Assistant	45,000	55,250
1102	Budget Analyst	65,000	75,000
1103	Clerk	50,000	60,500
1104	Division Director	95,000	109,950
1105	Janitor	28,000	33,595
1106	Principal Investigator	75,000	89,000
1007	Security Guard	48,000	64,000

Source: Created by the Author.

Like most things related to government, a salary range classification is approved by a legislative body and serves many purposes. A few of these purposes are listed below.

- Provides government officials data that may be useful in accounting, payroll and personnel processes.
- Ensures that salaries are reasonable and equitable relative to the responsibilities of the employee.
- Limits opportunities to discriminate.
- Allows the government to remain competitive in an open market and retain experienced employees.
- Acts as a control over salaries when new positions and raises are considered.

JUSTIFYING A NEW POSITION

Growth in responsibilities of an agency and personnel are fairly standard in most governments. As a result, it is necessary on occasion to request one or more new positions. There is never a guarantee that a request for a new position will occur. Nonetheless, it is important that agency heads ensure that they adequately review the old and new responsibilities of the agency in order to make sure that they can thoroughly justify new positions and maintain the previous positions. There are several items that go into a request for a new position that will facilitate the process (Riley and Colby 1991). The agency can:

- Justify the creation of the new position(s) by outlining the responsibilities of the person(s) relative to increases in workload or expanded programs.
- Describe the qualifications of the employee(s) with a notation as to whether it fits the current salary pay classification.
- Show how this position(s) will make the agency more efficient and effective.
- Show how the new position(s) will enhance new assignments or enhance current responsibilities.
- Program changes follow the same logic as a position request. Show how the program will make operations more efficient and effective.

CALCULATING A PERSONAL SERVICES BUDGET

Preparing a new budget can be difficult for the budget officer. In fact, this period causes a fair amount of trepidation for the entire staff. However, the process can be eased with several items. First and foremost is accurate information. It is very important that agency directors and the personnel office provide the budget officer with reliable data that corresponds with known facts. Second, a computer can expedite the budgeting process, but it cannot read minds. Hence, it does not notice mathematical errors in data entry for example. In most cases, budgets are inaccurate because of human error. Specific items needed by the budget office include:

- A manual to review budget requests. The manual would normally contain management policy information (the direction the agency is headed and potential areas to cut or expand).
- Budget preparation forms along with instructions.
- Salary information related to personnel (includes information on projected salary increases as well as fringe benefits).
- Operating and capital outlay instructions.

Beginning with the previous year's base, the budget officer can put the new projected salary information (based on *budget projections*) into a computer spreadsheet program for each position classification. Budget projections are based on projected revenue, which are unknown versus what is known. *Budget estimates* are based on more concrete information. Assuming that no changes occurred, the computer will automatically calculate the fringe benefits associated with the salary. In some cases, the percentage or dollar amount of fringe benefits may change. Exhibit 3.5 is an example of an *Agency Salary Projection Report*.

Exhibit 3.5. Agency Salary Projection Report						
FY 2020 (General Fund) Agency: *Police Department* – Division: *Homicide*						
Title	Salary	FICA	MED	Pension	Health	Total
Director	$69,569	$4,313.26	$1,008.75	$6,956.90	$3,500	$85,347.91
Captain	45,230	2,804.26	655.84	4,523.00	3,500	56,713.10
Detective	38,987	2,417.19	565.31	3,898.70	3,500	49,368.20
Detective	35,789	2,218.92	518.94	3,578.90	3,500	45,605.76
Assistant	27,123	1,681.63	393.28	2,712.30	3,500	35,410.21
TOTAL	$216,698	$13,435.26	$3,142.12	$21,669.80	$17,500	$272,445.18

Source: Created by the Author.

This report allows the viewer to determine the exact cost associated with a position or an individual. Social Security, Medicare, and retirement funds are based on formulas while health care cost for the individual employee is the same for everyone that has a particular characteristic, such as single, married with one dependent, and married with multiple dependents for health care benefits. Each of the employees listed here are current employees. The total cost included in exhibit 3.5 is the total cost to the government. The employee contribution is considered a part of the entire budget. That is, the employee contribution is not considered in the FICA and Medicare columns because their contribution is ultimately deducted from their salary. Hence, it is not necessary to show the contributions of both the employee and employer on a line item personnel budget.

If there are a number of employees who have the same salary, the budget officer may simply want to list the position by title and put the number of employees who correspond to that position/grade. This format saves time and space. However, this format only works when there are a number of employees who have the exact same salary.

A request for a new position along with salary projection follows the same format. However, there should be a justification for the new position at the bottom of the budget request (see exhibit 3.6). The justification should indicate why the position is needed along with any supporting evidence that would substantiate the request. Data are particularly useful in a position justification. Since the agency is not making a verbal argument for the new position, the justification should be carefully prepared.

A separate form should be used for each new position request. If the administrative position code does not indicate whether the position is an FTE or PTE, then it should be included on the personnel request form. Since positions are based on class, the requested salary for the new employee should fall within the legal pay range that was set by the legislative body. These forms normally come with complete instructions dictating what should be included. Specifically, these instructions should indicate the current rates for FICA (12.4 percent), Medicare (2.9 percent), and retirement (18 percent). In addition, it should contain the cost of health insurance ($1,800) and any other pertinent information.

Exhibit 3.6. New Personnel Request Form							
FY 2020 (General Fund) Agency: *Police Department*, Division: *Homicide*							
Position Title	Position Code	Base Salary	FICA	Medicare	Pension	Health	Total Costs
Dispatcher	1011	$22,500	$1,737.94	$3,26.25	$4,0500	$1,800	$30,414.19

Justification:

Due to an expansion in 911 services the number of incoming phone calls has proved to be a burden for one person. As a result, we had to hire a temporary employee and use patrol officers to aid in this effort. Therefore, it is economically feasible to have a full-time employee to carry out these responsibilities.

Source: Created by the Author.

PREPARING AN OPERATING BUDGET

As stated earlier, the personnel budget makes up the bulk of expenditures in the budget process. However, operating costs are just as important. These requests are reviewed and justified each fiscal year. *Operating costs* include items such as travel, telephone services and other utilities, pencils, paper, adding machines, rent or any other item that recurs. In simple terms, these are items needed by an agency to conduct business. Equipment, such as vehicles, can also be included as an operating expense if the agency is not requesting a large number of new vehicles every year. Further, if vehicles were to be replaced over a number of fiscal years, this might not be the best category to include them. It would depend on the policy of the government. Other exclusions would include high cost items such as super computers and buildings. These are *capital expenditure* items.

When making a request for operating expenditures, an agency has to indicate how these items will be used to meet the mission of the agency and any new activities that the executive or legislative body may have. The agency director submitting the budget should indicate in the budget transmittal letter how the requests are tied to the goals of the agency. In addition, data showing how expenditures are tied to programs and performance is very useful. Despite the inclusion of these items, operating budgets are not examined as much as personnel budgets. The few exceptions are training and travel.

There are three basic ways to present an operating budget proposal. The first is the incremental method. An *incremental operating budget* essentially shows a modest increase in the budget due to inflation and other naturally occurring economic factors. A lot of agencies tend to use this type of budget because it links spending directly to a service or item (see exhibit 3.7 for an example).

Exhibit 3.7. Incremental Operating Budget Proposal			
Object Code	Item	FY 2020 Cost (est.)	FY 2021 Cost (prop.)
2003	Travel	$5,000	$6,000
2004	Utilities	2,569	3,000
2005	Printing	12,904	15,000
2006	Misc. Supplies	459	600
2007	Pens	245	300
2008	Paper	2,349	3,600
2009	Adding Machine	299	150
2010	Telephone	1,349	2,800
TOTAL		$25,174	$31,450

Source: Created by the Author.

Also, this budget is particularly useful when there have been no new requests in the personnel budget and when there is no indication of changes in the agency. In addition, it is easy to convey the budget in this manner when the agency can show that it has efficiently and effectively pursued the mission of the agency. The incremental operating budget has four main components: an object code, item/service, current year cost, and estimated cost for the upcoming fiscal year. Where appropriate, it may also be useful to indicate the number of items requested (for example, the number of adding machines).

The estimates in FY 2020 should be based on the appropriation. That is, the estimate would not exceed the appropriation, but could be less based on costs as of the date of budget preparation. The agency could add an additional column with FY 2019 actual spending to give the reviewer a better trend analysis.

This method is also good to use when there is a drastic change in the cost of an item. For example, let's assume the cost of telephone usage has increased by 5 percent each fiscal year for the last five years and the amount for FY 2020 is a 15 percent increase over the previous year (exhibit 3.8). This increase would require a justification since it does not follow the previous trend. The same would be true for the 2021 proposed budget. Ideally, the justification would indicate what policy change or other events precipitated the increase in phone service costs. Clear crisp explanations to changes expedite the approval process (Riley and Colby 1991).

Exhibit 3.8. Police Department Program Operating Budget Proposal						
Program	*Travel*	*Utilities & Fuel*	*Printing*	*Telephone*	*FY 2020 (est.)*	*FY 2021 Request*
911 Service	$79,999	$3,985	$175	$10,785	$80,546	$94,944
DARE	1,459	350	100	150	1,643	2,059
Patrol	359,999	15,899	150	987	338,456	377,035
Annual Ball	450	600	1,200	100	1,789	2,350
TOTAL	$441,907	$20,834	$1,625	$12,022	$422,434	$476,388

Justification:

(a) *DARE Program*: In harmony with the Mayor and City Council's mission to expand the program into every school, we have increased the number of officers who go into the schools and the amount of information that they disseminate.

(b) *911 Service*: Due to the expansion of emergency services into the newly annexed suburbs of Mt. Vernon and Taylorville, we are requesting two new patrol officers and thus need to provide them with adequate training and other amenities.

Source: Created by the Author.

The second and third types of operating budgets are *performance* and *program budgets* (see chapter 1). A performance or program operating budget would link the operating expenditures to performance and programs (Kelly and Rivenbark 2015; Riley and Colby 1991). The budget examiner should be able to look at this budget along with the justification and see exactly where and what the funds are used for.[5]

CONCLUSION

Personnel services and operating budgets appear to be more or less operational functions. However, there is still a degree of negotiation that takes place. Positions are not always guaranteed despite arguments indicating the need. Budget personnel officers should ensure that they are meticulous with their data entry skills. A computer is only as good as the operator. It is very easy to put in the wrong number and throw off the entire budget. Budgets must balance to the last penny. Hence, rounding errors must be minimized.[6]

IMPORTANT TERMS AND PHRASES

Accrual Accounting
Actuaries
Annual Benefit
Ave. Final Compensation
Medicare
Budget Estimates
Budget Projections
Capital Budget
COLAs
Defined Benefit Plan
Defined Contribution Plan
Dividends
Equity Securities
Fixed Income Securities
Fringe Benefits
Full-Time Employee
Full-Time Equivalent
Fungibility
Grant
Health Insurance

Incremental Operating Budget
Life Insurance
Medicare
Monthly Benefit
Operating Budget
Part-Time Employee
Pay-as-you-go
Pension
Pension Board of Directors
Pension Plan
Performance Operating Budget
Personal Services Budget
Program Operating Budget
Prorated Benefits
Retirement
Salary/Wage
Salary Range Plan
Social Security
Vesting

CHAPTER 3 HOMEWORK EXERCISES

Directions: Templates for answering questions are found in the appendices. Use Excel formulas to calculate the answers. All of the responses should be completed and/or copied and pasted into a MS Word document. Email your Excel spreadsheet to your instructor and turn in the MS Word document in class.

(1) Research and define each of the following terms:

    (a) Actuaries
    (b) Dividends
    (c) Vesting
    (d) Pensions
    (e) Cost of Living Adjustment

(2) The city council for Jefferson City decided to create a new Tourism Department in FY 2021. The department has a director, secretary, marketing director, two van drivers, and three tourism officers. As the budget officer for the city, your job is to create a personnel budget for the department using the information listed below. Only consider the items that are listed. Read each bullet prior to beginning the assignment (See appendix 3A).

- Complete the FTE column.
- The director has a salary of $120,000 and is a FTE.
- The secretary has a salary of $54,000 and is a FTE.
- The marketing director has a salary of $68,500 and is a FTE.
- Each driver has a salary of $42,000 and is a FTE.
- Each tourism officer has a salary of $20,000 and works part-time (PTE). Although they each work six months out of the year, they are paid over a twelve-month period.
- FICA is 12.4 percent and Medicare is 2.9 percent for all employees.
- Health insurance costs are $4,000 per year for each FTE.
- Each tourism officer has a clothing budget of $500.
- Each driver has a clothing budget of $750.
- Each tourism officer is eligible for 50 percent of the fringe benefits (health insurance premium, life insurance and pension).
- Training costs associated with each tourism officer is $500.
- Training costs associated with each driver is $800.
- Life insurance premiums are $25 per month for each FTE.
- Pensions are 9.5 percent of salary for each FTE and the city pays the full amount.

(3) Prepare a salary projection report for the Jefferson City Fire Department for FY 2021 using the actual budget for FY 2020 as a model along with a budget request for two new fire fighter (2a) positions. Use the following information in your FY 2021 Salary Projections and budget requests (see appendix 3B). Note that the budget has the number of employees in each position grade rather than listing each employee. Also, you should calculate the total cost of employment for each staff person.

- The salary of the chief increased 7 percent while all other employees received a 5% increase.
- FICA is 12.4 percent and Medicare is 2.9 percent for all employees.
- The cost of health insurance increased 5 percent.
- The cost of uniforms increased 2 percent.
- The fire fighter's pay range is $60,000–$80,000. The new fire fighters should be paid (2a) $70,000.
- The new fire fighters (2a) will receive the same benefits package as the other FY 2020 employees.
- The cost of training the new fire fighters is $6,000 per employee.
- The pension rate in FY 2021 is the same as it was in FY 2020 (20 percent).
- The clerical staff member works a half day schedule 12 months per year (.5 FTE).
- Complete the FTE column.

(4) Three employees are retiring from Jefferson City. Your job as the human resource officer is to calculate their pension payments using the following information. Use the model in exhibit 3.1 to assist you in completing this problem. Calculate: Total percent value PP, Average Final Compensation, Annual Benefit, and Monthly Benefit. Turn in the short version Excel worksheet to your professor (See appendix 3C).

Employee 1 Mary Rademacher

- Has thirty-one years of service and is sixty-three years of age.
- Five highest years of salary are: $20,904; $21,398; $22,198; $34,239; & $36,908.

Employee 2 Steffanee Richardson

- Has thirty-two years of service and is sixty-four years of age.
- Five highest years of salary are: $29,504; $30,698; $32,798; $36,839; & $38,508.

Employee 3 Charlie Parker

- Has thirty-four years of service and is sixty-nine years of age
- Five highest years of salary are: $49,904; $51,899; $57,678; $61,742; & $64,108.

(5) As the budget officer for Alexander State Prison you have to prepare the FY 2021 Operating Budget projections for the Security Division based on the FY 2020 budget estimates. Below you will find one portion of the budget history for the prison. Here are a few facts that you should know about the prison when preparing the operating budget. First, there are thirty staff members in the division. Twenty-seven of the staff persons are equal in rank (guards). The warden, budget officer and secretary are the last three staff members. Other than what is stated, why do think these changes occurred (see exhibit 3.5)? Be rational and creative in your responses and justify the changes. Use bullet points to relay your justifications. Round all of your projections to the nearest dollar amount. Hint: You can round numbers in Excel using the round function as well as the "Decrease Decimal" function in the "Home" tool bar.

- Ten of the guards need training. Thus, training cost will increase by 34 percent.
- Energy costs are expected to rise 25 percent due to changes in global oil and gas prices.
- The cost of printing, pens, and pencils decreases by 2 percent from FY 2020.
- The cost of paper will increase by 5 percent.
- Telephone costs are expected to increase 4 percent.
- No new adding machine, but we need a new printer which will cost $500.
- Miscellaneous supplies will increase 25 percent.

Operating Budget				
Object Code	Item	FY 2019 (act)	FY 2020 (est)	FY 2021 (proj)
2004	Training	$32,000.00	$36,800.00	
2005	Utilities	15,550.50	17,176.56	
2006	Printing	11,500.00	13,225.00	
2007	Misc. Supplies	960.00	1,200.00	
2008	Pens and Pencils	150.50	155.02	
2009	Paper	3,800.00	4,999.00	
2010	Adding Machine	376.00	189.50	
2011	Telephone	4,200.50	4,347.52	
2012	Printer	0.00	0.00	
TOTAL		$68,537.50	$78,332.60	

(6) Optional In-Class Assignment: Defending Budget Justifications (45-minute exercise).

(a) *Before Class Assignment*: Each student should address the following proposal: The Warden of Roan State Prison wants to expand the number of guards by five and create an assistant warden position within the prison. He has requested that you, the prison budget officer, write the justifications for the positions. Using the information in the chapter on "Justifying a New Position," write a justification for the six positions. You should include a brief narrative describing the positions (guards are equal in rank) and their basic duties. Then, using at least five bullet points, describe why they are needed.

(b) *In-Class*: Split the class into groups of four or five and have each person summarize their justifications in no more than five minutes. Each student should bring additional copies of their response to distribute among the group members. When all of the group members are finished, a group justification should be created for each group and presented to the entire class.

NOTES

1. Although income taxes are considered a part of the personnel budget, they are intentionally excluded from this chapter because the payment of income taxes completely falls upon the burden of the employee. The tax rate can change for different individuals based on a number of different items that are not directly correlated with this discussion. These taxes are however discussed in detail in chap. 5, "Funding State and Local Budgets."

2. Despite the fact that these two items frequently comprise more than 50% of the budget, it is very difficult to cut the personnel budget. This is particular true during periods of low economic activity. Personnel service is the only portion of a budget that is likely to increase every fiscal year (COLAs, or cost of living adjustments). Along with this increase is also an increase in fringe benefits.

3. See Robert L. Bland (2005). *A Revenue Guide for Local Government*, 2nd ed. (Washington, DC: ICMA), for more information. See also Marvin Friedman (1983), "Calculating Compensation Costs," in *Budget Management: A Reader in Local Government Financial Management*, ed. Jack Rabin, W. Bartley Hildreth, and Gerald J. Miller (Athens, GA: Carl Vinson Institute of Government, University of Georgia), 116–27, for a discussion of calculating compensation costs.

4. In 2004, the State of Oregon issued $2.1 billion to cover the shortfall in their retirement system (Oregon [2004], "State Budget Update: November 2004," National Conference of State Legislatures, Denver, CO, https://www.ncsl.org/print/fiscal/sbu2005-0411.pdf.

5. A performance budget is similar. See exhibit 1.3 for an example. The only thing that would change are the items listed under operating expenses.

6. Large governments may prepare budgets to the nearest thousand dollars, omitting the last 000s.

Appendix 3A
Jefferson City Tourism Department

Jefferson City Tourism Department

Position	FTE	Salary	SS	Medicare	Pension	Health	Life Ins	Training	Clothing	Grand Total
Program Director										
Secretary										
Marketing Director										
Driver										
Tourism Officers										
TOTAL										

Source: Created by the Author.

Appendix 3B

Jefferson City Tourism Department

Jefferson City Tourism Department, Personnel Services Budget

FY 2020

Position	FTE	Salary	SS	Heath Ins	Pension	Medicare	Uniforms	TOTAL
Chief	1	$97,000	$6,014	$2,160	$19,400	$1,406.50	$750	$126,730.50
Shift Commander	3	150,000	9,300	6,480	30,000	2,175.00	2,250	200,205.00
Fire Fighter 1a	12	420,000	26,040	25,920	84,000	6,090.00	9,000	571,050.00
Fire Fighter 1b	26	650,000	40,300	56,160	130,000	9,425.00	19,500	905,385.00
Clerical (PT)	0.5	45,000	2,790	0	9,000	652.50	0	57,442.50
TOTAL	42.5	$1,362,000	$84,444	$90,720	$272,400	$19,749.00	$31,500	$1,860,813.00

FY 2021

Position	FTE	Salary	SS	Heath Ins	Pension	Medicare	Uniforms	TOTAL
Chief								
Shift Commander								
Fire Fighter 1a								
Fire Fighter 1b								
Clerical (PT)								
TOTAL								

New Position Budget Request

Position	FTE	Salary	SS	Health Ins.	Pension	Medicare	Uniforms	Training	TOTAL
Fire Fighter 2a									
TOTAL									

ALL POSITIONS

FY 2021	FTE	Salary	SS	Health Ins.	Pension	Medicare	Uniforms	Training	TOTAL

Source: Created by the Author.

Appendix 3C

Long Version

Long Version			
MARY RADEMACHER	*% Value Per Years of Service*	*Total Years of Service*	*Total % Value Per Plan (TVPP)*
Retirement up to age 62 or 30 years	1.60%		
Retirement up to age 63 or 31 years	1.63%		
Retirement up to age 64 or 32 years	1.65%		
Retirement up to age 65 or 33 years or more	1.68%		
Step 2: Average Final Compensation (AFC)			

Source: Created by the Author.

Chapter 4

Preparing a Capital Budget and a Capital Improvement Plan

OVERVIEW

One of the most critical responsibilities of a government is to provide citizens with a sound infrastructure and equipment capable of helping the government to be efficient and effective. There are two items that can be used to facilitate that goal: a capital budget and a capital improvement plan. This chapter is dedicated to discussing both of these items in detail. This includes a discussion of financing capital projects. Users of this text will learn how to write a: capital budget, capital improvement plan; create a finance structure for capital projects; and justify and defend capital projects.

CAPITAL BUDGETS VERSUS A CAPITAL IMPROVEMENT PLAN

While there is a definite correlation between a capital budget and a capital improvement plan, they are not the same. A *capital budget* is merely an expenditure list of high cost items such as buildings, bridges, highways and other large-scale items that are expected to provide benefits and services over a considerable period of time. A *capital improvement plan* (CIP) on the other hand is a spending plan that will take place over a three to five-year period. In some instances, the first year or current year of the capital improvement plan can become the capital budget. This decision is determined by a number of items, including the size of the budget and the size of the government. Some governments include the capital budget in their operating budget.[1]

CAPITAL BUDGETS

Unlike a personnel and operating budget, a capital budget only includes high cost non-routine items such as public buildings, equipment, infrastructure, and land purchases. Public buildings include: police stations, court houses, public schools and government offices. Equipment includes: vehicles, computers, and office furniture. Infrastructure includes roads, bridges, sewers, and water lines. It is however possible that some of these items can be included in an operating budget. For example, the purchase of a single computer would not require a long-term plan. However, the purchase of several computers tends to be more costly and cause a greater burden on the funding source. By placing the computers in the capital budget, a budget office may be more creative in financing the item (Gianakis and McCue 1999; Srithongrung 2010). Further, a city can have a separate infrastructure replacement budget to replace existing sewers, streets, etc. Most often, the determination of what is included in the capital versus the operating budget is a function of the government's capitalization policies. For example, if the government requires all equipment with a unit price greater than $5,000 to be capitalized, then all equipment with a unit price less than $5,000 would be included in the operating budget.

During times of budget shortfalls equipment can and often is the first thing cut out of the budget. This occurs because it is easier to cut equipment than people. Further, budget officials assume that agencies can get by one more year with the equipment that they have rather than replacing it. These cuts are facilitated when agencies seek to replace functional older equipment with newer equipment which may in fact improve efficiency and effectiveness.

When an agency is preparing a budget for new expenditures, analysts should realize that *start-up costs* are often expensive even though additional efforts lead to lower *unit costs*. In these circumstances *marginal costs* may be lower. When considering a comparable increase in the budget because of the new expenditure, the analyst should remember that marginal costs should not increase proportionally.

When performing this function, expenditures should be split into one-time *fixed costs* and *recurring costs*. One-time fixed costs include the up-front costs, and include: research cost, evaluations, land, construction labor, construction materials, legal fees, freight and shipping costs, and training. Recurring costs are those costs associated with providing the service on an annual basis. These include utilities, personnel, supplies, etc. As more units of service are added, recurring costs increase. As more services are added the unit cost goes down.

Let's assume for a moment that the municipal golf course is submitting their capital budget request. Since the golf course is more or less self-sufficient, funding is not a big issue. The first mistake that the golf course officials could make is to assume that since money is available that they can do a lack luster job in justifying the new requests. A budget officer should never take a surplus or a "guaranteed" increase in their budget for granted.

Unlike an operating and personnel budget, a capital budget may not be incremental in nature. The budget essentially reacts to the items within it. For example, during periods of relative inactivity a capital budget may appear to be incremental in nature. However, when agencies have large projects underway, the budgets can change drastically from year to year.

For example, take a look at exhibit 4.1. The Post Office has purchased items using a capital improvement plan that began a few years earlier. In FY 2020, they estimate that they will spend $20,000 on computers and are requesting $30,000 in FY 2021 to complete their system. According to the justification, this purchase is the final stage of a multiyear plan to replace

Exhibit 4.1. Simple Line Item Capital Budget for the Post Office				
Object Code	*Item*	*Quantity*	*FY 2020 Cost (est.)*	*FY 2021 Cost (proposed)*
3003	Computers	10	$20,000	$30,000
3004	Security System	1	500	34,000
3005	Copy Machine	1	4,000	4,000
3006	Mail Sorter	2	3,000	6,000
3007	¾ Ton Trucks	8	75,000	120,000
3008	Office Desks	10	1,500	3,000
TOTAL			$104,000	$197,000

Brief Description:

The Post Office is going through a normal update of its computer systems and vehicle fleet. The new security system will bring the Post Office into compliance with the last round of federal statutes. The new trucks will not only replace some of the aging fleet, but also provide for two new trucks to handle our expanding population in the southern region of the city.

Justifications:

(1) Installing and Implementing the New Security System: The old system is outdated and does not offer the level of security that we need for our new equipment. Further, over time, this new equipment is cost effective and more efficient. The monthly up keep cost is 60% less than the old system. Last, the system will bring the office into federal compliance.
(2) New Computers: These computers will allow us to complete our overhaul of the network. Our workload capacity will increase 20%. Thus, we will be more efficient and effective.
(3) Copy Machine: This purchase is the second and last phase of our office equipment update.
(4) Trucks: These five trucks are the final vehicle purchases in updating our fleet for the foreseeable future.
(5) Desks: The ten desks will hold the ten new computers. They are ergonomically designed and should improve the overall health of the users.

Source: Created by the Author.

older computers with new computers. The justification for purchasing the new trucks also follows the same logic. Unlike an operating and personnel budget, it is not necessary to elaborate in detail when justifying items in a capital budget that is following a CIP. However, thorough justification is needed if the plan is changed in any way.

Last, agency heads must remember that operating budgets are affected by capital budgets in the long term. As capital projects come to fruition, maintenance and personnel cost fall back into operating and personnel budgets. So, it is important that agency heads ensure that staff and additional resources needed to manage the capital project are in place prior to the completion of the project. These projects often provide a considerable strain on operating budgets when checks are not put in place.

WHY SEPARATE A CAPITAL BUDGET FROM AN OPERATING BUDGET?

On the surface, it may not seem important to separate these two funds. However, the bullet points below highlight some important reasons why this is important and necessary.

- Capital outlays are financed and often paid from one-time, earmarked sources such as debt proceeds and grants. Segregating the funds from operating budgets ensure that they are spent for their original purpose.
- The decision process differs in a capital budget. Frequently, projects are ranked and funded as revenue becomes available. As projects are funded, other projects are added to the list.
- The time frame for spending funds varies between the two funds. Capital budgets are rarely completely executed in a single fiscal year.
- Capital budgets often exceed budget projections and thus require close scrutiny.[2]
- Capital budgets can stabilize tax rates when individual capital projects are large relative to the tax base of the city (Mikesell 2018).
- Financial mistakes (underestimation of costs) made with capital budgets can linger for many years and these errors should not be tied to operating budgets which must balance each year.[3]

CAPITAL IMPROVEMENT PLANS

When cities are expanding their capital infrastructure or simply planning for the future they will frequently put together a long term spending plan called a *capital improvement plan* (CIP) as well as the sources for funding the plan. C. Bradley Doss Jr. (1993) defines a CIP as, "a comprehensive document that enables local governments to budget for immediate capital projects, evaluate the condition of existing projects, and assess the future capital needs for either expansion, renovation or construction of new capital stock" (272). This plan is a list of high cost expenditures that occur over several fiscal years. This process often begins with a request from the budget office for project proposals (See appendix 4A). Concurrently, the chief executive officer along with the legislative body will begin to develop their list of spending priorities (Bland and Rubin 1997; Kittredge and Ouart 2005; Lee, Johnson, and Joyce 2013; Mikesell 2018; Vogt 2004). Why develop a CIP?

Advantages

- Establishes agency long-term priorities.
- Provides a mechanism for coordinating various agency projects.
- Helps to prevent duplication.
- Maximizes the distribution of public resources.
- Can stimulate private investment and economic development (excerpted from Riley and Colby (1991), 105).

Disadvantages
- Items that should be placed in the operating budget sometime end up in the CIP because of high cost.
- Assumes that officials will continue to reevaluate project proposals as the environment changes.
- The amount of funds may distort the ranking of projects. Some projects create their own funding, which may make them seem more practicable and appealing than non-revenue producing ventures.
- At some point, it is necessary to eliminate projects from consideration. The availability of funds plays a perennial role in this process, but politics does as well. Decisions should be made objectively with the greater interest of the community.[4]

THE CAPITAL BUDGETING PROCESS

The capital budgeting process presented here occurs in three stages. The first stage is *planning*. Several important items must occur during this stage. First, some basic identification, classification and analysis of capital requests should occur. Then, a preliminary ranking of projects should occur, along with a time frame in which the work should be completed, (*capital budget calendar)*. According to Susan L. Riley and Peter W. Colby (19991), a budget calendar is "useful in coordinating the work of all the players and identifies who does what and when?" (107). Exhibit 4.2 provides an example of a capital project request form.

Stage two is concerned with *budget analysis, project evaluation* and *budget adoption*. In this stage, evaluators examine the status of current capital projects and capital facilities. Further, they select new projects and determine which projects require funding from the general fund or other sources, and which projects will create revenue. In addition, an assessment of infrastructure changes and the construction or purchase of buildings can be done (Bland and Clarke 1999). At this juncture, budget forecasts can be made. A.

Exhibit 4.2.   Capital Budget Project Request Form

Directions: Complete this form for each capital request (includes new projects, repairs, or modifications).

(1) Title of Project: Construction of Newburg Elementary School
(2) Location of Project: Jefferson City

Description of Project: The school will serve the southwest part of the city. It will fit the standard model that we have used for the last five years in school construction. Should the region continue to grow at the current rate, this building model will allow the school to expand at minimal cost.

Justification of Project: The population in southwest Jefferson City is growing at an extremely fast rate. Hence, this is the best location for the school. The other schools in the city are overwhelmed with students and the bus system is being stretched thin due to long bus rides to the schools.

Estimated Cost of Project

Project Cost Components		Projected Annual Cost	
(1) Land (3 acres)	$10,000	(1) FY One	$175,000
(2) HVAC	$35,000	(2) FY Two	$100,000
(3) Construction	$315,000	(3) FY Three	$25,000
(4) Plumbing	$20,000	(4) FY Four	$75,000
(5) Equipment	$20,000	(5) FY Five	$50,000
(6) Other Costs	$25,000		
Total Costs			$425,000

Current Status of Project: The project has not begun.
Estimated Project Life: 15–20 years once the school is open.
Possible Sources of Funding: School Bond

Source: Created by the Author.

John Vogt (1983) suggests that quantitative analysis be used in this process (see chapter 6 of this text). Once these decisions are made, *implementation* of the CIP can begin.

In stage three, funds are acquired, managed, and invested in the CIP. Equipment is bought, land is purchased and the construction begins (Vogt 1983). Lastly, a *post evaluation* has to be conducted shortly after the project has been completed (Mikesell 2018). The purpose of the evaluation is to ensure that goals and objectives were met (See appendix 4A).

IDENTIFYING AND PRIORITIZING PROJECTS

Selecting a group of people to identify projects for a capital improvement plan is not as simple as it appears. Robert L. Bland and Irene S. Rubin (1997) point out that the selection of participants will largely determine what comes out of the process (Bland and Clarke 1999). Vogt (2004) argues that experience should play a major role in prioritizing projects. Experienced citizens who are in touch with citizen's need should play a vital role.[5] Bland and Rubin (1997) offer three possible scenarios for prioritizing plans. Plan 1 is a planning oriented process where priorities are assigned by the planning or capital budget office based on need or technical standards. Priorities in Plan 1 can be categorized as follows:

- *High*: These are projects that are vital and impending. They should be ranked at the top and funded in the early years of the Capital Improvement Plan (CIP). These are items that *must be* done.
- *Medium*: These are projects that are also vital, but do not have to be funded immediately. They should be in the middle to latter years of the CIP. These are items that *should be* done.
- *Low*: These are projects that have great benefit to the city, but not to the extent that they should receive higher priority. That is, they will not adversely affect critical areas immediately. These are items that *could be* done. Elected officials may have a peripheral role in the plan.

Plan 2 is a less planning oriented process and may have the input of elected or bureaucratic officials as well as citizens. Hence, it becomes more politics based than strategically based on need. It could also follow the previous model.

In Plan 3, a group of elected officials and technical staff would identify and prioritize projects. Since the implementation of a capital improvement plan is a multi-faceted process involving different areas of expertise, it seems quite reasonable that the process is not limited to elected officials and bureaucrats.

In fact, it may be necessary to consult with professionals in the private sector (see also Bland and Clarke 1999; Kittredge and Ouart 2005).

David Nice (2002) argued that "need" should be the prevailing character-istic when prioritizing projects. For example, the building of a new landfill to offset an old one that is operating at the maximum capacity should take precedence over a new recreational park. A long-term assessment of a local-ity's needs would be very useful when prioritizing projects. Bland and Rubin (1997) suggested two methods for prioritizing projects. In the first method, "projects are generated and ranked through a technical planning process, possibly overseen by the planning department" (179). One way to prioritize projects using this method is to address the following issues:

- Legal Mandates: Is the project required by federal or state statute, court order, etc.?
- Removes or Reduces Hazards: Does it remove hazards or improve public safety?
- Legislative or Executive Goals: Does the project advance stated goals and objectives?
- Efficiency: Does the project improve productivity and lower operating costs?
- Standards of Service: Does the project maintain or extend current service levels?
- Economic Development: Does the project support or benefit economic development?
- New Service: Does the project offer new services or programs?
- Quality of Life: Does the project improve the quality of life for citizens?
- Convenience: Does the project make it easier for citizens or government officials to manage activities?[6]

At the other end of the spectrum, "projects are generated by departments and examined and ranked by variously structured committees" (Nice 2002, 179). Unfortunately, politics plays a role in this process. Most projects tend to show characteristics of both methods. In either case, a level of economic and political parity much be reached (Aronson and Schwartz 2004; Axelrod 1995; Mikesell 2018).

NEEDS ASSESSMENTS AND THE SELECTION OF PROJECTS

Prior to implementing a capital improvement plan, a *needs assessment* should be conducted. A needs assessment allows all concerned parties to examine the current status of the capital infrastructure. That is, the assessment should indicate the condition of all capital assets. By showing the positive benefits of previous investments in the infrastructure, you can legitimize new investments. Needs assessments should be comprehensive and conducted by a neutral unbiased party. Why? An agency can only look at its own needs over some period of time. Citizens and elected officials often have their own agendas and fail to see the big picture and as a result overlook conflicting or competing needs.

At the tail end of this process, someone has to decide what projects will be selected for funding. Nice (2002), Bland and Rubin (1997), Gerasimos A. Gianakis and Clifford P. McCue (1999), and Donald Axelrod (1995), offer a number of suggestions and questions that should be answered prior to making a final decision on capital projects. Vogt (1983) offers a two-dimensional matrix to establish priorities based on a numerical score. The matrix and the items included in table 4.1 are quite consistent.

Table 4.1. Other Factors to Consider Prior to Selecting Capital Projects
(1) Prepare an inventory of current fixed capital assets. What is the life expectancy of these assets and how much are they currently worth?
(2) What is the fiscal impact of each new project for the current and future years? How will the project impact the personnel and operating budget on a year-by-year basis? Will the project generate revenue on a year-by-year basis? Is the project a continuation of an earlier project? Are there any legal liabilities that will impact the project?
(3) Assess the impact of the project on the community. Are there any special energy requirements? How will the project affect the aesthetic value of the community (noise, air, commuters, households, recreation and quality of life)? Are there any health and safety issues?
(4) Determine possible health and safety effects (accidents, illness, sewage, etc.).
(5) Estimate how the project will disrupt day-to-day activities in the community.
(6) What is the impact of the project on the various populations in the community? Consider the following factors: race, income, single parent households, age and disabled.
(7) Ascertain the level of public support for the project. Is the project consistent with the master plan for the community?
(8) If the project is not funded or deferred, what impact will this have on the community (i.e. higher costs, inconvenience)?
(9) Will the project benefit or adversely impact other localities?
(10) Will the project benefit or adversely impact other capital projects?

Source: Created by the Author.

FINANCING CAPITAL IMPROVEMENT PROJECTS

In most state and local governments where funds are limited, a decision to pursue a project and the decision to fund a project occur relatively close together. While it is possible for a project to create revenue, a lot of projects do not generate revenue. In either case, the budget officer should make at least four revenue projections relative to funding capital outlay: current operating revenue and expenditures, current outstanding debt, annual debt-service payments and intergovernmental grants and aid. Every attempt should be made to determine how the economy and other environmental and demographic changes have affected these items (Bifulco, Bunch, Duncombe, Robbins, and Simonsen 2012; Vogt 1996; 2004).

Funding a capital project, to a large extent, depends on the project. For example, it is feasible to fund the construction of a new highway from a toll on the highway. However, it would not be feasible to use a highway toll to fund the construction of a new school. This is illegal. A bond may be a better alternative.

Bland and Rubin (1997) offer two basic strategies for financing capital improvement projects. The first is *pay-as-you-go* financing. In this method, officials may use current revenues, federal or state grants, reserve funds, revenue from leases or other revenue such as utility charges to fund projects. Vogt (1983) points out several advantages to using this method. First, "it encourages responsible spending by requiring the same officials who approve projects or outlays also to levy taxes to pay for them," "it avoids paying the interest charges that are involved with bonding; and it avoids the accumulation of large, fixed principal and interest payments in the operating budget" (139). It also, "sidesteps bond and debt markets" as well as improves the financial position of the local government by holding down debt and lowering debt service cost (Solano 2004; Vogt 2004, 144). Pay-as-you-go financing is particularly effective if a government has a consistent need for infrastructure maintenance. For example, a mature state or local government needs to replace and maintain its streets, waterlines, and sewer lines. Dedicating a set amount annually for this purpose avoids the extra interest charges (Wang and Hou 2009).

Vogt (2004) offers a second *pay-as-go* or cash method for financing capital projects by creating a capital reserve. Essentially revenues would be diverted from other sources into this capital fund which could be used when the time arose. Spending does not occur until a sufficient amount of revenues have been collected to meet the needs of the expenditure. For example, a city might want to construct a new city park and have a five-year plan to save the funds to pay for it. A *capital reserve* would be the perfect tool to facilitate this process. A note to the wise, it is better to separate the *capital reserve fund* from other funds. This prevents *fungibility* from occurring easily (Aronson and Schwartz 2004).

The second method is *pay-as-you-use* financing. This includes bonds or other debt instruments, assessments on recipients of the service, or mortgages or bank loans. Robert L. Bland and Wes Clarke (1999) point out two advantages to debt financing. First, it allows a government to acquire capital as needed yet devote a relatively stable amount of current revenue each year for debt service. Second, it also removes capital acquisition decisions from the operating budget process, which is often completed under a tight time constraint. This also allows officials to better plan for the future (see also Aronson and Schwartz 2004; Vogt 1983). Another advantage of pay-as-you-use financing is that the taxpayers who are receiving the benefit of the project are paying for it. The taxpayers are contributing annually to the payment for debt service.

Riley and Colby (1991) offer several methods to the pay-as-you-use financing method. The first method is to issue *bonds*. A bond is basically money that is borrowed from an individual(s) with the assurance that the bond can be cashed in a given period of time for a sum of money (principal and interest). State and local governments use bonds to finance projects that cannot be financed from the current revenue sources. The interest earned on bonds is not taxable by the United States government.

Bonds can be issued through public entities to assist in private development activities, if they further the objectives of a particular agency (e.g., economic development, energy conservation, affordable housing). These bonds can either be *revenue bonds*, which are a type of *municipal bond* where principal and interest are secured by revenues such as charges or rents paid by users of the facility built with the proceeds of the bond issue. The issuer of a revenue bond is not obligated to use any other funding source to pay back the bond. Projects financed by revenue bonds include turnpikes, airports, and not-for-profit health care and other facilities.

The more common approach is to use *general obligation bonds* (GO), which may be taxable or tax-exempt bonds which are backed by the general "faith and credit" of the issuing entity to assure repayment of the bonds. Because the backing for revenue bonds is limited to the revenue stream that is used to support the bonds, they have a higher interest rate than general obligation bonds. General obligation bonds can make up more than a third of the long-term debt issued by state and local governments (Vogt 2004).[7]

Prior to securing any type of bond, a local government may need to be rated. *Bond ratings* are quite similar to an individual credit report that you or I may get prior to buying a house or a car. Vogt (2004) describes it this way:

> A bond rating evaluates a debt issuer's strength or weakness on factors that bear on the issuer's ability and willingness to make principal and interest payments on the debt when due and to comply with other obligations that the issuer assumes under the debt contract. A rating addresses not only the probability that the issuer will make debt service payments but also the legal protection afforded to investors by laws, regulations, and the debt contract. Such protection or security varies by type of debt and also depends on state and federal laws and regulations. (Vogt, A. John. 2004. *Capital Budgeting and Finance: A Guide for Governments*. Washington, DC: ICMA)

As shown, the emphasis is on the ability of the entity to repay the amount borrowed with the interest and the protection afforded to the investors (see Aronson and Schwartz 2004; for a description of bonds and ratings; Krueger and Walker 2010; Srithongrung 2008; Vogt 2004).

Some governments are precluded from issuing general obligation debt because of legal restrictions or debt limitations. Other types of financing instruments have been created to allow governments to construct capital facilities. For example, a government might enter into a lease-purchase arrangement with a private contractor to build a water treatment plant. The government makes lease payments to the contractor until the project is paid off. At that point, it is turned over to the government. Another financing option is a *certificate of participation*. A government contacts one or more financial institutions and a pool is formed. Each participant in the pool receives a certificate of participation. The project is financed using the resources in the pool and the resulting facility is leased to the government. Each participant receives a share of the debt service based on its participation in the pool.

A municipality may also secure *short-term notes* or use a *line of credit* (LOC) where "money is made available for the local government to use on an "as needed" basis (Riley and Colby 1983, 110).[8] Short-term notes are used during the construction phase of a project because of arbitrage restrictions established by the Internal Revenue Service (IRS). Since debt issued by state and local governments is exempt from federal taxes, the IRS requires funding of a capital project to be undertaken as cash is needed. For example, if a government is building a facility that costs $10 million, issuing $10 million in bonds when the project is approved would allow the government to invest the proceeds and earn substantial interest for some period of time. Under the arbitrage rules, a government now has to reimburse the federal government for such arbitrage earnings. Thus, governments finance the projects during the construction period by using short-term notes. City and counties can also *joint finance* projects that will be shared.[9]

CONCLUSION

While there are some similarities between an operating and a capital budget, it is clear that the differences substantiate separating the two. It is important for the reader to understand that investments into capital infrastructure and the use of public resources to fund capital projects play a major role in economic development and growth in states and municipalities. Hence, time and resources devoted to the process should not be taken lightly. Chapters 5 and 6 in this text will further this topic with a discussion of payment options and maximizing the use of capital facilities through analytical models and techniques.

IMPORTANT TERMS AND PHRASES

Bond
Bond Rating
Budget Adoption
Capital Budget
Capital Budget Calendar
Capital Improvement Plan
Capital Reserve
Capital Reserve Fund
Certificate of Participation
Fixed Cost
Fungibility
General Obligation Bonds (GO)
Implementation
Internal Revenue Service (IRS)

Joint Finance
Line of Credit (LOC)
Marginal Cost
Municipal Bond
Pay-as-you-go
Pay-as-you-use
Planning
Post Evaluation
Project Evaluation
Revenue Bonds
Recurring Cost
Short Term Note
Startup costs
Unit Costs

CHAPTER 4 HOMEWORK EXERCISES

Directions: Templates for questions 3, 4, and 5 are found in the appendix. Please turn in your Excel worksheets and the MS Word file with the pasted worksheets to your instructor.

(1) Research and define each of the following terms:

    (a) Marginal Cost
    (b) Recurring Cost
    (c) Indirect Cost
    (d) Direct Cost
    (e) Fixed Cost
    (f) Up Front Cost
    (g) Variable Cost
    (h) Unit Cost
    (i) One Time Cost
    (j) Operating Cost
    (k) Step Cost

(2) Based on your research and the material in this text, why would a city prefer to use a municipal bond to finance a long term capital project versus creating a new tax?

(3) As the new chief of Jefferson City's Fire Department, it is your job (budget analyst) to write the justifications for the department's proposed FY 2020 capital budget. Specifically, you must prepare justifications for the proposed new fire station near the New Loudon Subdivision. Remember, you are trying to convince the city's elected officials that the construction of a new fire department will allow your department to be more efficient and effective. Further, your justifications should show that you have considered the long range plans of the city's elected officials to expand public services.

    The items needed to construct the fire department are listed below the table. Land that could be used for the station was purchased in FY 2019. Although some of the items in the estimated and proposed budgets are for existing services, the majority of the items are for the new station. This is particularly true in FY 2020. Exhibit 4.1 serves as a point of departure.

    Also, there is an example of a proposal in appendix 4A and 4B. Your proposal should have: a *project summary* and a *project description* in your justification along with the *proposed capital budget* that is listed below. While there can be legal reasons to build the station, remember: economic growth, population growth, and other factors contribute to the need to build the station. Use logic and creativity when writing your justifications (use paragraphs). Include your justifications within the project description (also include comments on the individuals items in the budget).

Jefferson City Fire Department's FY 2021 Proposed Capital Budget				
Object Code	Item	Quantity FY 2019	FY 2020 Cost (Est)	FY 2021 Cost (Proposed)
3003	Computers	5	$5,000	$5,000
3004	Security System	1		30,000
3005	Copy Machine	2	4,000	4,000
3007	¾ Ton Truck	1		25,000
3008	Office Desks	3	1,500 (10)	450
3009	Pumper	1		95,000
3010	Tanker	1		125,000
3011	New Fire Station	1		756,000
3012	Water Well	1		195,000
3013	Land	4 acres	4,500.00 (acre)	9,000
TOTAL			$15,000	$1,244,450

Items Needed for the Fire Station:

- Computers
- Copy Machine
- Fire Station
- Land
- Office Desk
- Pumper
- Security System
- Tanker
- ¾ Ton Truck
- Water Well

Note: A Tanker and Pumper are large fire trucks

(4) Jefferson City has several capital projects that the mayor wants to complete over the next two to three years (FY 2020–2022). She has asked you, the city manager, to prioritize the eight projects and justify each placement based on some sort of rational methodology. Your rankings will determine where the project will be placed in the final CIP which will be completed by another group. Hence, review, rank, and justify the list of projects on a scale of 1 to 8. The most important project should be listed first (include the projected cost with the name of the project). In addition to considering the information in the text, pay special attention

to the list of questions in table 4.1. I have included some background information on the city that should be useful in your rankings and justifications. Your justifications should be logically creative. See appendix 4C.

Projects and Costs:

- *CBD Sewers*: Add 5 miles of sewers in the central business district ($6.2 million).
- *ERA Sewers*: Add 2 miles of sewer lines in the eastern residential area ($4.53 million).
- *NRA*: Build a new waste treatment lift station in the northern residential area ($6.8 million).
- *Beltway Project*: Complete the final stage of the beltway around the city (3 miles) ($6.3 million).
- *Storm Water Project*: Construct two storm water management ponds ($2.5 million).
- *Library Renovation:* Update the entry to the building, remodel the circulation department and install a new book checkout system ($850,000).
- *Downtown Garage*: Construct a downtown parking garage for city employees and public use ($4.5 million).
- *Downtown Artery*: Landscaping the main downtown artery ($950,000).

Background Information:

- The population of the city has grown an average of 3% a year for the last five years.
- The number of public service employees has increased an average of 1% a year for the last ten years.
- Ten new corporations have moved into the city over the last three years employing 3,450 new employees. Roughly half of them are located in the southern region and the other half in the northern region. However, those in the southern region tend to be more dependent upon water given the nature of the business.
- The city has 107,000 residents and lies in between two large cities exceeding 1 million residents.
- The land selected for the construction of the ponds is located near a school and a public park.
- The average household income in the city is $79,000 per year.

(5) You have been hired by the state of Alexander as a budget analyst to develop a capital improvement plan. The state had an economic windfall with the collection of revenue from the gaming industry and wants to

make good use of some of these funds to improve the states' infrastructure among other public institutions in the state. You have been given a budget of $600 million to develop a five-year CIP. You cannot spend more than your total allotment under any circumstance. Here is some useful information that you should use in developing your FY 2020–2024 CIP. The state assumes that you will not be able to solve all of the problems in the state over a five-year period, but they do expect a lot.

First, complete the spreadsheet showing that you have spent no more than $600 million. Second, briefly justify your spending patterns using the two headings: High Priority Tasks and Low Priority Tasks. The projects that you expect to complete should be justified in the *High Priority Tasks* section. The projects that you will not complete should be justified in the section *Lower Priority Tasks*. Read all of the information before you begin to work on the justifications.

The bullet points below provide all of the information that you need in order to complete your CIP. See appendix 4D for a copy of the spreadsheet.

- The state's primary and secondary educational facilities can essentially be split into two types: Functional and Dysfunctional. Dysfunctional educational facilities are located primarily in the economically depressed Schaefer Delta. There are forty-five schools in this area that are identical and each is in need of repair and renovations. Repair and renovation cost average $250,000 per school. School renovations should be completed within the first three years of the CIP (equal amounts spent each year). The Functional schools are completely up to date and require no repair or renovations.
- The state is plagued with a number of two-lane highways that cross the state. The first highway is *Highway 66* and it goes south of the Davisville state line through the Alexander Delta to Brownsville (240 miles in length). It is the main north-south route. Given the low economic productivity in the state, it is vital that this highway be completed at some point. Should you decide to expend funds to complete Highway 66, you must complete at least 90 percent of the highway.
- *Highway 87* is the second major highway in the state and it goes from the Arkadelphia border to the Columbia border (eighty-five miles that is currently two-lane). It is the main east-west corridor. Improvement to the highway system should reap multiple economic benefits. Particularly in the Delta Region. Should you decide to expend funds to complete the highway, you must complete at least 95 percent of Highway 87. It will cost $2 million per mile to complete the four-lane highway system (Highway 66 and 87).

- The state has eighty-seven county health departments. Thirty-six of these building are in need of repair. Three additional buildings should be constructed adjacent to existing health departments in Desoto, Simms and Bolivar counties. The construction estimates for each building is $300,000. Repair costs are estimated to cost a total of $10 million. Bolivar County has the greatest need followed by Jackson and Desoto County respectively.
- The Supreme Court building is in need of repair. Given the nature of the repair, at least two fiscal years will be involved with the same amount spent each year. The repairs cost $5 million.
- For the sake of beautification, the state has also decided to build six new Welcome Centers in the state. These fully functional centers will cost the state $1 million each. The Welcome Centers will be located at both ends of the border for Highway 66, Highway 87 and Interstate 55. With the new highways under construction, the Welcome Centers should improve the image of the state.
- You can spend up to the following amounts per fiscal year: 2020, $115 million; 2021, $110 million; 2022, $40 million; 2023, $165 million; and 2024, $180 million.

The chart below shows the total costs of all projects fully funded. However, please remember that you are limited to *$600 million* in your CIP budget.

Fully Funded Projects	Cost
Dysfunctional Schools	$11,250,000
HWY 66	480,000,000
HWY 87	170,000,000
Welcome Centers	6,000,000
New Health Departments	900,000
Health Department Repair	10,000,000
Supreme Court BDLG	5,000,000
TOTAL	$683,150,000

(6) Optional In-class Exercise: Discussing CIP Items in the Jefferson City Council Meeting (1- hour exercise)

   (a) *Before Class Assignment*: Each student should examine and make copies of a city's CIP plan in order to see how projects are justified for different departments. In addition, print out the Excel spreadsheet for question 4.

(b) *In-Class Scenario*: The City Council has planned a hearing to discuss the CIP for FYs 2020–2024 and each of the city's departments must present their individual CIP to the council. The city has $400 million to fund projects over the five year CIP with no spending caps in any particular year. A template with the total amount of funds requested from the city's department in each fiscal year is provided below. Hence, you should keep this in mind as you plan your spending priorities. You should also remember that it is your objective to fully fund all of the items in your agency CIP. Please review the spreadsheets in appendix 4E (and below) for the agency line-item requests.

Fully Funded Allocations by Fiscal Year (Amounts in millions)						
	FY 2020	FY 2021	FY 2022	FY 2023	FY 2024	TOTAL
Public Works	$39.75	$44.75	$44	$38	$38	$204.5
Engineering	55.7	32.7	34.2	32.2	30.7	185.5
Parks & Rec.	17.5	32.5	15	15	5	85
Police Dept.	8	9.5	15.5	15.5	10.5	59
Housing & Com. Dev.	10	15.5	23.5	16	10	75
TOTAL	$130.95	$134.95	$132.2	$116.7	$94.2	$609.0

Step 1: Divide into small groups (4–6 students). One group will represent the City Council (4–5 members) while the remaining groups will represent bureaucratic departments/agencies within the city. One person should be selected to serve as the City Council Chairman. In addition, one person in each bureaucratic group will serve as Department Head to coordinate and record the outcome of the meeting with their staff. Reduce the number of group members as needed to ensure that all five departments are represented.

Step 2: Using the data provided below, each bureaucratic group should prioritize (numerically) the items listed for their agency capital improvement plan (The amount listed below for each item is the total amount budgeted for the item). This priority list will be presented by the department head to the city council. Although the agency head will have the final say in their department, all group members should feel free to offer their recommendations. Remember, your job is to convince the city council that all of your projects should be included in the final CIP. You have twenty minutes to prioritize and justify your projects.

Step 3: Each department head will present their priority list to City Council. The Council will listen and ask the department heads questions and eventu-

ally adjourn to decide whose projects will be added to the CIP. Each department will have five minutes to present their plan with no more than five
questions from the Council to each agency.

Step 4: The Council will take fifteen minutes to contemplate the plan and
then reveal the final CIP to the department heads and their staff. They should
include justifications for their actions. Under no circumstances should the
CIP be extended to more than five years and no additional funds should be
added to the CIP ($400 million maximum).

ADDITIONAL INFORMATION AND SUGGESTIONS

- Agencies should rank each of the bulleted items from highest to lowest.
- Groups should request the full amount listed.
- There are five districts in Youngstown. The population is growing in dis-
  trict 1, 2, and 3 at a faster rate than in districts 4 and 5.
- Industrial growth is occurring in districts 4 and 5 at a faster rate than the
  other districts.
- New schools are needed in district 1 and 2.
- Roughly 75 percent of the housing and community development projects
  are in district 3 and 5.

DEPARTMENT INFORMATION AND PROJECTS
(TOTAL COST IN PARENTHESIS)

(1) Public Works ($204.5 million)

- Road Resurfacing ($35 million spent equally over the five year CIP)
- Curb Ramps at Intersections ($15 million spent equally over the five
  year CIP)
- Vehicles ($5 million spent equally over the first two years of the CIP)
- Equipment ($15 million spent equally over the five year CIP)
- Information Technology ($30 million spent equally during the latter
  three years of the CIP)
- Safety Enhancement on School Pedestrian Route ($500,000 spent
  equally during the first two years of the CIP)
- Contract Construction ($75 million spent equally over the five year CIP)
- Land Acquisition (widen roads and create storm water funds) ($18
  million spent equally over the first two years of the CIP)
- Street Lights Replacement and Expansion ($1 million in FY 2020)

- Expand Airways Rd to accommodate industrial growth ($10 million spent equally in FY 2021 and 2022)

(2) Engineering ($185.5 million)

- Street Repair ($50 million spent equally over the five year CIP)
- Replacement Bridge at County Road and Hwy 4 ($25 million in FY20)
- Land Acquisition ($10 million spent equally over the five year CIP)
- Traffic Signals ($3.5 million spent equally over five year CIP)
- Contract Construction ($75 million spent equally over four years of the CIP)
- Pedestrian Walking Trails ($4 million spent equally over the second and third fiscal years of the CIP)
- Bike Riding Lanes ($3 million spent equally over third and fourth fiscal years of the CIP)
- Vehicles ($15 million spent equally over the latter four fiscal years of the CIP)

(3) Parks and Recreation ($85 million)

- Vehicles ($15 million spent equally over the latter three years of the CIP)
- Equipment ($15 million spent equally over the first two years of the CIP)
- Zoo Major Maintenance ($20 million spent equally over years three and four of the CIP)
- City Museum Major Maintenance ($10 million during year one of the CIP)
- City Park Rehabilitation and Maintenance ($25 million in year two of the CIP)

(4) Police Department ($59 million)

- Vehicles ($25 million spent equally over the five year CIP)
- Equipment ($15 million spent equally over the five year CIP)
- New Station with furniture, fixtures, equipment and information technology ($1.5 million in year two of the CIP)
- Main Office Renovations ($5 million spent equally in years four and five of the CIP)
- Helicopter ($2.5 million in year three of the CIP)
- Traffic Light Cameras ($10 million spent equally in years three and four of the CIP)

(5) Housing and Community Development ($75 million)

- Vocational and Rehabilitation Center ($10 million spent equally during the first year of the CIP)

- Young Public Housing Complex ($24 million spent equally during the middle three years of the CIP)
- Boone Gardens Housing Complex Renovations ($15 million spent equally during the second and third years of the CIP)
- Boone Gardens Housing Complex Swimming Pool Renovations ($2 million in FY 2024)
- Anderson Housing Complex ($24 million spent equally during the last three years of the CIP)

Note: If the class is too small to complete the full blown project, simply reduce the CIP Budget to $300 (maximum) and only use the first two items in the list or reduce the budget to $250 million and use items (1) and (5). The remaining items in the directions would remain the same.

NOTES

1. Review Robert L. Bland and Wes Clarke (1999), "Budgeting for Capital Improvements," in *Handbook of Government Budgeting*, ed. Roy T. Meyers (San Francisco: Jossey Bass), 653–77; John L. Mikesell (2018), *Fiscal Administration: Analysis and Applications for the Public Sector*, 10th ed. (Belmont, CA: Wadsworth Cengage Publishers); J. Richard Aronson and Eli Schwartz (2004), "Cost-Benefit Analysis and the Capital Budget," in *Management Policies in Local Government Finance*, 5th ed., ed. J. Richard Aronson and Eli Schwartz (Washington, DC: ICMA), 133–53; Thomas D. Lynch, Jinping Sun, and Robert W. Smith (2017), *Public Budgeting in America*, 6th ed. (Irvine, CA: Melvin & Leigh); Paul L. Solano (2004), "Budgeting," in *Management Policies in Local Government Finance*, 5th ed., ed. J. Richard Aronson and Eli Schwartz (Washington, DC: ICMA), 155–206; and A. John Vogt (2004), *Capital Budgeting and Finance: A Guide for Governments* (Washington, DC: ICMA), for additional information on capital budgets and capital improvement plans.

2. Review Donald Axelrod (1995), *Budgeting for Modern Government*, 2nd ed. (New York: St. Martin's Press), 104–5; Robert L. Bland and Irene S. Rubin (1997), *Budgeting: A Guide for Local Governments* (Washington, DC: ICMA), 169–74; Bland and Clarke (1999), "Budgeting for Capital Improvements," 654; and R. Mark Musell (2009), *Understanding Government Budget: A Practical Guide* (New York: Routledge), 41–56, for additional material discussing capital budget and budget projections.

3. Capital budgets include financing provisions and must be balanced. However, there are a number of things that can and do occur on capital projects that cause cost overruns.

4. This material was taken from David Nice (2002), *Public Budgeting* (Stamford, CT: Wadsworth/Thompson Learning), 123–27; Bland and Rubin (1997), *Budgeting*, 171–75; and Susan L. Riley and Peter W. Colby (1991), *Practical Government Budgeting: A Workbook for Public Managers* (Albany: State University of New York Press), 105–6; and Mikesell (2018), *Fiscal Administration*.

5. This includes experienced managers, service professionals, budget and finance staff, governing board members, other officials, and citizens.

6. Excerpted from: A John Vogt's (2004), "Prioritizing Capital Projects," in *Capital Budgeting and Finance: A Guide for Local Government* (Washington, DC: ICMA).

7. Many governments are not allowed to issue debt. So, instead they use other means such as certificates of participation and lease-purchase arrangements.

8. See the debt administration section of chap. 7 for more information on financing debt using bonds.

9. Review chaps. 6, 7, and 8 of Vogt (2004), *Capital Budgeting and Finance*, for a thorough discussion of these items.

Appendix 4A

City of Alexandria, Virginia Health Department

Alexandria Health Department's (AHD) mission is to protect and promote health and well-being for all Alexandria communities and includes serving other Virginia residents and others as required by Virginia Department of Health and/or federally funded services. AHD Public Health Specialty Clinics are essential elements of Alexandria's safety net system. The Prenatal Clinic offers pregnancy and post-partum care and the Nurse Case Management Program serves high-risk pregnant women, infants and children. Preventive Clinic services and programs, unique to AHD, include the Nutrition/WIC Program, Immunization Clinic, Family Planning, Sexually Transmitted Infection Clinic, HIV/AIDS services, and the Tuberculosis Program. The Teen Wellness Center provides health services to Alexandria youth. AHD's Environmental Health Division operates Food Safety, Vector Control and Aquatic Health programs. AHD's Public Health Emergency Management helps Alexandria communities prepare for, respond to and recover from public health emergencies and includes the Medical Reserve Corps, a program to recruit and retain volunteers. AHD's Epidemiology Program investigates, monitors, and offers guidance to prevent and control, communicable diseases; it also analyzes and interprets data to guide program and policy development. AHD's Community Partnerships Program provides research, policy development, and public health leadership to Alexandria organizations and communities so all Alexandrians have an equal opportunity for health.

STRATEGIC PLAN INDICATORS
SUPPORTED BY THIS DEPARTMENT

- Increase the percentage of residents who feel they are in very good or excellent health from 73 percent (fiscal year).
- Reduce obesity among city residents from 16 percent in 2013–2014 to 13 percent (calendar year) (reported using two years of data).
- Reduce the teen pregnancy rate from 23 per 1,000 in 2016 to 10 (calendar year).

- Reduce the City's infant mortality rate from 5.1 per 1,000 live births in 2014 to 3.1 (calendar year).

		Strategic Plan Indicators			
Key Department Indicators	FY 2014 Actual	FY 2015 Actual	FY 2016 Actual	FY 2017 Estimate	Target
Percent of Health Department programs achieving an average rating from clients of at least an 8.5 out of 10 regarding satisfaction with services received (1= Very Dissatisfied; 10 =Very Satisfied)	—	100%	100%	100%	100%
Total number of registered client visits to the Health Department	65,823	65,800	63,664	65,812	66,500
Number of immunizations given to the public	15,930	14,618	10,234	11,380	12,200
Number of food facility inspections	2,675	2,490	2,257	2,300	2,650
Number of maternity (prenatal/OB) clinic visits provided for uninsured/ underinsured women	5,097	5,436	5,288	5,267	5,267

		Revenue & Expenditure Summary			
	FY 2016 Actual	FY 2017 Approved	FY 2018 Proposed	$ Change 2017–18	% Change 2017–18
Expenditures by Character					
Personnel	$1,398,406	$1,834,336	$1,877,421	$43,085	2.3%
Non-Personnel	$4,808,296	$4,991,295	$4,994,795	$3,500	0.1%
Capital Goods Outlay	$0	$46,457	$0	($46,457)	–100%
Interfund Transfer	$26,811	$0	$0	$0	0.0%
Depreciation	$4,484	$0	$0	$0	0.0%
TOTAL	$6,237,998	$6,872,088	$6,872,216	$128	0.0%
Expenditures by Fund					
General Fund	$6,144,794	$6,825,631	$6,872,216	$46,585	0.7%
Non-Fiscal Year Grants	$88,720	$0	$0	$0	0.0%
Internal Service Fund	$4,484	$46,457	$0	($46,457)	–100%
TOTAL	$6,237,988	$6,872,088	$6,872,216	$128	0.0%
TOTAL Department FTEs	15.43	15.63	15.63	0.00	0.0%

There are no major changes to the Health Department's FY 2018 budget. Personnel spending increases $43,085 or 2.3 percent due to merit pay increases and benefits. Non-personnel expenditures increase by $3,500. Capital Goods Outlay decreases by $46,457 due to no planned vehicle replacement in FY 2018 for the Health Department.

Department Changes to City Services			
Program	Adjustments	FTE	Amount
TOTAL FY 2017 APPROVED ALL FUNDS BUDGET		15.63	$6,872,088
All	Current Service Adjustment	0.00	$128
	Current Services adjustments reflect the change in cost of continuing the current level of service into the next fiscal year and includes increases and/or decreases in salaries & benefits, contracts, and materials		
Leadership & Management an Maternal & Child Health Care Services	Funding Shifted Between Department Programs	0.00	$0
	In FY 2017, $142,539 was added to the Health Department's budget to supplant the lost Title X Family Planning Grant. The funds were initially placed in the Leadership and Management Program and were subsequently transferred to the Maternal & Child Health Care Services Program. No service impact.		
TOTAL FY 2018 PROPOSED ALL FUNDS PROGRAM BUDGET		15.63	$6,872,216

Source: Amended from a budget obtained from the following website: City of Alexandria Virginia, (2018), "Proposed Operating Budget, Fiscal Year 2018," https://www.alexandriava.gov/uploadedFiles/budget/info/budget2018/FY%202018%20Proposed%20Operating%20Budget.pdf (accessed January 4, 2020).

Appendix 4B

Jefferson City Fire Department Capital Budget Process

As the new director of Jefferson City's Fire Department, it is your job to improve the department's capital budget process for your office. Your first job is to prepare justifications for the capital budget requests suggested by your predecessor. Below is the department Budget Request (Hint: Be creative in your justifications. Economic growth, population growth, and the age of equipment are examples of reasons for expansion, improvement or replacing equipment). Remember, you are trying to convince the city that these items will allow your department to be more efficient and effective. Further, your justifications should show that you have considered the long range plans of the city's elected officials to expand public services. The items of interest are listed below the table. The number of computers, copy machines and office desks are the same from the previous year as well as the value of the land to acreage ratio. Exhibit 4.1 can serve as a point of departure for you, but remember, there are numerous ways to write justifications, so be professionally creative in your use of space, charts, graphs, etc.

Justifications:

    (1) Computers
    (2) Security System
    (3) Copy Machines
    (4) ¾ Ton Truck
    (5) Office Desk
    (6) Pumper
    (7) Tanker
    (8) New Fire Station
    (9) Water Well
    (10) (10) Land

Appendix 4C

Jefferson City Project Justification

Rank	Project Name	Cost	Justification
1			
2			
3			
4			
5			
6			
7			
8			

Jefferson City Project Justifications

Appendix 4D

Preparing a Capital Budget and a Capital Improvement Plan

State of Alexander, Capital Improvement Plan FYs 2020–2024								
	# In Grade	FY 2020	FY 2021	FY 2022	FY 2022	FY 2023	FY 2024	TOTAL
Dysfunctional Schools	45							
HWY 66	240 miles							
HWY 87	85 miles							
Welcome Centers	6							
New Health Depts.	3							
Health Depts. Repair	36							
Supreme Court Building	1							
TOTAL								

List High Priority Tasks:

List Lower Priority Tasks:

Appendix 4E

Capital Improvement Plan

Capital Improvement Plan

	FY 2020	FY 2021	FY 2022	FY 2023	FY 2024	Total	
Public Works							
Engineering							
Parks and Recreation							
Police Department							
Housing & Community Development							
TOTAL							

Public Works	FY 2020	FY 2021	FY 2022	FY 2023	FY 2024	Summary of FYs	Total Cost
Road Resurfacing	$7,000,000	$7,000,000	$7,000,000	$7,000,000	$7,000,000	$35,000,000	$35,000,000
Curb Ramps	3,000,000	3,000,000	3,000,000	3,000,000	3,000,000	15,000,000	15,000,000
Vehicles	2,500,000	2,500,000	0	0	0	5,000,000	5,000,000
Equipment	3,000,000	3,000,000	3,000,000	3,000,000	3,000,000	15,000,000	15,000,000
Information Technology	0	0	10,000,000	10,000,000	10,000,000	30,000,000	30,000,000
Safety Enhancement	250,000	250,000	0	0	0	500,000	500,000
Contract Const.	15,000,000	15,000,000	15,000,000	15,000,000	15,000,000	75,000,000	75,000,000
Land Acquisition	9,000,000	9,000,000	0	0	0	18,000,000	18,000,000
Street Lights	0	0	1,000,000	0	0	1,000,000	1,000,000
Expand Airways	0	5,000,000	5,000,000	0	0	10,000,000	10,000,000
TOTAL	$39,750,000	$44,750,000	$44,000,000	$38,000,000	$38,000,000	$204,500,000	$204,500,000

Engineering	FY 2020	FY 2021	FY 2022	FY 2023	FY 2024	Summary of FYs	Total Cost
Street Repair	$10,000,000	$10,000,000	$10,000,000	$10,000,000	$10,000,000	$50,000,000	$50,000,000
Replacement Bridge	25,000,000	0	0	0	0	25,000,000	25,000,000
Land Acquisition	2,000,000	2,000,000	2,000,000	2,000,000	2,000,000	10,000,000	10,000,000
Traffic Signals	700,000	700,000	700,000	700,000	700,000	3,500,000	3,500,000
Contract Construction	15,000,000	15,000,000	15,000,000	15,000,000	15,000,000	75,000,000	75,000,000
Pedestrian Routes	0	2,000,000	2,000,000	0	0	4,000,000	4,000,000
Bike Routes	0	0	1,500,000	1,500,000	0	3,000,000	3,000,000
Vehicles	3,000,000	3,000,000	3,000,000	3,000,000	3,000,000	15,000,000	15,000,000
TOTAL	$55,700,000	$32,700,000	$34,200,000	$32,200,000	$30,700,000	$185,500,000	$185,500,000

Parks and Recreation	FY 2020	FY 2021	FY 2022	FY 2023	FY 2024	Summary of FYs	Total Cost
Vehicles	$0	$0	$5,000,000	$5,000,000	$5,000,000	$15,000,000	$15,000,000
Equipment	7,500,000	7,500,000	0	0	0	15,000,000	15,000,000
Zoo Maintenance	0	0	10,000,000	10,000,000	0	20,000,000	20,000,000
Museum Maintenance	10,000,000	0	0	0	0	10,000,000	10,000,000
Park Maintenance	0	25,000,000	0	0	0	25,000,000	25,000,000
TOTAL	$17,500,000	$32,500,000	$15,000,000	$15,000,000	$5,000,000	$85,000,000	$85,000,000

Capital Improvement Plan (Continued)

Police Department	FY 2020	FY 2021	FY 2022	FY 2023	FY 2024	Summary of FYs	Total Cost
Vehicles	$5,000,000	$5,000,000	$5,000,000	$5,000,000	$5,000,000	$25,000,000	$25,000,000
Equipment	3,000,000	3,000,000	3,000,000	3,000,000	3,000,000	15,000,000	15,000,000
New Station	0	1,500,000	0	0	0	1,500,000	1,500,000
Main Office Renovations	0	0	0	2,500,000	2,500,000	5,000,000	5,000,000
Helicopter	0	0	2,500,000	0	0	2,500,000	2,500,000
Traffic Division	0	0	5,000,000	5,000,000	0	10,000,000	10,000,000
TOTAL	$8,000,000	$9,500,000	$15,500,000	$15,500,000	$10,500,000	$59,000,000	$59,000,000

Housing & Community Development	FY 2020	FY 2021	FY 2022	FY 2023	FY 2024	Summary of FYs	Total Cost
Voc. & Rehab Center	$10,000,000	$0	$0	$0	$0	$10,000,000	$10,000,000
Young Complex	0	8,000,000	8,000,000	8,000,000	0	24,000,000	24,000,000
Boone Gardens Comp ex	0	7,500,000	7,500,000	0	0	15,000,000	15,000,000
Boone Gardens Pool	0	0	0	0	2,000,000	2,000,000	2,000,000
Anderson Complex	0	0	8,000,000	8,000,000	8,000,000	24,000,000	24,000,000
TOTAL	$10,000,000	$15,500,000	$23,500,000	$16,000,000	$10,000,000	$75,000,000	$75,000,000

Source: Created by the Author.

Chapter 5

Funding State and Local Budgets

OVERVIEW

While the previous chapters have more or less focused on the expenditure side of the budget, this chapter concentrates on *revenue*. Revenue is the life blood of governments and a very important factor for government officials and citizens to consider when making policy decisions. In FY 2017, thirty-one states began the year predicting budget shortfalls (Gleason 2017). In some cases, these deficits were projected well into the hundreds of millions of dollars. In FY 2018, forty states had revenues higher than their projections (NASBO 2018). Hence, it is quite important that government officials closely examine potential revenue sources and spend quality time conducting accurate revenue forecasts. Due to limited revenue sources it is also important that government engage in *revenue management*. This chapter begins with a general discussion of revenue sources for all levels of government followed with a more detailed examination of state and local revenue sources. This includes the newest form of revenue sources: medicinal and recreational marijuana, lotteries and gaming.

SOURCES OF REVENUE

The number one source of revenue for state and local governments is *taxes*. Taxes are "compulsory charges made against the public by a government to obtain the money it needs to finance its activities" (Mendonsa 1983, 63; see also Rose 2010). Taxes come in various forms and differ somewhat from one governmental unit to the next. For example, the federal government depends heavily upon *federal individual income taxes* and *social insurance* receipts while state governments depend a lot on *sales* and *individual state income taxes*. Local governments are more dependent upon *property taxes* (Bartle, Kriz, and Morozov 2011). Some taxes are considered *regressive* while others are considered *progressive*.[1] However, taxes are not the only source of revenue for state and local governments. Revenues are also collected from *user fees; intergovernmental transfers; licenses and permits; and excise taxes on motor fuels, gaming, recreational and medicinal marijuana, alcohol sales and tobacco sales;* and various other charges (fines, forfeitures). Many cities work under the auspices of a charter and this document dictates what sort of taxes will be collected. For example, some cities collect income from earning.[2] However, legislative approval is often needed to add an additional tax. Table 5.1 shows the major categories of revenues for the federal, state and local government along with budget representation estimates. These estimates can differ by state and local governments for any particular year (Carroll 2009; Kioko 2011; Mikesell 2014).

As shown below, the federal government is heavily dependent upon individual income taxes and social insurance payments. However, social insurance is not used to fund any federal program, since it is considered a trust. State and local governments are much more diverse and balanced in their sources of revenue. Most notable with these latter two levels of government is the dependence upon intergovernmental transfers.

Table 5.1. Major Sources of Revenues in the United States				
	Element	*Federal*	*State*	*Local*
1	Individual Income Taxes	44%		2%
2	State Income Taxes		18%	
3	Corporate Income Taxes	11%	2%	
4	Sales Taxes		23%	7%
5	Property Taxes			30%
6	Excise Taxes	3%		
7	Social Insurance	36%		
8	Intergovernmental Transfers		33%	36%
9	Insurance Trust Revenues		20%	
10	Charges, Fees and Miscellaneous		18%	23%
11	All Other	6%	5%	2%

Note: These are all rough yearly estimates. *Source*: The exact dollar amounts can be found at the following location: Tax Policy Center (2018), "The Tax Policy Center Briefing Book: A Citizen's Guide to the Tax System and Tax Policy," Washington, DC.

Further, state governments are modestly dependent upon sales and income taxes, and *insurance trust revenues.* Insurance trust revenues are "taxes and fees that finance various insurance trusts to support unemployment compensation programs, state employee pensions, and other programs" (Nice 2002,

26). Lastly, local governments depend on property taxes, charges and fees. Taxes are traditionally evaluated using the following dimensions:

(a) Yield: How much money can be raised using the tax?
(b) Stability: How much does the revenue fluctuate based on changes in the economy?
(c) Equity: Do similarly situated people pay the same level of tax? Do those who have a greater ability to pay more contribute more?
(d) Efficiency: Does the tax distort economic activity? How much does it cost to administer the tax and who covers those costs?

Given the fact that states and local governments have a plethora of revenue sources at their disposal, one can use the following formula to determine the level of revenue needed:

$$Yield = Rate * Base$$

(e) Yield = Revenue.
(f) Rate = The rate is levied against the base (i.e., higher incomes are taxed at a higher rate).
(g) Base = Property value, income, subject sales, etc.

In order to change the yield, you simply need to change the definition of the base as well as the rate.

TAXES

Taxes fall into three basic categories: income, consumption, and wealth. In some cases, several categories may be involved in a transaction. Taxes here are split into four general categories: (a) Property, (b) Income Taxes, (c) Sales Taxes, (d) Alcohol, Tobacco, Marijuana, and Petroleum, (e) User Charges and Impact Fees, (f) Intergovernmental Transfers, (g) Licenses, Permits, and Franchise Fees, (h) Gaming and (i) Other Revenues (see also Swain and Reed 2010).

(a) Property Taxes

A major source of revenue for local governments is *property taxes*. These are taxes levied against real property, personal property and the property of a privately owned utility. Real property consists of land, homes, businesses, and other permanent fixtures. Personal property is property that can be moved from one location to another. It can be inventory, vehicles, and equipment. Privately owned utilities include real and personal property

(Kittredge and Ouart 2005; Mikesell 2014; Rubin 2006). The assessed value of these categories is usually determined by a state or local government or by judicial decision. Under normal circumstances, the market will play a role in this value. This process is very complicated to say the least.[3] However, Arthur A. Mendonsa (1983) offers the following principles when assigning value to property.

- Uniform procedures should be in place when assigning value to property. Property that are similar should be assessed the same. That is, property that have "equal market value should be assigned approximately equal taxable values" (63).
- Assessed values should be adjusted periodically to keep pace with market value. When market values decrease, the assessed value should likewise decrease and vice versa.
- Officials should make every effort to tax all property. This includes using "aerial photographs, field surveys, comparing utility customer records with personal property tax rolls, and other search and find techniques" (64).

According to Gerasimos A. Gianakis and Clifford P. McCue (1999) property taxes is one of the most unpopular taxes in the United States even though it is considered by most to be progressive.[4] One reason for such a poor ranking is based on the principle of capital gains. That is, as the value of the property increases, so does the amount of the tax unless the rate is reduced. Since the gain in wealth is not realized until the property is sold the tax seems unfair since the property tax is paid each year. The tax can also be used to balance the budget of a local government when other options do not appear to be feasible.[5] Even though a large number of tax bills are escrowed, the bill comes once a year and thus is highly visible to the taxpayer. Infrequent reassessments may also have a negative impact on property during periods of economic downturn. Lastly, taxpayers see the value of their property as subjective and arbitrarily set by the government (Lynch, Sun, and Smith 2017).

Setting the Property Tax Rate

There are quite a few items that are considered when setting the property tax rate. These include items such as the location (city vs. rural) of the property and what the property is used for (business vs. residential). There are three basic operations used when setting the tax rate: *assessment of property value* (*tax assessor*), establishing the *tax rate* (*millage rate*), and collecting the tax (*tax collector*). The legislative body sets the tax rate while assessment and collection can be done by the same or separate institutions.

Tax Assessments and Tax Rates

The *tax assessors* office normally identifies and classifies property. Property can be classified as: residential versus business; farm versus non-farm; or farm, residential, commercial or industrial. Farmland is taxed at a much lower rate than non-farm land and businesses tend to be taxed at a much higher rate than residential areas unless they are new to the area (Lynch et al. 2017). Another important characteristic in this process is to determine the role of exemptions. An exemption is the "amount deducted from the assessed value of property for tax purposes" (Riley and Colby 1991). Homestead exemptions are very common. However, there could be exemptions for widowers, senior citizens, handicap residents, etc.

The *market price/value* of the property is also very important when establishing the tax rate. Market price is the price that a seller and buyer are willing to accept without coercion. Normally, this is the price used in the assessment. After the assessor places a value on the property, the tax rate is established. While the government expects other revenue, the tax rate is still influenced by the amount of revenue needed to run the government. If expenditures are not balanced, the property tax rate can increase or the budget can be cut (Raphaelson 2004).

A local government can either decide how much money it needs from property taxes or simply set the property tax rate. In method one, let's assume that the government needs $200,000 from individual property taxes and the tax assessor has determined the total assessed value of individual property taxes is $4,000,000. So, if you divide the amount of funds needed by the total assessed valued, you will get the *fixed or nominal tax rate*. In this case, the rate would be 0.05 or 5 percent ($200,000 / $4,000,000). Therefore, a home assessed at $55,000 would yield $2,750 in property taxes (0.05 × $55,000). The tax rate typically changes for business and personal property.

In the second method, property tax rates are set up front and then applied to property. This rate is commonly assessed using a *millage rate* or a "cents on the dollar method. A millage rate is expressed in terms of mills. One mill yields (1/1000 of one dollar) $1.00 of tax liability for every $1,000 of assessed value. Again, the rate would vary depending on the type of property assessed. For example, let's consider a business that has a market value of $100,000 and an assessed value of $45,000. The millage rate is 5 percent (or 50 mills / dollar). So, you multiply the assessed value by the millage rate and determine the estimated tax ($45,000 × 0.05 = $2,250). Another way of looking at this assessment is to use the following calculation: Taxes = 50 mills / $1 × $45,000 = 2,250,000 mills = $2,250.[6]

The *most effective tax rate* (METR) can be calculated by dividing the tax assessment (estimated) by market value ($2,250 / $100,000 = 0.0225 or

2.25%). When calculating multiple units, add all of the tax rates (METRs) together and divide by the total number of properties. All calculations are done after all exemptions are considered (Rabin, Hildreth, and Miller 1996).

Consider the Jefferson City Autoplex in table 5.2. As shown, the applied millage rate is 3 percent, but the question is: what is the most effective tax rate? The table shows that the METR is 2.32 percent for the cities' auto businesses.

Table 5.2. Most Effective Tax Rate Jefferson City Autoplex					
Business Entity	*Market Value*	*Assessed Value*	*Millage Rate*	*Est. Tax*	*METR*
A&B Auto	$135,000	$90,000	3%	$2,700	2.00%
Gomez's Car Repair	$200.000	$155,000	3%	$4,650	2.33%
Amber's Autos	$175,000	$150,000	3%	$4,500	2.57%
Hybrid Express	$355,000	$300,000	3%	$9,000	2.53%
McClain's BMW	$650,000	$475,000	3%	$14,250	2.19%
TOTAL	$1,515,000	$1,170,000	—	$35,100	2.32%

Source: Created by the Author.

In the above example, the estimated tax is the sum of the assessed value multiplied by the millage rate (in Excel: "=90,000*.03"). The METR for A&B Auto is calculated by dividing the estimated tax times the market value (in Excel: "=2,700/135,000"). The total METR is calculated by adding each of the individual METR together and dividing them by the total (2.00 + 2.33 + 2.57 + 2.53 + 2.19 = 11.62; 11.62 / 5 = 2.32%).

An extremely important event in property tax administration involves the date on which the property value is to be fixed. Property changes hands constantly. As a result, failing to fix a date means the government is aiming at a moving target. So, a government specifies that the value of the property will be determined as of a particular date, such as January 1st. This is known as the *lien date*. The government places a lien on the property as of that date if the tax is not paid. Thus, the government is entitled to the tax. The date on which the actually *levy* of the tax is made by the legislative body is usually later in the year. For example, the levy date might be April 1st. Unlike virtually all other taxes, a property tax is levied to support the activity of the government during a fiscal year. In this example, the fiscal year is July 1st–June 30th.

Another event that takes place is the reappraisal. Governments have different ways of *reappraising property*. Some require that an actual appraisal take place by an appraiser. This might be done every three years or more. Others allow for estimates every two or three years followed by an actual appraisal the next cycle. Estimates are usually done by analyzing housing sales in the neighborhood during the past two years. The assessor would also look at permits to see if any improvements were made.

The reappraisal process is one of the most unpopular actions that affects a property owner. An increase in the property tax bill results from an inflationary increase in the value of the property without any increase in the rate. For example, a home that had a value of $100,000 and a rate of $20 per thousand would receive a bill for $2,000. When the property was reappraised, it was valued at $120,000. Now the bill was $2,400. The most famous instance of taxpayer revolt was *Proposition 13* in California. Its passage required the rate to be reduced so that the amount paid after appraisal was substantially the same as the amount paid before. Many states have enacted similar provisions.

Coefficient of Dispersion

Let's assume for a moment that the tax assessments are questionable. That is: Were the properties assessed based on market price? Are there biases in the assessment based on the type of property? Are some properties under or over assessed? In order to answer the first question, the *coefficient of dispersion* should be checked. This test allows the examiner to determine how close are assessed values are to each other, relative to the market. Exhibit 5.1 provides an example of this test (partially excerpted from Lynch et al. 2017).

Exhibit 5.1. Coefficient of Dispersion Test				
Property	*Sales Price*	*Assessed Value*	*Assessment Ratio*	*Average Deviation*
Property 1	$100,000	$55,000	55%	55%–63%=[–8%]
Property 2	100,000	64,000	64%	64%–63%= 1%
Property 3	100,000	70,000	70%	70%–63%= 7%
TOTAL	$300,000	$189,000	189%	16%

Step 1: Individual Assessment Ratios:
$55,000 / $100,000 = .55 or 55%
$64,000 / $100,000 = .64 or 64%
$70,000 / $100,000 = .70 or 70%

Step 2: Average Assessment Ratio of Properties:
(Total Assessment Ratio / Total Number of Properties)
= Average Assessment Ratio (189 % / 3) = .63 or 63%

Step 3: Average Deviation:
(Sum of the Absolute Value of Average Deviation / Number of Properties)
= Average Deviation 8% + 1% + 7% = 16%, 16% / 3 = 5.3%

Step 4: Coefficient of Dispersion:
(Average Deviation / Average Assessment Ratio of Properties)
= 5.3% / 63% = .08 or 8%

Source: Created by the Author.

A coefficient of dispersion less than 10 percent suggest a minor problem with the assessed values. A coefficient higher than 10 percent suggests a problem and the magnitude of the problem increases as the coefficient increases. Hence, a coefficient of 8 percent does not indicate a substantial problem with the assessed values in the exhibit 5.1. The closer the coefficient is to zero the better the assessments are to each other.

Price Related Differential

Another test that can be used with the coefficient of dispersion is the *price-related differential*. This test determines if higher priced properties are under assessed. Exhibit 5.2 provides an example of this procedure (The example and subsequent steps in exhibit 5.2 were excerpted from Lynch et al. 2017, 348).

Exhibit 5.2. Price Related Differential Test			
Step 1: Calculate the individual aggregate assessment-sales ratios which are weighted by the values of the parcels in the sample. In the example below, you divide the assessed value by the sales price (i.e. $20,000 / $100,000 = 0.20 or 20% / assessed value/sales price).			
Property	*Sales Price*	*Assessed Value*	*Assessment Ratio*
Property 1	$100,000	$20,000	20%
Property 2	10,000	4,000	40%
Property 3	10,000	4,000	40%
Property 4	10,000	4,000	40%
TOTAL	$130,000	$32,000	140%

Step 2: The aggregate assessment-sales ratio is:
($32,000 / $130,000) = 0.246 or 24.6%.

Step 3: Calculate the average of the assessment ratios of the separate parcels. The average assessment ratio of properties is: 140% / 4 = 0.350 or 35%.

Step 4: Divide the mean of the assessment ratios by the aggregate assessment-sales ratio to determine the price-related differential. The price-related differential is: 35 / 24.6 = 1.42 or 142%.

Step 5: Interpreting the results. Deviation from 100% is the important figure in this analysis. A price-related differential that is 100% indicates that there is neither over assessment nor under assessment. However, if the differential is more than 100% then there is under assessment of the higher priced properties. If the differential is less than 100% then there is an under assessment of the lower priced properties. In this case, the deviation is 142% indicating the higher priced property is significantly under assessed. Mathematically, the differential indicates that the collective disparity between the sales price and the assessed value of the higher priced properties is greater than the collective disparity between the sale price and assessed value of the lower priced properties.

Source: Created by the Author.

Tax Collection

The last step in the process is tax collection. In a lot of local governments, tax collection is handled by the Tax Collector or in some instances the Sheriff's office. The Sheriff's office becomes particularly important when property is foreclosed. If property taxes are not paid, the property can be sold in order to collect the taxes. Delinquency rates normally do not exceed 5 percent. However, it is wise to assume that everyone is not going to pay their taxes when preparing property tax revenue estimates.

Tax assessors assume that the property tax will be paid yielding a one to one ratio. That is, if your taxes are $956, then you will pay $956. However, property tax payments frequently come in schedules based on months. For example, let's say that your payment is due by November 30th. The bill might have a payment schedule for October, November, December, and January. The property owner could save money by paying the bill early (October date) or pay the actual tax amount by the November 30th deadline. By delaying payment, the property owner can be penalized with a 1 percent penalty in December, 2 percent in January and then become delinquent in February with a flat 3–5 percent penalty. Although it is not a good accounting practice, you can budget for the penalties. Arguments for doing so should be based on strong historical trend analysis.

(b) Income Taxes

For a lot of states, *income taxes* make up a large proportion of taxes collected. In 2017, forty-three states collected state income taxes.[7] These taxes tend to follow the same format as federal income taxes. That is, income is defined as all income rather than just wages. An income tax is considered to be a *progressive tax*: the greater the income, the higher the tax rate. Individual income taxes make up about 18 percent of all revenue collected in a state (Tax Policy Center 2018).

Local governments can also levy and collect income taxes (*payroll taxes*). Some local governments limit the tax to earned income, such as salary and wages, rents and royalties; and lottery and other gambling winnings. In other instances, the tax is only applied to wages and salaries earned and are deducted directly from individual earnings. The tax rate is usually 1–2 percent of earned wages. Generally speaking, these taxes are considered to be *regressive taxes* because all individuals pay the same rate regardless of their salaries or wages. Thus, the rate for the CEO is the same as the rate for the mail clerk. Hence, the impact is more significant for the lower income individual. Payroll taxes also have an impact on commuters who do not live in the jurisdiction where they work, since they are also required to pay the tax. Commuters essentially pay a tax for services that they receive associated with their place of employment, such as police, fire, and road maintenance. This is particularly important for cities that have large employment centers, but whose employees live in the suburbs.

Since income and payroll taxes are taxpayer assessed, they have a low administrative overhead. That is, the tax is collected by the employer and sent to the state or local government.

Some state governments also allow local governments to collect a *corporate income tax*. However, this tax can be detrimental to promoting the business industry unless other local governments also have the tax (Bland 2005). Payroll taxes are not as stable as property taxes and are very susceptible to the business cycle. The majority of local governments do not collect payroll taxes. However, this aspect is very regional in nature.[8]

In 2019, as in most years, tax rates shifted. Exhibit 5.3 shows the tax rates for the federal government.

	Exhibit 5.3.	**Federal Tax Rates in 2019**	
Tax Rate	*Single*	*Married, Filing Jointly*	*Married Filing Separately*
10%	$0 to $9,700	$0 to $19,400	$0 to $9,700
12%	$9,701 to $39,475	$19,401 to $78,950	$9,701 to $39,475
22%	$39,476 to $84,200	$78,951 to $168,400	$39,476 to $84,200
24%	$84,201 to $160,725	$168,401 to $321,450	$84,201 to $160,725
32%	$160,726 to $204,100	$321,451 to $408,200	$160,726 to $204,100
35%	$204,101 to $510,300	$408,201 to $612,350	$204,101 to $306,175
37%	$510,301 or more	$612,351 or more	$306,176 or more

Source: IRS.gov.

Let's consider the example in exhibit 5.4. There are four employees listed in Jefferson City's legal affairs office. Note that two of the employees are listed by label while the other two are not. If you have several employees who make the same salary, it is easier to put them into one category listed by their title

	Exhibit 5.4.	**Income Tax Payments**			
Employee	*FTE*	*Salary*	*Federal Income Tax*	*State Income Tax*	*Payroll Tax*
Lei Nie	1	$97,000	$17,453.92	$5,290	$1,697.50
Lincoln Brown	1	90,000	15,773.92	4,905	1,575.00
Exec. Assistant	2	100,000	13,716.32	5,410	1,750.00
TOTAL		$287,000	$46,944.16	$15,605	$5022.50

Source: Created by the Author.

rather than listing them separately. This format does not work if you want to identify a person by name, nor does it work if and when their salaries change.

In this example, there are two executive assistants who make the exact same salary. Therefore, the amount of taxes owed would be the same after any exemptions. This method is much more efficient and effective than listing each employee.

Income taxes are normally graduated. As salary increases, so does the *tax rate*. For example, the following tax rates were used with the example in exhibit 5.3 (all of the calculations are rounded to two digits to the right of the decimal).

While this process may seem complicated, it is really quite easy. The one thing that you should remember is that employees who make lower salaries pay fewer taxes and as their salaries increase, so does the rate on the tax. However, do not make the mistake of taking the entire salary and applying one tax rate. For example, Lei Nie's federal income tax, in the above example, was calculated as follows. First, take the first $9,700 of his salary and apply a 10 percent tax rate to that amount. Second, apply a 12 percent tax rate to the next amount that falls within the second tax bracket {$29,774 ($39,475–$9,701)}, then, apply a 22 percent rate to the amount that falls within the next tax bracket {$44,724}, and finally apply a 24 percent tax rate to the last $12,799 ($97,000–$84,201) of his salary. If you calculate the math using the data for a single tax filer, it would essentially look like table 5.3:

Table 5.3. Salary and Tax Calculations		
Salary Range	Calculations	Taxes Owed
$0–$9,700	= $9,700 x 10%	= $970.50
$9,701–$39,475	= $29,774 x 12%	= $3,572.88
$39,476–$84,200	= $44,724 x 22%	= $13,487.50
$84,201–$160,725	= $76,524 x 24%	= $27,930.00
$160,726–$204,100	= $43,374 x 32%	= $74,266.50
$204,101–$510,300	= $306,199 x 35%	= $594.65
$510,301+	= ?$ x 37%	= ?$

Source: Created by the Author.

In Excel, you can use the formula: =9700*10%+(39475–9701)*12%+(84200–39476)*22%+(97000–84201)*24% to calculate Mr. Nie's taxes. As a point of reference, note that $97,000 is Mr. Nie's maximum salary.

As you can see, Mr. Nie would owe $17,453.92 in taxes. It is important to note here that the federal government rounds numbers. So, he would actually owe $17,454. If there are multiple persons considered on the salary line, you cannot use the cell number (C8), you must divide the salary by the number of people. Hence, you should write a formula to determine the taxes owed by one person and then multiply the total by the number of individuals.

An example of a formula in Excel with two persons, who make the same salary ($50,000), on one line could look like this: =(9700*10%+(39475–9701)*12%+(50000–39476)*22%)*2, or you could use: =(9700*10%+(39745–9701)*12%+((C9/B9)–39476)*22%)*2, where C9 is the total salary and B9 is the number of persons on the line / in the position description. The second formula is more efficient and effective because you do not have to change the formula to compensate for changes in the number of persons or the salary in the future. This format is very useful in estimating taxes.

In order to calculate state income taxes, you would follow the same format as the federal model. Last, since the payroll tax is a flat rate, it can be computed by simply multiplying the rate times the total salary for each employee. In this example, the state income tax is calculated at 4 percent on the first $3,000 of the employee's salary and 5.5 percent on the remaining salary (In Excel the formula is "=3000*4%+(97000–3000)*5.5%").

(c) Sale and Use Taxes

One of the largest sources of income in a state is the *sales tax*. Sales taxes are funds collected at the retail transaction stage. They are collected when goods and services are sold. One advantage for the government is that retailers bear the burden of handling most of the paperwork. The government is concerned with timely and accurate payments from the retailer. Once the taxes are collected by the state, they redistribute the funds to the appropriate local government. Many local governments also have the discretion to levy a *local option sales tax* (Wang and Zhao 2011). In many states, only counties are able to levy a sales tax. In others, a municipality may levy a tax if the county chooses not to. In still others, both the county and municipality may levy the tax. Local governments should consider all other options prior to making this decision because it could have a negative impact on revenue collections.[9] To lessen the burden on retailers, local government sales taxes are added to state sales taxes and remitted to the state.

Sales taxes are *regressive taxes* because citizens pay the same sales tax rate regardless of their income level. They also are not as stable as property because of fluctuating business cycles. Citizens will stop buying "luxury items" and reduce discretionary purchases when the economy slows down. Each state sets its own sales tax rate. States and localities also have some discretion as to what sales taxes will be applied to. For example, sales taxes are not applied to the sale of un-prepared food in Kentucky. Other products that may be exempt from sales taxes are medicines and clothing. An additional item for a state to consider is collecting the tax from the retailer. The Department of Revenue in the state of Tennessee has officers who are charged with collecting delinquent sales tax payment from retailers who collect, but choose not to send in the payments.

A *use tax* differs slightly from a sales tax. A use tax is imposed by a state to compensate for the sales tax lost when an item is purchased outside of the state, but is used within the state. For example, let's say that you buy a car in a state that has no sales tax, but you live across the border in a state that does have a sales tax. When you bring the car home and register it in your state, the state taxing authority will bill you for the sales tax it would have collected had you bought the car within the state. Otherwise, you are not able to legally use the car in the state where you live (Kittredge and Ouart 2005).

(d) Alcohol, Tobacco, Marijuana, and Motor Fuel Taxes

Alcohol, tobacco, marijuana, and motor fuel taxes are also collected at the time of sale. These are also called *excise taxes* because a rate is applied to a specific product on a per unit basis. In many cases, such as alcohol and tobacco, the purpose of the tax is used to curtail the use of the product. Excise taxes are also applied to luxury items such as luxury boats and cars and hotel rooms. In some cases, these funds are also returned to the locality where they were collected. Further, they may be *earmarked* for a specific purpose. For example, motor fuel taxes are commonly used for building and maintaining roads and highways. The advantage to this tax is that it is benefit-based. The citizens that pay the tax reap the benefit of improved highways and roads. Unfortunately, these funds may be needed in other areas, but there is no chance of diversion given the rigid nature of the funds (Mikesell 2004; 2018).

One of the newest sources of revenue for states and local governments comes from the cultivation and sale of medicinal and recreational marijuana as well as edibles made from marijuana. In 1996, California legalized marijuana for medical use followed by Alaska, Oregon, and Washington in 1998. As of 2019, thirty-three states and the District of Columbia had legalized medicinal marijuana and eleven states had legalized recreational marijuana (Governing 2019). Taxes collected on marijuana is very lucrative for state and local governments for a variety of reasons (Yan 2012). Sales totaled over a billion dollars in 2019 and is expected to grow exponentially as more states legalize the product. From the view of the state and local governments who have legalized the product, it is a win-win situation. The system is set up to tax the industry at every step, from seed to retail sale. During this process, the cultivator, distributor, retailer and consumer all pay taxes in various forms. These include, excise taxes, sales taxes, license fees, and application fees.

As you can see, sales taxes, license fees, and application fees are discussed in other sections. However, *excise fees* are different. In this example, the taxes are "imposed on the first sale or transfer from a retail marijuana cultivation facility to a retail store or retail manufacturing facility" (Colorado. Department of Public Safety 2018). Excise rates on cannabis/marijuana vary across states depending on it use, medicinal or recreation. In general, the rates range from 0%–37% in the thirty-three states. Excise taxes are collected at the point of sale by the business owner, thereby reducing some of the administrative burden on the government.

(e) User Charges and Impact Fees

A *user charge* is a fee charged to individuals who voluntarily use a publicly provided service. For example, large municipalities may implement a toll charge to pay for the construction of a new road. If you do not use the new road, then you do not pay the charge. The purpose of a user charge is to relieve the financial burden placed on the general revenue system. In most cases, user charges are geared toward the population that is benefiting from public service. User charges are useless if they are not enforceable and the charge must cover the cost of the service without disrupting other revenue sources.

A more common example of a user fee is the funds collected for police and fire protection or a school district. Charges for this service will often appear on a utility or cable television bill. The address on the utility bill essentially alerts government officials that a new customer has moved into the jurisdiction.[10] Likewise, small towns often operate one or more utilities where they can charge fees. This includes water, gas, and electrical utilities. These government businesses have little or no competition (*monopoly*). Mendonsa (1983) points out that "utility charges are calculated by applying a predetermined rate to a measured volume of service received by a utility consumer. Thus, the amount of revenues due from the utility charges is known before the payments are actually received" (66).

Impact fees are charges that are passed on to developers in order to offset the cost to community resources and the infrastructure. According to Thomas D. Lynch, Jinping Sun, and Robert W. Smith (2017), these fees are more popular in high-growth areas and larger cities. Development frequently causes wear and tear on the roads in these areas, requires additional water resources, sewage and so forth. Further, the increase in the population that results from development impacts the local parks, community centers, and libraries.

Setting a User Fee Rate

While it may be clear to government officials that they should implement a user fee, it might not be clear how much that amount should be. One method to determine the amount is to use *cost-volume profit* (CVP) or *break-even analysis*. This tool assesses how price, volume, and variable and fixed costs interface. At some point, revenue and cost equal (Bierhanzl and Downing 2004; Lynch et al. 2017).

Let's consider an example. A local government has decided to charge individuals driving a motor vehicle a fee to use a newly constructed four-lane road that will save the user 100 miles of travel. Government officials expect that 75,000 vehicles will pass through the road on a yearly basis, the traceable fixed costs (for example, permanent salaries, insurance equipment, and utilities) are projected at $400,000, and the allocated fixed costs (for example toll overhead and general government overhead) are $80,000. The variable costs (for cleanup, supplies, and part time workers) are projected at $3 per car. A subsidy of $100,000 is budgeted from the city's general fund (figure 5.1).

The CVP equation is: $P = VC + \dfrac{[(TFC + AFC) - S]}{Q}$

P = The correct user fee charge per vehicle
VC = Variable Cost per car
TFC = Traceable Fixed Costs ($400,000)
AFC = Allocated Fixed Costs ($80,000)
S = Subsidy ($100,000)
Q = Total number of vehicles (75,000)

$P = 3 + \dfrac{[(400,000 + 80,000) - 100,000]}{75,000}$

$P = 3 + \dfrac{380,000}{75,000}$ $\quad P = 3 + 5.07 \quad P = 8.06$ or $8.07 per car

Figure 5.1. Cost-Volume Profit (CVP) Calculation

Let's go a step further and add another caveat to this scenario. For twelve weeks in the summer, city officials perceive that the amount of traffic on the highway will increase by 100,000 cars per week. In the past, the city has used its current police force to manage any increases in traffic. However, they have concluded that they cannot continue with this practice. As a result, they are interested in hiring more police officers to two of the shifts 7 days a week for the twelve-week period. So, how many police officers will be needed to provide 16 hours of coverage for the 3-month period or 90 days?

The first thing that we must do is calculate the number of hours that could be gained by each additional employee over the 3-month period. If each employee works 40 hours per week for 12 weeks, the number of paid hours (P) is 480. Let's also provide the following benefits over the period: (1) Two sick days, (2) One paid holiday, and (3) Four paid days off. Assuming that the five paid days are taken, the following would apply: 5 × 8 hours = 40 hours (A). Hence, figure 5.2 is an example of the effective hours per employee (E) is:

Effective Hours Per Employee (E)

$$E = P - A$$
$$E = 480 - 40 \text{ hours}$$
$$E = 440 \text{ hours}$$

P = Paid Hours
A = Hours of Paid Leave/Time Off
E = Effective Hours per Employee

The formula for calculating a single shift is:

$$\text{Staffing Factor (SF)} = \frac{\text{Hours per year of operation}}{E}$$

$$SF = \frac{8 \text{ hours per day x 90 days}}{440}$$

$$SF = \frac{720}{440}$$

SF = 1.64 (single shift)
SF = 3.28 (double shift 1.64 x 2)

SF = Staffing Factor

Figure 5.2. Employee Effective Hours Calculation

If you want to double the shift, you simply need to double the number of hours to 16 per day. This would bring the total to 3.28 officers per day (see also Ammons 2002). Unlike other numbers (such as income or average age), it is more difficult to round people. For example, if we use the data in the above example and traditional rounding methods, we would round 1.64 to 2 employees and 3.28 to 3 employees. However, if the formula is indeed valid, we would have too many employees or not enough. So, what do you do in these circumstances? Research by David N. Ammons (2002) suggests that you round to the nearest whole number (i.e., 1 full time employee) or hire a part time employee. In the above example, 1.64 would be rounded to 1.5 persons and 3.28 would be rounded to 3.5 persons. If the number of person is less than 0.5, it may be more feasible to simply provide overtime to the new or existing employees rather than use resources to hire an additional person. A cost-benefit analysis can help you to make this decision.

(f) Intergovernmental Transfers

A large percentage of a state's revenue comes in the form of *federal grants*. The amount of a grant varies and is quite dependent on federal activities. During the 1960s and 1970s, federal grants to states increased as the federal government sought to expand the role of the states. By the early 1980s, grants leveled out and then rose again in the late 1980s. Grants come in two major forms: categorical and block. *Categorical grants* make up the largest type of grants that a state receives.

A categorical grant is used for a specific program and has very strict guidelines for the activities to be carried out within a specific time period. Medicaid and food stamps are included in this category. Categorical grants exploded during President Lyndon B. Johnson's Great Society programs in the 1960s. Formula and project grants fall within the umbrella of categorical grants. *Formula grants* use a distribution formula to determine the amount to be allocated to the state or locality. Population, geography, income and education are variables that are used in formula grants. A *block grant* is used for broad policy areas. It can be used in a variety of programs and activities by state and local governments. States prefer this type of grant due to fewer restrictions on the funds (Axelrod 1995; Riley and Colby 1991).

Local governments receive grants directly from the federal government or passed through from the state government. Local governments also receive grants from the state. In many cases, the grants from the state are a form of revenue sharing. For example, the state will share income and sales tax collections with local governments on some formula basis. School districts receive major funding from the state, along with additional funding from the federal government. Transportation agencies also receive significant funding from the federal government to purchase capital equipment.

(g) Licenses, Permits, and Franchise Fees

Another source of revenue for local governments comes from licenses and permits. A *license* or *permit* is defined as "special rights or privileges granted to an individual or business by a governmental unit in return for the payment of designated fees" (Mendonsa 1983, 65). Licenses are provided to businesses and individuals to conduct an array of different activities. These include, operating a street side kiosk to operating a restaurant. Permits allow individuals and businesses to build structures and to authorize other regulated actions. The cost of the license fee differs by activity. For example, the cost of a hunting license is different from that of a license to operate a restaurant. Without a license, an individual or business is forbidden to engage in the activity legally. The owner of a license does not receive any specific government service by having the license. Under normal circumstances, everyone who applies for a license receives it if they are qualified. However, a person does receive services from a permit. For example, the issuance of a building permit will result in a number of inspections by the government. The purpose is to ensure that the building or improvement meets the building code requirements established by the government.

One positive aspect of a license and permit is that they are easy to track. Because each license and permit is numbered; government officials can monitor, measure and control the process. It also allows the government to audit the revenue source with little effort. When problems occur, they can be easily pinpointed. For example, if building permits are decreasing, officials can determine whether the drop is the result of a dip in the economy or some other factor.

A *franchise fee* is closely related to a license fee, but there are some subtle differences. Franchises are provided on a limited basis. A franchise presupposes that the business will serve the entire community, operate with a certain quality and rate, and outline the responsibility of the owner and the government. It also may involve the use of the government's rights-of-way. In certain parts of the country cable companies operate on a franchise fee basis. Other examples could include telephone services. These fees can generate large amounts of funds.

(h) Gaming

States and local governments began engaging in games of chance in the mid-1960s, but in the last fifteen years they have become very popular as an alternative source of revenue as a result of opposition to tax increase. Since New Hampshire first adopted the lottery in 1964, forty-eight states and the District of Columbia have legalized some form of gaming. These institutions come in the form of state lotteries, bingo, riverboat gambling, casinos, and slot machines. Despite the social and moral concerns that residents have with gaming, they tend to support these measures because they raise funds voluntarily versus compulsory taxes. In addition, proponents of lotteries often argue that lotteries are preferable to raising taxes when it comes to issues such as funding education. As a result, states have been able to generate millions of dollars in revenue. However, there is a fair amount of overhead associated with the gaming industry. In each case, state and local governments have established bureaucratic structures to regulate the industry. Some states, however, see minimum economic benefits from casino operations. This is the case in states where casinos are owned and operated by Native American tribes on reservations. They are exempt from taxes and other fees.[11] However, these states do reap benefits in other ways. Many American Indian casinos contribute payments-in-lieu-of-taxes to the government. Others provide substantial support to schools within the reservation, thus reducing state support.

(i)   Other Revenues

Occasionally governments will receive funds from sources that do not fit into any of the above-mentioned categories. For example, gifts, donations, and sales of equipment and assets fit into this category. There are no tax levies and there is no method to distributing the funds. Cities and states can also collect funds from investments and leasing of property to the private sector or other governments. Governments that operate jails may charge smaller governments that do not have such facilities for the housing of prisoners.

Governments also receive monies from fines, forfeits, and penalties. These funds usually come from the actions of police departments and the courts. Since these activities are well documented and are standardized, it is fairly easy to keep track of them (Mendonsa 1983).

REVENUE MANAGEMENT

Gianakis and McCue (1999) define revenue management as "the assessment and maintenance of a local government's capacity to generate sufficient funds from all available sources to support policy decisions regarding service levels" (102). Revenue management attempts to establish revenue performance standards, compare actual with expected performance, record revenue performance, initiate corrective change, and constructs a support system that facilitates that model. There are three general components to proactive revenue management: *revenue development*, *revenue analysis*, and *revenue support systems*. Revenue development is mainly concerned with developing a tax structure that considers short and long term funding. A lot of revenue management techniques are time limited and tend to reflect election cycles and short term political needs rather than long term strategic planning. Revenue analysis systematically examines each revenue source with an eye to achieving the optimal benefit from the source. This includes issues such as equity, yields, and the cost of administration. Lastly, revenue support systems examine the day-to-day management of revenue (Gianakis and McCue 1999).

Let's consider a simple example. Jefferson City was considering passing a law increasing the millage rate on business property for FY 2020 in order to balance the proposed budget. If passed, the law would increase the amount of property taxes by $598,000. However, when the law was examined, it was found that it would have a negative impact on the tax structure for small businesses. The city has thirty-five businesses, but one business (Business X) employs 65 percent of the private workforce. As a result of the increase, Business X would see a 3 percent increase in taxes owed while the remaining thirty-four businesses would owe the balance. So, is it feasible to pass on 97 percent of the cost to the remaining small businesses despite the fact that they represent only 35 percent of the private workforce? Businesses can pass on tax increases to customers or the land owner, but this can also have a negative domino effect on the cost of doing business. In this example, the equity issues raised by the law did not seem to affect the city council since small businesses were the fastest growing industry in the city.[12] While the decision on paper would have a positive impact on the city's budget, the council members did not consider the long-term effect of the law on the city's small business sector.

Situations like this one bring value to revenue management. It is crucial that a budget manager communicate to elected officials the value of revenue management. In order to properly implement a revenue management system, it is important that the organization's culture is understood. That includes a good understanding of the social, political and economic dynamics associated with a city or state.

Revenue management is a proactive approach concerned with "establishing revenue performance standards, documenting revenue performance, comparing actual with expected performance, initiating corrective action and creating a support structure that facilitates the approach" (Gianakis and McCue 1999, 103). This means that elected officials and agency heads need to:

- Develop a commonly accepted method for funding services in the short and long term.
- Identify where the city currently stands in relation to its revenue capacity.
- Explore other options for achieving vision.
- Institute a program for measuring progress.

There are several items that must be considered when evaluating revenue structures and determining the revenue management strategy. Consider the questions in exhibit 5.5 when thinking about the previous example. Essentially, as a budget officer, you are asking yourself whether any particular factor will affect the tax structure and vice versa. For example, if we consider the current example, the budget director would want to know: will the increase in the rate generate the needed funds, who is going to be affected by the property tax increase, how that change will affect their ability to pay and still make a profit, will that cost be passed on to other individuals, will it hurt our tax structure and so on. As an elected official, you want to know if

Exhibit 5.5.   Developing a Revenue Management Plan
Political Questions
(1) What are the dominant political attitudes (party/council unity)?
(2) What is the dominant political culture (mixed or unified)?
(3) Is raising taxes feasible right now (election year)?
Tax Questions
(4) Can user fees or special districts solve the tax deficit?
(5) Should funds be earmarked from the current budget?
(6) Can taxes be raised legally?
Demographic Equity Questions
(7) Is a particular group benefiting from the tax increase?
(8) Will increasing taxes have an adverse economic impact on a particular sector (business, personal, education, etc.)?
(9) What is the level of education in the city?
(10) What is the age of residents?
(11) What type of industries exists and are we facilitating their growth?
Administrative Questions
(12) Is there a cost associated with the decision?
(13) If yes, what kind (payer cost, convenience cost, administrative cost)?

Source: Created by the Author.

your chances of reelection will be impacted, will you get support from other elected officials, will the tax adversely impact your constituents and so on.

These and other questions address political, efficiency, effectiveness and equity issues. However, equity and equality are not synonymous. Decision makers can also: (a) Divide the number of users by the total cost and spread the burden evenly without concern for impact and equity, (b) Apply the *ability to pay rule* where those who can afford to pay more are taxed at a higher rate, and (c) Apply the *benefits received principle* where those that receive the benefit bear the cost associated with the benefit.

CONCLUSION

This chapter shows that there are several different ways in which state and local governments finance the administration of government. Some of the methods discussed are political in nature while others apply across the board to everyone. Effective revenue management models must consider a plethora of important political, cultural, economic, demographic and administrative questions. Even though no one really wants to pay more taxes, financial decisions are more palatable when the decisions that lead to the tax structure are well thought out and developed based on good questions and answers.

IMPORTANT TERMS AND PHRASES

Ability to Pay Rule
Aggregate Assessment-Sales Ratio
Allocated Fixed Cost
Assessed Value
Benefits Received Principle
Block Grants
Categorical Grants
Coefficient of Dispersion
Cost-Volume Profit (CVP)
Earmarked Funds
Excise Taxes
Federal Grants
Federal Income Taxes
Fines
Forfeitures
Formula Grants
Franchise Fees
Impact Fees
Insurance Trust Revenues
Intergovernmental Transfer
License
Market Price / Value
Millage Rate
Monopoly

Payroll Taxes
Permit
Price-Related Differential
Progressive Taxes
Property Taxes
Public Utilities
Regressive Taxes
Revenue
Revenue Analysis
Revenue Development
Revenue Management
Revenue Support Systems
Sales Taxes
State Income Taxes
Tax
Tax Assessment
Tax Assessor
Tax Collector
Tax Rate
Traceable Fixed Cost
User Fees
Use Tax
Variable Fixed Cost

CHAPTER 5 HOMEWORK EXERCISES

Directions: Questions 1–7 should be completed in Excel. Question 8 can be completed in a word processing program. Round all of your data in the same fashion as it is done in the text. Unless noted otherwise, dollar amounts should be rounded to two digits to the right of the decimal (cents). See the appendix for Excel templates. Please turn in your Microsoft Excel worksheets and the word file with the pasted Excel worksheets to your instructor.

(1) You are an intern at the Tax Assessor's Office for Jefferson City and your supervisor has asked you to prepare the following:

(a) First, complete a property tax estimate for a newly constructed sub-division. You should apply a 12 percent millage rate on the assessed value of each house and the park. The land that the house sits on is included in the market value of the property. Also, calculate the total assessed value of all the units/properties and the total estimated tax (see appendix 5A).

- The new subdivision has 100 units and a park. The prices provided below are based on assessed value.
- There are 15 two-bedroom houses on 5 acres of land valued at $95,000 each.
- There are 15 two-bedroom houses on 20 acres of land valued at $85,000 each.
- There are 60 three-bedroom houses with a two-car garage on 75 acres of land. The houses are valued at $210,000 each.
- The last 15 houses are four-bedroom units with a two-car garage on 15 acres of land. They are valued at $170,000.
- Lastly, the subdivision has a park with a swimming pool, tennis court, and a basketball court. The park and green space is valued at $105,000.

Note: Assessed value is: Individual Unit Value multiplied by the Number of Units

(b) The city also needs $1,700,000 in individual property taxes and the tax assessor indicated that the total assessed value of individual property is $20,000,000. What should the fixed or nominal tax rate be set at to collect the $1,700,000 in property taxes?

Tax rate = _____.

(c) The city has set the millage rate at 3.5 percent for all businesses. The spreadsheet in appendix 5A has a partial listing of the city's businesses. Calculate the amount of taxes that can be expected along with the most effective tax rate (METR) for each business and an average tax rate using the partial list of businesses provided. (See appendix 5A)

- The millage rate for each of the seven properties is 3.5 percent.
- Franklin's Clothing has a market value of $625,000 and an assessed value of $525,000.
- Payton's Tax Service has a market value of $575,000 and an assessed value of $475,000.
- Stacie's Lawn Care has a market value of $285,000 and an assessed value of $175,000.
- Eva's Finishing School has a market value of $400,000 and an assessed value of $325,000.
- Tiffany's Day Care has a market value of $250,000 and an assessed value of $175,000.
- Yiesha's Hair Care has a market value of $370,000 and an assessed value of $300,000.
- Myron's Boys Club has a market value of $650,000 and an assessed value of $575,000.

(2) Calculate the coefficient of dispersion using the following information. Should the assessor reapportion the assessed property values (use average assessment)? Explain (see appendix 5B).

(a) There are five pieces of property that sold for $165,000 each and were assessed at $125,000, $130,000, $125,000, $110,000, and $95,000.

(b) There are ten pieces of property that sold for $115,000 each and were assessed at $39,500, $90,900, $68,000, $65,000, $92,000, $90,000, $85,000, $75,000, $89,250, and $65,000.

(3) Using the price related differential test, calculate the individual assessment sales ratios, aggregate assessment sales ratio, average deviation, and the price related differential using the data provided below. Are the higher priced properties or the lower priced properties under assessed? (see appendix 5C).

Assessment Ratio Worksheet			
Property	*Sales Price*	*Assessed Value*	*Assessment Ratio*
Property 1	$165,000	$190,000	
Property 2	145,000	125,000	
Property 3	25,000	20,000	
Property 4	30,000	25,000	
Property 5	25,000	18,000	
Property 6	200,000	170,000	
Property 7	150,000	125,000	
Property 8	135,000	125,000	
Property 9	30,000	22,000	
Property 10	25,000	15,000	
Property 11	25,000	19,000	
Property 12	35,000	28,000	
TOTAL	$990,000	$892,000	

(4) Calculate the revenue collected from federal income taxes, state income taxes, and the local pay roll tax for FY 2020 and prepare a revenue estimate for Jefferson City's Public School System for FY 2021 based on the following information. Assume that no other deductions came from the employee's salary other than what is listed in the spreadsheet. Hint: New employees are not eligible for raises, which are based on performance measures from the previous fiscal year (see appendix 5D).

(a) FY 2020 Facts:

- The school system currently has thirty-four full time employees. There is one superintendent, two principals, three janitors, ten kitchen staff, and eighteen teachers (including coaches).
- The superintendent has a salary of $99,000.
- Each principal has a salary of $75,000.
- Four of the teachers (Teacher A) have salaries of $55,000; six teachers (Teacher B) have salaries of $45,000; and six teachers (Teacher C) have salaries of $40,000.
- The remaining two teachers (A Level) are also coaches. The football coach receives an additional $5,000 in salary and the basketball coach receives an additional $7,000 in salary each year.
- Mr. Jones manages the kitchen. His FY 2020 salary is $45,000.

- The remaining kitchen staff make $28,000 each in FY 2020.
- The three janitors make $25,000 each in FY 2020.

The federal income tax rates are.

Salary Range	Calculations
$0–$9,700	= $9,700 x 10%
$9,701–$39,475	= $29,774 x 12%
$39,476–$84,200	= $44,724 x 22%
$84,201–$160,725	= $76,524 x 24%

- The federal tax rates are the same in FY 2020 & FY 2021.
- The state income tax rate is 4 percent for the first $3,000 of the employee salary and 5.5 percent on everything above that amount. The rate is the same in both years.
- The local payroll tax is 1.75 percent in FY 2020 and 1.85 percent in FY 2021.

(b) FY 2021 Facts:

- In FY 2021, the school system hired 2 more teachers at the Teacher D level. They will begin work in FY 2021 at a salary of $35,000.
- In FY 2021, each school employee received a 5 percent raise except the principals and superintendent. They received a 2 percent raise. Note, new employees do not receive a raise.

(5) Using the information that is listed below, prepare a revenue estimate and revenue projection for Jefferson City in FY 2020 and FY 2021 respectively using the actual budget data from FY 2019. All of the changes to the FY 2021 budget are based on FY 2020 estimates. Hint: Complete each of the FY 2020 estimates, based on FY 2019 actuals, prior to beginning the FY 2021 projections. Round all data to the nearest dollar amount since these are estimates (see appendix 5E).

- Property tax collections have been quite stable. A modest 2 percent increase is expected in FY 2020 and a 3 percent increase in FY 2021. News alert: The new Kollipara subdivision will be completed in FY 2020. So, property tax receipts should increase an addition 1 percent in FY 2021, for a total of 4 percent in FY 2021.
- User fees in FY 2020 are expected to increase 5 percent. In FY 2021 the fee will increase 5 percent due to an increase in the number of street meters.
- Franchise fees and permits are expected to increase 2 percent in FY 2020 and 1 percent in FY 2021 because of new development near the mall.

- Utility fees / charges are expected to decrease 5 percent in FY 2020 and 5 percent in FY 2021.
- Intergovernmental transfers are expected to increase 4 percent in FY 2020 and 2 percent in FY 2021.
- Sales tax collections are also expected to increase 4 percent FY 2020 based on the expanded business sector. It is expected to increase 11 percent in FY 2021.
- Impact fees remain unchanged.
- Storm water management is expected to increase by 5 percent each year.

(6) Jefferson City constructed a swimming pool in FY 2020 and you have been asked to calculate the user charge based on an estimate of 10,000 swimmers. Since the pool is inside a building it will remain open all year. Household income in Jefferson City is $100,000 per year (see appendix 5F).

(a) After you calculate the user fee, explain the impact of the fee on the population. Use the cost-volume profit formula, the information in the directions, and the items listed below to construct your user charge.

- Employee salaries, insurance, fringe benefits, equipment maintenance, and utilities are projected at $65,000.
- The city received a one-time gift of $55,000 to subsidize the first year of operation.
- Allocated fixed costs are projected at $25,000.
- Variable costs are projected at $3.00 per swimmer.
- Using the same figures, estimate the user charge for FY 2021 as well. However, assume that the number of swimmers increased by 2,000 and the local government will take $60,000 from the general fund to subsidize the pool. What can the government do to maintain the current user fee?

(b) Using question (6a) as a point of departure, the city has to determine how many additional life guards it needs to operate the pool during the summer when children are out of school. Due to the sheer volume of children and city codes, the city cannot ask the existing employees to work additional shifts. Hence, they are interested in hiring lifeguards for *three* of the shifts. Each lifeguard will work a four-hour shift seven days a week for the twelve-week period. They cannot work more than one shift per day. The new lifeguards will get three paid days off over the twelve-week period. So, how many life guards are needed to provide twelve hours of additional coverage for the 84-day period? This problem can be completed in a word processing program.

(7) Jefferson City has appointed you to work on the FY 2021 budget. Your job is to modify the FY 2020 budget according to these guidelines. Print a hard copy of the completed assignment for your instructor and save the new file under a new file name. Assume that FY 2020 revenue collections are identical to those collected in FY 2021 unless the information indicates something different. Hint: Funds should be placed in funds that have jurisdiction. The fund transfers for FY 2021 is the exact amount as it was in FY 2020 (see appendix 5G).

(a) Revenue

  • Revenue created as a result of changes in these areas goes into the General Fund.

    (i)   Property taxes increased 3.5 percent.
    (ii) Business licenses increased 4.7 percent.
    (iii) Vehicle stickers decreased 1.3 percent.
    (iv) Insurance taxes increased 2 percent in the general fund only.

  • The total amount of user charges increased 10 percent in FY 2021. The new revenue from the user charges went into the Water & Sewer Fund and the Natural Gas Fund. Each Fund received half of the new revenues from the user charges.
  • The remaining funds maintained their FY 2020 revenue funding levels.

(b) Expenditures

  • General Fund Modifications

    (i)   Half of the new revenues (dollar amount change in Total Revenue from FY 2020 to FY 2021) in the General Fund went to Public Safety.
    (ii) General Government received 3 percent of the new revenues in the General Fund.
    (iii) Public Works received 17 percent of the new revenues in the General Fund.
    (iv) Sanitation and Capital Expenditures each received 15 percent of the new funds in the General Fund.

  • Water and Sewer and Gas System Operations (Natural Gas) received increases in expenditures as a result of increased revenues in their departments/funds.
  • The remaining departments and funds went unchanged. That is, expenditures were the same as they were in FY 2020.
  • Note: Revenues and expenditures should be the same amount for each fund in the worksheet.

(8) Jefferson City is contemplating the construction of a football arena near the down town main artery and the city administrator has requested that you (finance officer) develop a tax plan to fund the construction of the structure. The proposed structure will cost the city $40,000,000 to construct and could bring in over a $3,500,000 a year in revenue. Your job is two-fold. First, prepare a funding structure with the percentage and dollar contribution of each entity. Second, develop a set of political, equity, and economic questions that are likely to arise in the city council meeting concerning your plan. You should also provide answers to these questions. Also, you cannot use more than two outside funding source (i.e., naming rights, private donors, advertising, etc.).

    (a) Funding Structure: Amount   Percentage
    (b) Economic Questions (c) Equity Questions and (d) Political Questions

(9) Optional In-Class Exercise: Defending Funding Structure Plan (45-minute exercise)

    Step 1: Split the class into groups of four or five and have each person defend the funding structure that they created in question 8. Hence, it will be necessary for each person to bring four copies of their response to question 8 to distribute among the group members.

    Step 2: Each participant in the group should be given no more than four minutes to explain their funding structure. Then, group member should question the impact of the funding structure on the city, citizens, tourists, stakeholders, etc. (four minutes max). By majority vote, each individual tax plan should be approved as viable or denied based on the structure as well as the presenter's ability to respond to the questions.

    Step 3: While several plans may be good, the group should select one as the best alternative and that person should briefly describe their plan to the entire class at the end of the group meetings.

NOTES

    1. A progressive tax provides for rates that increase as the tax base (the value of the property or the amount of income being taxed) increases. A regressive tax remains constant or declines as the tax base increases.

    2. For example, cities in Ohio, Pennsylvania, and Maryland can collect income taxes on earnings.

    3. See Gerasimos A. Gianakis and Clifford P. McCue (1999), *Local Government Budgeting: A Managerial Approach* (West Port, CT: Praeger); and Thomas D. Lynch, Jinping Sun, and Robert W. Smith (2017), *Public Budgeting in America*, 6th ed. (Irvine, CA: Melvin & Leigh), for additional information.

4. The yield on property tax is based on the value of the house, not the income of the owner. There are many senior citizens who are house-poor. They live on fixed incomes, but live in houses with high property taxes. So, this would invalidate the progressive claim.

5. In many New England local governments, the property tax is the balancing factor. They first determine all other sources of revenue. Whatever is needed becomes the property tax levy.

6. Another way to think about millage rates is in terms of assessments. If we apply the one mill being one tenth of a percent—meaning one mill rate equals $1 of revenue for every $1,000 of assessed value, then a property tax rate of 67.5 mills as applied to a $110,000 property assessed at 25 percent percent of market value would yield $1,856.25 (110 × .25 × 67.5 = $1,856.25).

7. Alaska, Florida, Nevada, South Dakota, Texas, Washington, and Wyoming had no state income tax as of January 1, 2020. Tennessee and New Hampshire have a state income tax that is limited to dividend and interest income, see Sandra Block (2019), "9 States with No Income Tax," *Kiplinger*, October 1, https://www.kiplinger.com/slideshow/taxes/T054-S001-states-without-income-tax/index.html (accessed January 31, 2020).

8. See Gianakis and McCue (1999), *Local Government Budgeting*; Lynch et al. 2017; and Jonathan Gruber (2005), *Public Finance and Public Policy* (New York: Worth Publishers), for a discussion of payroll taxes.

9. Review Gianakis and McCue 1999; Mikesell 2014, 2004; Lynch et al. (2017), *Public Budgeting in America*; William P. Kittredge and Sarah M. Ouart (2005), *Budget Manual for Georgia Local Government* (Athens, GA: Vinson Institute, University of Georgia); and Irene S. Rubin (2006), *The Politics of Public Budgeting: Getting and Spending, Borrowing and Balancing*, 5th ed. (Washington, DC: C Q Press), for a discussion of sale taxes.

10. See also Paul B. Downing (1983), "User Charges and Service Fees," in *Budget Management: A Reader in Local Government Financial Management*, ed. Jack Rabin, W. Bartley Hildreth, and Gerald J. Miller (Athens, GA: Carl Vinson Institute of Government, University of Georgia), 73–82; John L. Mikesell (2004), "General Sales, Income, and Other Nonproperty Taxes," in *Management Policies in Local Government Finance*, 5th ed., ed. J. Richard Aronson and Eli Schwartz (Washington, DC: ICMA), 289–314; and John L. Mikesell (2018), *Fiscal Administration: Analysis and Applications for the Public Sector*, 10th ed. (Belmont, CA: Wadsworth Cengage Publishers); and Rubin (2006), *Politics of Public Budgeting*; for a discussion of user fees and charges.

11. Review Mikesell (2018), *Fiscal Administration*; Edward J. Clynch, Douglas G. Feig, and James B. Kaatz (2001), "Local Government Casino Gaming Tax Receipts in Mississippi: An Impact Appraisal," Paper presented at the Southeastern Conference for Public Administration Conference, Baton Rouge, Louisiana; and David Nice (2002), *Public Budgeting* (Stamford, CT: Wadsworth/Thompson Learning), for additional information on gaming revenues.

12. Equity is defined in terms of the impact on small businesses versus all businesses.

Appendix 5A
Property Tax and Millage Rates

Property Tax Estimate, Walters Subdivision, Jefferson City, FY 2020					
Items	Number of Units	Individual Unit Value	Assessed Value	Millage Rate	Total Est. Tax
Two BR on 5 Acres	15	$95,000		12%	
Two BR on 20 Acres	15	85,000		12%	
Three BR on 75 Acres	60	210,000		12%	
Four BR on 20 Acres	15	170,000		12%	
Green Space and Park	1	105,000.00		12%	
TOTAL	106				

Millage Rate, Jefferson City, FY 2020					
Business	Market Value	Assessed Value	Millage Rate	Tax Est.	METR
Franklin's Clothing	$525,000.00	$525,000.00	3.5%		
Payton's Tax Service	575,000.00	475,000.00	3.5%		
Stacie's Lawn Care	285,000.00	175,000.00	3.5%		
Eva's Finishing School	400,000.00	325,000.00	3.5%		
Tiffany's Day Care	250,000.00	175,000.00	3.5%		
Yiesha's Hair Care	370,000.00	300,000.00	3.5%		
Myron's Boys Club	650,000.00	575,000.00	3.5%		
TOTAL	$3,055,000.00	$2,550,000.00			

Appendix 5B

Coefficient of Dispersion

Coefficients of Dispersion				
	Sales Price	*Assessed Value*	*STEP 1 & 2* *Assessment Ratio*	*STEP 3* *Average Dev.*
Property 1	$165,000	$125,000		
Property 2	165,000	130,000		
Property 3	165,000	125,000		
Property 4	165,000	110,000		
Property 5	165,000	95,000		
STEP 4	Coefficient of Dispersion =			
Explanation:				
	Sales Price	*Assessed Value*	*STEP 1 & 2* *Assessment Ratio*	*STEP 3* *Average Dev.*
Property 1	$115,000	$39,500		
Property 2	115,000	90,900		
Property 3	115,000	68,000		
Property 4	115,000	65,000		
Property 5	115,000	92,000		
Property 6	115,000	90,000		
Property 7	115,000	85,000		
Property 8	115,000	75,000		
Property 9	115,000	89,250		
Property 10	115,000	65,000		
STEP 4	Coefficient of Dispersion =			
Explanation:				

Source: Created by the Author.

Appendix 5C

Price Related Differential

Price Related Differential			
STEP 1	Individual Assessment-Sales Ratios		
	Sales Price	*Assessed Value*	*Assessment Ratio*
Property 1	$165,000	$190,000	
Property 2	145,000	125,000	
Property 3	25,000	20,000	
Property 4	30,000	25,000	
Property 5	25,000	18,000	
Property 6	200,000	170,000	
Property 7	150,000	125,000	
Property 8	135,000	135,000	
Property 9	30,000	22,000	
Property 10	25,000	15,000	
Property 11	25,000	19,000	
Property 12	35,000	28,000	
TOTAL	$990,000	$892,000	
STEP 2	Aggregate Assessment-Sales Ratio		
STEP 3	Average Deviation		
STEP 4	Price Related Differential		
STEP 5	*Explanation*		

Appendix 5D

Jefferson City Public School System

Projected Revenue: Jefferson City Public School System, FY 2020						
Position Description	# in Grade	FY 2020 Salary	Fed. Inc. Tax	State Inc. Tax	Payroll Tax	Total Taxes
Superintendent	1					
Principal	2					
Teacher A	4					
Teacher B	6					
Teacher C	6					
Janitor	3					
Kitchen Manager	1					
Kitchen Staff	9					
Football Coach	1					
Basketball Coach	1					
TOTAL	34					
Revenue Estimate: Jefferson City Public School System, FY 2021						
Position Description	# in Grade	FY 2021 Salary	Fed. Inc. Tax	State Inc. Tax	Payroll Tax	Total Taxes
Superintendent	1					
Principal	2					
Teacher A	4					
Teacher B	6					
Teacher C	6					
Teacher D	2					
Janitor	3					
Kitchen Manager	1					
Kitchen Staff	9					
Football Coach	1					
Basketball Coach	1					
TOTAL	36					

Source: Created by the Author.

Appendix 5E

Jefferson City Revenue

Jefferson City Revenue Estimate, FYs 2020–2021			
Items	*FY 2019 (act.)*	*FY 2020 (est.)*	*FY 2021 (proj.)*
Property Taxes	$710,000		
User Fees	30,000		
Franchise Fees	5,600		
Permits	3,600		
Utility Fees	115,000		
Intergovernmental Transfers	255,000		
Sales Taxes	180,000		
Impact Fees	4,500		
Storm Water Mgt.	9,500		
TOTAL	$1,313,200		

Source: Created by the Author.

Appendix 5F
Jefferson City Swimming Pool City Estimate

Cost Volume Profit Formula	P=VC+[(TFC+AFC)–S]/Q
	Data
2020 est. Swimmers	
2021 est. Swimmers	
Variable Cost (per swimmer)	
Traceable Fixed Cost	
Allocated Fixed Cost	
2020 Subsidy	
2021 Subsidy	
2020 User Fees	
2021 User Fees	
b. Additional Staffing	
Effective Hour Formula	= P–A
Staffing Formula	Hrs. per year of operation / Effective hours per employee
Additional shifts	Data
Pool operation days	
Pool operation hours	
Number of Days	
Hours per shift	
Days per week	
Paid time off (PTO) in days	
Effective hours per Employee	
Staffing Factor	

Source: Created by the Author.

Appendix 5G

Jefferson City Budget Summary

Jefferson City Budget Summary, FY 2020

REVENUE SOURCE	General Fund	Cemetery Fund	City Tax Aid	911 Fund	Central Garage	Water & Sewer	Sanitation	Natural Gas	Capital Exp.	GRAND TOTAL
Property Taxes	$,483,000	$0	$0	$0	$0	$0	$0	$0	$0	$1,483,000
Insurance Taxes	885,000	0	0	0	0	41,500	0	0	0	$926,500
Vehicle Stickers	420,000	0	0	0	0	0	0	0	0	$420,000
Business Licenses	350,000	0	0	0	0	0	0	0	0	$350,000
User Charges	0	27,500	0	0	116,250	3,421,500	1,884,000	5,375,000	0	$10,824,250
Special Assessments	0	0	215,000	94,000	0	195,000	50,000	285,000	0	$839,000
Other & Misc.	662,779	1,000	4,000	7,500	0	0	0	0	0	$675,279
Fund Transfers	0	47,800	0	0	0	0	0	0	1,037,200	$1,085,000
TOTAL Revenues	$3,800,779	$76,300	$219,000	$101,500	$116,250	$3,658,000	$1,934,000	$5,660,000	$1,037,200	$16,603,029
Fund Balance	$650,000	$7,500	$40,000	$170,000	$0	$0	$50,600	$0	$0	$918,100
TOTAL Available Funds	$4,450,779	$83,800	$259,000	$271,500	$116,250	$3,658,000	$1,984,600	$5,660,000	$1,037,200	$17,521,129

(continued)

Jefferson City Budget Summary, FY 2020 (Continued)

EXPENDITURES	General Fund	Cemetery Fund	City Tax Aid	911 Fund	Central Garage	Water &Sewer	Sanitation	Natural Gas	Capital Exp.	GRAND TOTAL
General Government	$1,309,454	$0	$0	$0	$0	$0	$0	$0	$0	$1,309,454
Public Safety	2,781,100	0	0	271,500	0	0	0	0	0	$3,052,600
Public Works	360,225	0	165,000	0	0	0	0	0	0	$525,225
Central Garage	0	0	0	0	116,250	0	0	0	0	$116,250
Sanitation	0	0	0	0	0	0	1,984,600	0	0	$1,984,600
Water &Sewer Oper.	0	0	0	0	0	3,658,000	0	0	0	$3,658,000
Cemetery Operations	0	83,800	0	0	0	0	0	0	0	$83,800
Gas System Oper.	0	0	0	0	0	0	0	5,660,000	0	$5,660,000
Capital Expenditures	0	0	94,000	0	0	0	0	0	1,037,200	$1,131,200
TOTAL Expenditures	$4,450,779	$83,800	$259,000	$271,500	$116,250	$3,658,000	$1,984,600	$5,660,000	$1,037,200	$17,521,129

Source: Created by the Author.

Chapter 6

Budgeting Techniques
and Analytics Models

OVERVIEW

By definition, budgeting requires some level of technical analysis. This fact has become more realistic today as an increasing number of state and local governments deal with a variety of problems ranging from budget deficits to urban sprawl to a lack of economic development. In a lot of cases, governments provide services that cannot be performed or are too large to be provided by the private sector or through normal market forces. As a result, it is imperative that budget analysts apply various analytical techniques and models to their analysis in order to determine the most efficient and effective approach to solving issues and providing services.

This chapter discusses several practical techniques and analytical models that are useful in assisting state and local budget analyst in dealing with expenditure issues from an array of different perspectives. The chapter begins with a simple method of understanding policy problems and analysis. Next, there is a discussion of various forecasting techniques. Last, some specific techniques are discussed. These include: discounting, cost benefit analysis, cost-effectiveness analysis, internal rates of returns, payback method, productivity analysis, and multiple regression analysis.

UNDERSTANDING THE METHODS
AND TECHNIQUES OF ANALYSIS

Once a decision has been made to solve a public problem or expand services, policy experts must ensure that the problem is fully understood along with the alternatives to solving the problem. David L. Weimer and Aidan R. Vining (1989) provide a succinct model to understanding the problem and examining the options to solving the problem. Bureaucrats and budget analysts can follow these steps in providing policy makers with viable policy options. In short, a decision has to be made to choose alternative (a) or alternative (b) or (c) below (see also McLean 2018; Swain and Reed 2010).

Problem Analysis

(1) Understanding the Problem

    (a) Receiving the Problem: Assessing the Symptoms
    (b) Framing the Problem: Analyzing Market and Governmental Failures
    (c) Modeling the Problem: Identifying Policy Variables

(2) Choosing and Explaining Relevant Goals and Constraints
(3) Choosing a Solution Method

Solution Analysis

(4) Choosing Evaluation Criteria
(5) Specifying Policy Alternatives
(6) Evaluating: Predicting Impacts of Alternatives and Valuing them based on a *Criteria*
(7) Recommending Actions

FORECASTING REVENUES

Good revenue estimations or forecasts are considered by most to be more of an art than a science. In addition to good judgment, economic savvy and a variety of methodologies go into the process. Any particular methodology will lead to a different estimate. To say the least, an analyst should understand the revenue system and have a good understanding of all the factors that have impacted past revenue collections. Revenue estimates are normally conducted out of the budget office or the comptroller's office (Axelrod 1995; Wang 2006). Most state and local governments will begin revenue projections about six months before the beginning of budget implementation. The advantage to starting early is that it allows analyst time to revise their estimates as they get closer to the actual day of implementation and determine whether revenue collections will exceed or fall short of expectations (Fleeter and Walker 1997). To say the very least, a state or local government should forecast revenues and expenditures over a couple of years regardless of the level of economic and political stability in the jurisdiction. Hence, forecasting is an integral part of any model assessing expenditure or revenue patterns over time. *Forecasting* is an attempt to predict future revenue collection based on present administrative, structural conditions, demographic and economic factors. For example, the federal government has predicted that the Social Security fund will practically disappear in the next twenty years based primarily on the number of persons currently contributing to the fund and those taking money out of the fund.

Depending on the size ($) of the budget in a jurisdiction, forecasters should begin the process anywhere from six to eighteen months prior to the beginning of the fiscal year. A good time frame is useful because it saves a lot of time and effort on the part of agency directors who are charged with preparing their budget. It is not efficient or effective to budget for funds that may or may not exist. Hence, budget forecasts should be modified as new information is added to the equation. The Office of Management and Budget (OMB) and the Congressional Budget Office (CBO) along with Presidential advisors estimate the federal budget, while state and local budget officials handle the responsibility at lower levels (Franklin, Bourdeaux, and Hathaway 2019; Lee, Johnson, and Joyce 2013; Mikesell 2014; Nice 2002).

Key Factors to Consider When Forecasting Revenues

- *Revenues should be projected separately.* Because each revenue source is distinct and has its own set of nuances it is rational to estimate them separately. By so doing, it limits the number of errors and may bring greater balance to the overall estimates due to over and under estimates for individual tax expectations.
- *Focus efforts on the large revenue sources.* As indicated in table 5.1, the property tax is one of the largest sources of income for a local government. Hence, it is important that great care be taken in this preparing this estimate. Small revenue sources do not have a great impact on the budget.
- *Historical data is the key to success.* Revenue projections do not tend to change dramatically over time. As a result, data and financial records should be closely examined. Once this data is examined, projections can be made after adjustments are made for other factors in the environment such as demographic shifts and economic development. Further, it is important that the analyst pay attention to items that may not reoccur. For example, the government may receive a grant for five years that is not renewable.
- *Underestimate rather than overestimate budgets.* Although budgets are based on solid economic factors, the ramification of budget deficits can be very political in nature. State and local elected officials do not want to explain budget deficits to voters because the repercussions could be felt in the next election cycle. Therefore, estimates should be somewhat conservative.
- *Good Judgment.* While a state or local government's tax base may seem stable, it is important that estimators keep an eye on other nearby jurisdictions that may have an impact on their revenue estimates. Further, estimators may receive estimates from other sources that are not in line with their estimates. Ultimately, it is up to the judgment of the estimator to decide what to consider in the estimate.

FORECASTING MODELS

Susan L. Riley and Peter W. Colby (1991) discuss five models that local governments can use when estimating revenue. Deciding which model to use can be determined by a number of factors. Particularly, the size of the city's budget and resources available to conduct the estimate are important. The first model is called a *simplistic model*. This model is based on historical data.

An analyst would simply use trend analysis and extrapolate the data for the current fiscal year. In addition, expected changes in the use of services that might be relevant to revenue collections are also considered. For example, a factory that closes with several hundred residents may have a disparate impact on revenue collections. The second model is a *multiple regression model*. A multiple regression model uses factors such as unemployment, population shifts, and changes in the economy to predict revenue. An *econometric model* synchronizes revenue estimates with a review of interdependent variables, such as the consumer price index, interest rates, cost benefit analysis, net present value (NPV), internal rate of return (IRR), and construction activity. The fourth model is called a *microsimulation model*. This model uses various forms of data such as a sample of IRS returns to predict future trends. The last model is an *input-output model*. This model uses purchase and sales data to ascertain where the revenue is produced.

Another model by J. Winn Decker and Bruce D. McDonald III (2019) is called *consensus forecasting*. In this model, a collection of parties is brought to the table to create the forecast. The goal of this model is to eliminate political disagreements, increase transparency and accuracy in the forecast.

Most local governments use the simplistic model because it is very clear-cut and uses data and financial resources that are readily available. Charles D. Liner (1983) argued that multivariate regression is not an appropriate tool for local government revenue projections. However, he does make a case for time series analysis since it makes use of internal data that is readily available and can be computed using simple equipment such as a calculator. A three to five-year period is typically used in the model (Bretschneider and Gorr 1999). Special attention should be paid to calculating property tax estimates. Liner (1983) suggested that revenue should be split into component parts and then the analyst has to decide whether to analyze actual revenues or the base of the revenue sources. Property tax revenue has assessed value (base), the tax rate, and the collection rate (actual). Further, it may be necessary to separate, real versus personal property. It may also be useful if the analyst can prepare graphs or charts showing the revenue trend over time. The amount of time designated to this process will clearly be dictated by the size and level of importance for the revenue source.

State governments are more likely to use one of the more sophisticated models because their budgets are larger and more complicated. Donald Axelrod (1995) argued, "the critical phase in revenue estimation is calculating the effect of the economic assumptions on the tax base for each tax" (78). For example, income taxes come from three major sources of income: wages and salaries, corporations, and other non-wage income such as rents, dividends and interests. Analysts can then use the set tax rates to estimate revenue. Lastly, they can adjust the estimate for various exemptions, deductions, refunds or expected delinquencies.

> For sales, excise, and other consumption taxes, it is necessary to estimate, tax by tax, the effect of economic activity on wholesale and retail sales. After deducting exemptions, analysts come up with a new tax base to which they apply the tax rates. Property taxes are determined by the assessed value of property and the appropriate tax rates, and adjusted to reflect exemptions, deductions, and statutory tax limits. (Axelrod 1995, 78)

Selecting the Best Forecasting Model

John L. Mikesell (2018) discusses six points that are useful as a guide to forecasting. First, the user should completely understand the revenue source. This includes administration and collection measures. Further, forecasters should ensure that the variables included in the model are as close to perfect as possible. Unreliable data for the dependent variable in particular compromises the validity of the estimate (Liner 1983). Second, the data should be plotted in a graph to show the movement of the revenue. Forecasters can use this information to determine the effects of other variables on the revenue. If possible, corrective measures can be taken to improve the administration or collection mechanisms.

The third point is honesty in reporting. Elected officials often have their own agendas and may seek to manipulate the process with low or high forecasts in an attempt to increase or decrease expenditures. Mikesell's (2018) fourth suggestion considered "what" the forecaster is trying to do with the revenue source. For example, if an annual forecast is needed, then a regression model would suffice. If a long-term forecast is needed, then a trend extrapolation model would work. Fifth, each revenue source should be estimated separately. There are too many factors that are indigenous to a particular revenue source that would inflate or deflate the total revenue source. It is easier to compensate for errors in separate revenue models. Lastly, revenue sources should be monitored throughout the year and compared with the projections. With that stated, the forecaster should be aware that a change in revenue projections for one month may or may not make a drastic difference for the rest of the year.

Regardless to what is found, the forecaster should use the information to improve the model (see also Liner 1983; Riley and Colby 1991).

Generally speaking, state and local governments initiate budget projections about six months prior to the beginning of the next fiscal year or budget cycle. The size of the budget and the number of factors affecting the budget are likely indicators of how much lead time is needed (Bretschneider and Gorr 1999).

Types of Forecasts

- *Status Quo Model*: This model assumes that the future will look a lot like the present. For example, if a state spent $75 million on capital expenditures last year, then it will cost approximately that amount this year. This model works well in stable governments. The major advantage of the model is that it is simple and easy to administer. The major disadvantage is that any shift in economic conditions will compromise the validity of the model (Nice 2002).

- *Extrapolation Model*: This model uses current trends (time-series data) in revenue and expenditures to explain future revenue and expenditure trends. Extrapolations can use constant increments, constant percent changes, simple growth models using the average annual compounding formula, or linear or nonlinear time trends in which revenue for the budget year is estimated as an arithmetic function of time ($R = a + bt$). For example, if property tax receipts have increased an average of 2% over the last five years, the model would assume that they would increase 2% during the forecasted year as well. While more accurate than the status quo model, it does have the same disadvantages. For example, the model does not examine cause and effect relationships between the revenue sources and a particular economic factor (Bretschneider and Gorr 1999; Mikesell 2018; Nice 2002).

- *Judgmental or Brainstorming Model*: In some instances, budget managers have substantive experience and knowledge of the nuances of a jurisdiction. They essentially use all of their contacts that also have longevity and the exact information that they need to project the budget. Initially, all sorts of data and information are generated. Then, these data and information are analyzed and scored for usefulness. Third, the best information and data are synthesized. Lastly, the best information and ideas are considered in the model. The obvious disadvantage to this model is dependence on the experts. While human judgment is important, it is enhanced tremendously with known facts that are quantifiable (Gianakis and McCue 1999).

- *Delphi Model*: In this model, experts discuss forecasts under the auspices of a moderator who handles only the logistical part of the discussion. Each participant is asked the same question by the moderator with the intent or hope that a consensus can be reached. The advantage of the model is that participants are not pressured to accept the position of other participants. This model also serves to allow minority views to be espoused (Gianakis and McCue 1999; Nice 2002).

- *Time-Series Model*: A time-series model can be simple or very complex. The model essentially attempts to break down and explain all of the component parts to the budget into four components: a long-term trend, seasonal variation, cyclical variation and irregular variation. The model addresses questions such as: When are the most property taxes, user fees, and sales taxes collected? When are public utilities the most heavily utilized? (Gianakis and McCue 1999; Liner 1983; Mikesell 2018; Nice 2002).
- *Multiple Regression Model*: A regression model is a more complex time series model that estimates revenue using several independent variables such as the unemployment rate and income levels. The advantage of this model is that it is relatively simple to estimate each revenue source separately (Bretschneider and Gorr 1999; Gianakis and McCue 1999; Mikesell 2018).
- *Econometric Models*: Econometric models estimate revenue within a simultaneous system of interdependent equations that express empirical and theoretical relationships between fiscal and economic variables (Mikesell 2018). The advantage to this model is that it allows the user to examine revenue sources that are not dependent on other revenue sources.

COST-BENEFIT ANALYSIS AND COST-EFFECTIVENESS ANALYSIS

These two techniques "attempt to relate the costs of projects or programs to performance, and both quantify costs in monetary terms. They differ, however, in the way they measure the outcomes of programs" (Lee et al. 2013, 494).

Cost-benefit analysis (CBA) compares the cost of a program with the benefits of the program. The alternative that yields the greatest net benefit at the least amount of cost is normally chosen. In addition to a dollar amount being placed on the variables in the analysis, benefits are also assessed from a quantitative perspective. Both of these techniques are quite dependent on data, so the analyst should ensure that he/she has the most reliable data available (Makowsky and Wagner 2009).

The main objective of these and other techniques is to improve internal and allocative efficiency in public spending. Spending today does not equate to spending tomorrow. As a result, it is necessary for budget analysts to be aware of items such as: present value, discount rates, recurring costs, and compounded interests when putting together cost-benefit models.[1]

There are some problems associated with cost-benefit models. One problem is with *free riders*. That is, some citizens enjoy the benefits of public service without paying for them. A second problem is the uneven distribution of benefits. David Nice (2002) used the example of a car licensing fee in Washington that offered the greatest reduction in the cost of the fee to those who owned the most expensive cars. From a political perspective, this proposal was not viewed as beneficial. A third example is political manipulation. In order to make a project look more attractive, the costs of the program can be lowered arbitrarily while the benefits can be increased (Axelrod 1995). Further, it is sometimes difficult to identify all of the costs and benefits associated with a program. There may be some spillover effects as well as other externalities that are hard to predict (Ammons 2002). There are also some benefits that are not necessarily considered when providing public services. For example, research shows that crime tends to decrease in neighborhoods when a police officer parks a squad car in the driveway at his/her private residence. Apparently, criminals avoid neighborhoods where police officers reside (Gianakis and McCue 1999).

Calculating cost-benefit analysis can be very complex since all of the factors involved in the process must be quantifiable and measurable over time. "Benefits are measured by the market price of the project outputs or the price consumers are willing to pay, while costs are measured by the monetary outlays necessary to undertake the investment" (Lynch, Sun, and Smith 2017, 160).

Let's look at an example of a municipality that wants to decrease the amount of non-violent crime in a particular part of the city. They look at three possible alternatives to improving the problem: (1) Increase the amount of time patrol officers spend in the neighborhood; (2) Place a police substation in the neighborhood and move six currently employed officers; and (3) Add a bicycle/foot patrol officers in the department whose jurisdiction would include that neighborhood.

Alternative 1: Increase Patrol Time (Budget: $0)

Cost: The first option is to increase the amount of patrol time in the neighborhood, while reducing the amount of time in other neighborhoods, using existing officers. Overall, patrol time will increase by 15 percent. There should be minimum, if any, increases in cost since we will use existing law enforcement personnel.

Benefit: Based on previous patterns, crime should decrease by 5 percent for every two hours added to the day patrol and decrease by 4 percent for every four hours added to the evening and night patrol. However, data suggest that shifting officers from one neighborhood to another is likely to shift crime from one neighborhood to another neighborhood over time.

Alternative 2: Add a Substation

Cost: The city has several options within this alternative. It is assumed that utility cost will be comparable in each of the alternatives.

Option A. Rent space from a private vendor. The most desirable area costs $750 per month plus utilities.

Option B. Purchase and refurbish one of the older buildings in the neighborhood. While the average building in the neighborhood is relatively cheap as a result of the crime level ($72,000), the cost to refurbish the site can range from $10,000 to $15,000 based on the condition of the building.

Option C. Build a new substation. The building, land and furnishing will cost the city $175,000 and take at least seven months to complete.

Option D. Purchase a building that is ready for occupation. Buildings that are ready for occupation tend to sell 10–15 percent higher than the average building. For example, a 700 square foot building that is completely ready for occupation will cost about $105,000.

Benefit: Based on previous crime patterns, we expect the crime rate to decrease by 50 percent within the first month of operation. Whether we lease, buy or build a substation will not affect this rate. However, the speed in which the officers occupy the space obviously will impact how quickly their presence will impact the crime rate.

Alternative 2 Budget			
Option A		*Option B*	
	FY1		FY1
Rent	$9,000	Building Purchase	$72,000
TOTAL	$9,000	Refurbishing Cost	15,000
		TOTAL	$87,000
Option C		*Option D*	
	FY1		FY1
Building	$100,000	Building	$105,000
Land	50,000	Benefits	50,000
Furniture	25,000	Equipment	32,000
TOTAL	$175,000	TOTAL	$187,000

Alternative 3: Add a Bicycle/Foot Patrolperson to the Area

Cost: The city would hire one new police officer at a cost of $50,000 per year, plus an additional $8,000 for training. Last, they will need a fully equipped bicycle ($1,000).

Benefit: One additional foot patrol would increase police visibility in the neighborhood by 100 percent. Crime decreased by 10 percent when the first foot patrol was hired last year. We expect that rate to increase an additional 15 percent since both officers will work simultaneously. Further, a citizen satisfaction survey indicated that citizens felt 75 percent safer as a result of the increased interaction with police officers that were on foot.

Alternative 3 Budget	
	FY1
New Policeman	$55,000
Benefits	15,000
Training	8,000
Bicycle	1,000
TOTAL	$70,000

Now that we have three alternatives, which one is the most efficient and effective? Let's look at each of the three alternatives. Alternative 1 is by far the most cost efficient, but is the worse in terms of benefits given the impact of moving an officer from one location to another location. Each of the options within Alternative 2 is an expensive choice.

In fact, Alternative 2 is the most expensive, but it has the greatest potential for good benefits. Alternative 3 falls squarely in the middle of Alternatives 1 and 2 in terms of costs and benefits. In this example, Alternative 3 is probably the best option given an assessment of costs and benefits. However, these decisions can and often become political decisions with little discussion of the budgetary ramifications.

Cost-effectiveness analysis (CEA) assumes that there are benefits and concentrates on spending the least amount of funds to achieve the objective. Another way to look at cost-effectiveness is to examine all viable policy options and determine which option is the most cost efficient. Gerasimos A. Gianakis and Clifford P. McCue (1999) pointed out that this model provides for technological efficiency, but not allocative efficiency "because no effort is made to determine whether the cost supports the pursuit of the goal" (89). Cost-effectiveness models are useful in both operating and capital budgets.

For example, exhibit 6.1 compares three options to reducing the number of cars in the downtown area of Jefferson City. Each of the options clearly has benefits, but the costs of exercising any particular option varies. Policymakers consider many more factors than what is included here. This would include questions such as: How many citizens will be affected by the option? Which option will allow for expansion in the future? Will the option generate revenue? How long will it take to complete the option? The quantitative techniques used in cost-effectiveness models are similar to those used in cost-benefits models (Axelrod 1995).

Exhibit 6.1. Cost-effectiveness Analysis Example (Transportation)		
Objective: Reduce the number of cars in the Jefferson City downtown area.		
Policy Option	*Cost*	*Estimated Users*
(a) Add two new bus lines emanating from a new garage near midtown.	$9.5 million	3,500 / day
(b) Add three trolley lines with parking lots near the three main arteries.	$8.2 million	3,000 / day
(c) Build an above ground train that circles downtown from each of the five suburbs.	$22.4 million	6,000 / day

Source: Created by the Author.

FINANCIAL DECISION MAKING TOOLS

Discounting to Present Value/Discount Rates

The term discounting has been traditionally used in the private sector. However, *discounting* to the present value is a very useful tool for public administrators because it considers the value of the dollar today relative to some other period in time. Analysts will find discounting useful when comparing two items that occur during different periods with similar financing methods. For example: leasing versus purchasing items or contracting out versus providing the service from within the government.

Robert D. Lee, Jr., Ronald W. Johnson, and Philip G. Joyce (2013) indicated that discounting serves two main purposes. First, funds are diverted from the private sector to the public sector. If these funds reap at least a dollar for dollar ratio, then it is feasible from an economic perspective to provide the service from within the government. Second, citizens prefer to reap the benefits of spending now rather than in the future. Hence, citizens are aware that the spending power of a dollar is greater today than it is in the future and are not inclined to endorse programs or invest money unless the interest is likely to reap greater future benefits (Wang 2006).

If we had a choice, we would like our money to increase in value over time, rather than decrease. Discounting works similar to compounded interest collected on a savings account in reverse. For example, if we were contemplating putting $10,000 in a saving account at a 6 percent interest rate, we would want to make sure that the spending power of the principal and interest ($10,600) will equal or exceed its current value in one year. If principal and interest does not equal or exceed the current value, then it would not be economically feasible to put money into the account. The 6 percent interest rate measures our willingness to trade $10,000 today (PV) for $10,600 in twelve months (FV). Interest rates calculate *future values*, while discount rates calculate *present value*.

$$\text{Future Value (FV)} = \text{Present Value (PV)} \times (\text{One} + \text{Interest Rate (IR)})$$
$$FV = \$10,000 \times (1 + 0.06)$$
$$FV = \$10,600$$

Present value is calculated using the same data as future value. However, the term discount rate is used rather than interest rate because the value of what we will receive in the future is smaller today because there is a delay in receiving the benefit. Hence, we subtract an amount to compensate us for that delay. We are, in effect, placing a value on time (Ammons 2002; Aronson and Schwartz 2004; Miller 1996). There is no hard and fast rule to determining what discount rate should be applied, but the process can be difficult. However, you should consider these rules relative to the public sector when considering a discount rate (Lee et al. 2013):

• The longer it takes for returns to occur, the more their value is discounted.
• Costs that occur earlier in the project are subject to less discounting.
• Total discounted benefits must exceed total discounted costs.

$$\text{Discount to the Present Value} = \text{Future Value} / (1 + \text{IR})$$

Let's consider an example that describes how discounting to the present values occurs:

Example 6.1

Jefferson City has a project that will take four years to implement from the day that construction begins. The city expects to save $5,000 a year once the project is implemented. Since funds will be spent prior to the completion of the project, time becomes a cost. Hence, it is feasible to use discounting. Using the PV formula and a 5% discount rate, the expected value of a $5,000 forecasted benefit for the project at the end of four years is $4,113.50. So, city officials can decide if the project is worth the investment based on this figure. That is, is it worth the effort to complete the project to save $4,113.50 a year?

Year 1 PV = $5,000 / (1 + 0.05) = $4,761.90
Year 2 PV = $4,761.90 / (1 + 0.05) = $4,535.14
Year 3 PV = $4,535.14 / (1 + 0.05) = $4,319.18
Year 4 PV = $4,319.18 / (1 + 0.05) = $4,113.50

A simple or short way to calculate the value of the savings in the fourth year is to use the Excel formula given below. By cubing the discount factor, you can calculate the present value the same way as you did with the long method above. However, you can expect the sum to vary slightly based on rounding error. You can decrease this error by not rounding the sum to two digits to the right of the decimal as you did in the long method. In this example, 1.05 raised to the fourth power is 1.21550625, which would give us a PV of $4,113.51. As you can see, this sum is only one cent off of the long method. In Excel, you can use the formula =(1+.05)^4 to calculate the answer. Note that the number four (4) in the preceding formula represents the number of years and .05 represents the discount rate.

$$\text{PV (of \$x over 4 years @ 5\%)} = \frac{\text{Future Value}}{(1 + .05)^4} = \frac{\$5,000}{1.21550625} = \$4,113.51$$

The second example below considers a leasing agreement versus a selling agreement for the city. In short, the city has to decide if it is financially better off selling the building versus leasing it for a finite period of time.

Example 6.2

Jefferson City has been offered $150,000 for a building that is leased to Barnett Real Estate. The real estate company pays $1,200 per month on a five-year lease with the option to buy the building at the end of the lease for $80,000. So, the city has to decide if it is better to sell the building now, or continue to lease it. Using a 5% discount rate, for a property that has annual benefits for n years, we can use the following formula to calculate the present value. Note: n = number of years.

$$\text{PV} = \text{Annual Value} \times \frac{[(1 + \text{Discount Rate})^n - 1]}{\text{Discount Rate} (1 + DR)^n}$$

(a) Leasing/Purchase Option

- Annual Benefit   = $14,400.00 ($1,200.00 x 12 months)
- One Time Benefit   = $80,000.00
- PV Annual Benefit   = $14,400.00 $\quad \text{x} \dfrac{(1.276 - 1)}{.05\ (1.276)}$

  (Add the math to calculate 1.276)

                        = $14,400.00 $\quad \text{x} \dfrac{(.276)}{.064}$

                        = $14,400.00 $\quad$ x 4.31

                        = $62,064.00

- PV One Time Benefit   = $80,000.00 $\quad / (1.05)^5$

                        = $62,695.92

  TOTAL Benefit   = $62,064.00 $\quad$ + $62,695.92

                        = $124,759.92

(b) Sale Option

- $150,000

(c) Comparing Options

It would seem feasible to sell the property given the small but positive disparity between the two sale options ($150,000–$124,759.92 = $25,240.08). If the difference was smaller, other items such as the current status of the lease holder, future plans of the city, and expenditure and revenue priorities should be closely scrutinized. More than anything, PV allows decision makers the opportunity to examine the current lease and assess what it is really worth ((([5 × $14,400] + $80,000) = $152,000).

Let's consider one more example where the city wants to invest funds into a new computer system. The question posed to the city is: Are the computers worth the investment?

Example 6.3

Jefferson City has determined that it is losing money in the billing department due to its inferior computer network. So, prior to spending $150,000 on new computers, city officials decided to use discounting to determine if it is worth the money to buy a new computer system. Specifically, is the expected $47,500 saved each year worth it in another six years when the cost of buying the computers is considered?

Depending on the item in question, it might be useful for a city to also secure bids and contract the project out to the lowest bidder if it is cost efficient. When leasing or contracting out a service/project, the analyst should pay close attention to the net present value (NPV). The NPV should be large (positive number) enough to justify the city providing the service. If the net present value is small, the city might want to seriously consider the lowest bidder.

Table 6.1 shows the results of the analysis using a 9 percent discount rate over a six- year period. When the amount invested is subtracted from the total present value of annual saving the net present value is $63,081.14 (where the sum of the NPV – Amount Invested: $213,081.14 – $150,000 = $63,081.14). This amount is over and beyond the cost of purchasing the computers. Hence, it would be a good investment for the city.

$$\text{NPV (Present Value)} = \frac{\text{Annual Savings}}{(1 + r)}$$

Table 6.1. Discounting Cash Flow Technique			
Year	Savings	NPV*	9% D.R.
1	$47,500	$43,577.98	.917
2	47,500	39,979.80	.842
3	47,500	36,678.72	.772
4	47,500	33,650.20	.708
5	47,500	30,871.74	.650
6	47,500	28,322.70	.596
TOTAL Present Value of Annual Savings (Sum of NVP for each year)	$213,081.14		
Amount Invested	$150,000.00		
Net Present Value (NPV)	= $63,081,14		
* Figures are rounded. Note: See also Kramer, Fred A. 1976. "The Discounting to Present Value Technique as a Decision Tool." *Special Bulletin.*			

Source: Created by the Author.

However, what if the NPV was smaller given the potential size of a city's budget? What if the savings were smaller and the discount rate was larger or smaller? What if the computers had a life span of seven years rather than six years? What if we had a private company offering the service at a lower amount? The NPV is ultimately affected by the data that is put into the equation. Hence, an analyst should be fully cognizant and understand this principle. Lastly, if the NPV is a negative number, it is a bad investment.

In order to get the figures in table 6.1, use the present value formula. After the first iteration, the sum becomes the new value. Over a six-year period, the city would save $213,081.14.

$$\text{NPV (Net Present Value)} = \frac{\text{Annual Savings}}{(1 + r)} = \frac{\$47,500.00}{(1 + .09)} = \$43,577.98*$$

$43,577.98 / $47,500.00 = .917 $43,577.98 / 1.09 = $39,979.80
$39,979.80 / $47,500.00 = .842 $39,979.80 / 1.09 = $36,678.72

*Figures are rounded.

Note: The formula that was used in Example 6.2 can also be applied to the problem discussed in Example 6.3. It is particularly useful in this setting because we are expecting annual benefits over several years.

Rate of Return

The *rate of return* (RI) is a private sector technique that solves for the rate of return on investments. In some instances, government officials have to decide if it is economically feasible to provide a service or contract the service out to the private sector. RI is calculated by dividing the net yearly/annual savings by the average investment in the project. There is an underlying assumption in this technique that government entities depreciate assets on an annual basis.

We can use the example in table 6.1 to explain and apply this technique. As shown previously, the city had yearly/annual savings of $47,500 by investing $150,000 into a new computer system. So, the first thing that we do is calculate annual depreciation using the following formula:

$$\text{I (Initial Investment) / EL (Expected Asset Life)} =$$
$$\text{AD (Annual Depreciation)}$$
$$\$150,000 / 6 \text{ years} = \$25,000$$

Next, we calculate the average investment (AI). We know that the computers will be worth $150k during the first year (FI) and $25k during the sixth year (LI) or the last year of the project. So, if we add the value of the computers in the first year to their value in last year and divide it by two, the average investment is $87,500. By the way, the last year value and the annual depreciation are the same.

First Year Value (FI) + Last Year Value (LI) /2 = Average Investment (AI)
$150,000 + $25,000 / 2 = $87,500

After doing the math, we see that the rate of return on the average investment is 53.7 percent using the formula:

Annual Savings (AS) /Average Investment (AI) = Rate of Return (RI)
$47,500 / $87,500 = .543 or 54.3 percent

City officials now have to decide if a rate of return of 54.3 percent is large enough to justify the project. While there is not an exact cut off for an acceptable rate of return, one can follow a basic rule, a larger rate of return is more acceptable than a smaller rate of return. In this case, 54.3 percent is not as good as 75 percent, but better than 40 percent.

Payback Method

The payback method is a tool that allows decision makers to examine the time needed to recover an investment through net annual savings. In simple terms, how much time is needed to recover the cost of the investment? In the private sector, the question is: how much time is needed to make a profit?

Let's use the data for Jefferson City in Example 6.3 where the city expected to save $47,500 annually by purchasing $150,000 in new computers for the Billing Department. The annual operating cost to the city is $25,000. The first thing that we must do is calculate the net annual cash flow saving.

Net Annual Cash Flow Savings (NSAV) =
Annual Saving (AS) – Operating Cost (OC)
$22,500 = $47,500–$25,000

Since we know the total dollar amount needed to complete the investment, we simply need to determine the expected life of the computers. Generally speaking, high end technology hardware and software is expected to have a life span of five years in the public sector. So, we can determine the payback period by dividing the annual investment (Ai) by the net annual cash flow saving (NSAV).

$$\text{Ai / NSAV} = \text{PP}$$
$$\$150{,}000 / \$22{,}500 = 6.6 \text{ years}$$

In this example, it is clear that 6.6 years is barely larger than the six-year expected life of the computers. Therefore, it would suggest that the computers are not a great investment. However, all is not necessarily lost. The city can also use this information to formulate other scenarios and ways to save money or reduce operating expenditures. For example, what would happen if the city received a lower bid on the computers or the life expectancy of the computers is extended one more year? The basic goal is to ensure that the expected life of the investment is greater than the payback period.

This model can be modified a bit to calculate the remaining life (RL) of an asset and actual savings (aS). Using the above example, we can calculate RL using this formula:

$$\text{EL} - \text{PP} = \text{RL}$$
$$6 - 6.6 = -0.6 \text{ years}$$

In this example, the computers fall 0.6 years short of the period needed to pay for them (Note: In Excel you should round this number to one digit to the right of the decimal. This will require you to round the RL in a separate cell). Again, this would support the previous finding that this would not be a great investment. It also supports the proposition that the city should ensure that they are getting the best possible estimates/bids on the computers. Actual savings can be determined using the formula:

$$\text{RL} \times \text{AS} = \text{aS}$$

In the above example ($-0.6 \times \$47{,}500 = -\$28{,}500$), we would have a net sum of zero since we are not saving any money. RL and AS must be positive numbers in order to reap savings (Round the remaining life years to one digit to the right of the decimal prior to calculating annual savings). Realistically, you want the item of expenditure to last longer than the period needed to pay for it (see Chapman 1996 for a nice snapshot of these three methods).

BREAKEVEN ANALYSIS

One tool that a city can use to determine if it is feasible to engage in an activity is called *breakeven analysis*. Greg G. Chen, Lynne A. Weikart, and Daniel W. Williams (2015) defined breakeven analysis as, "a method used to determine the volume or the number of products or services that must be sold or in some other way reimbursed at a given price in order for the operation's total revenue to be exactly equal to its expenses" (27). Breakeven analysis is a very useful tool in planning a new program or activity as it provides you the exact cost of engaging in the function. This of course is predicated on the information that is available.

Let's consider an example, Jefferson City has worked hard to ensure that the homeless population does not sleep on the streets and have a place to eat. After converting a recently closed school to a homeless shelter, the city needed to determine how much it would cost to feed the 250 men and women who reside there. In order to do so, they need to know a few things. First, what are the fixed costs (FC) to managing the shelter, maximum volume (Q), as well as the unit costs (UVC)? In addition, the city needs to know how many days the shelter can provide meals. In this example, they can serve meals, on average, thirty days per month. Since the shelter is currently operational, it will cost $25,000 per month in fixed costs to hire staff and secure equipment. The food will cost about $2.50 per meal (UVC).

In this example, we are solving for P, which is the price of each meal with respect to all of the other costs associate with feeding the homeless population.

$$P = \frac{FC + Q \times UVC}{Q} \qquad P = \frac{\$25,000 + 250 \times 30 \times \$2.50}{250 \times 30} \qquad P = \frac{43,750}{18,750}$$

$$P = \$5.83$$

As shown in the math above, the city should expect to spend $5.83 per meal to feed 250 homeless persons. This cost could be reduced or increased by changing any of the variables in the formula.

Depending on what you are looking for, you can also use this information to solve for maximum volume (Q) or total cost (TC) using the formulas below.

$$Q = \frac{FC}{P - UVC} \qquad TC = FC + Q \times UVC$$

PRODUCTIVITY ANALYSIS

The term *productivity* can be measured in a number of different ways, but the most common method compares the ratio of the quantity to the quantity of input used in the production of that output. The key question is: Can the work be completed more efficiently and effectively with the addition of more resources? Contrary to popular belief, governments do in fact make an attempt to do more with less. Using better work procedures, better equipment, and improving employee attitude toward the job can work toward achieving this end. Assessing productivity can be achieved through an examination of outputs and outcomes. However, it is better to examine the benefits to individuals and society (outcomes) rather than the product of the project (outputs). Performance audits make it easy to obtain outputs, but outcomes require value judgments to determine if society is better off. There are a number of factors that can affect the relationship between outcomes and outputs, so it is difficult to have a meaningful analysis of outcomes. Review the section in chapter 1 on program and performance budgets to see how expenditures are tied to outcomes and outputs. Further, an increase in production may suggest a decrease in cost, but a reduction in cost does not necessarily mean an increase in production. Programs may appear to be more efficient by cutting the budget without much regard for productivity.

One of the most commonly cited reasons for increased productivity are increased workload. Some employees are simply bored and unchallenged while others do not have enough to do. Others find their work too complex and thus do not perform. When the work is simplified, they tend to perform better. As a result, unit costs can be lowered. Improved training procedures, new equipment, better use of job evaluations, improved employee relations, and opportunities for mobility have also been shown to improve productivity.

Essentially, programs and projects must be evaluated on their own merits. Evaluators must understand the mechanics of the work performed and human behavior in order to provide good recommendations (Lynch et al. 2017).

MULTIPLE REGRESSION ANALYSIS

Regression analysis is used quite a bit as a forecasting method by most states and large local governments. Users of this technique should be familiar with statistical packages such as SPSS, Stata, R or SAS to conduct this sort of analysis. Regression analysis is particularly useful in budgeting when examining revenue and expenditure models. It allows the user to determine the effect of each independent variable on the dependent variable while controlling the other independent variables.

A simple regression model uses a straight line where $Y = a + bX$ to describe the relationship. In this model, Y is the dependent variable, a is the distance between the point where the regression line intercepts the Y axis and the origin, the slope b is the regression coefficient and measures the change in Y given one unit change in X (Lynch et al. 2017; Mikesell 2018).

Again, the technique works on the basic assumption that a change in a dependent variable (Y) is correlated with a change in an independent variable

(X). This change can be negative or positive. Regression analysis uses interval or ratio data. However, nominal or ordinal data can be converted to numbers and then the numbers are used as proxies (also called *dummy variables*). For example, let's think about the word region. The words south and north do not mean anything to a computer program. So, if we convert the terms to 0 and 1, where 0 = south and 1 = north, we can then use the numerical data in our analysis. However, the user has to remember not to make false claims with the data. For example, a mean score of 145 for south and 239 for north means absolutely nothing. Let's take a look at an example to clarify the concepts listed above.

In this example, Mrs. Joya Smith is the Secretary of Health and she is trying to make an argument that the federal government needs to continue supporting the Medicaid and SCHIP programs in their efforts to decrease the number of uninsured children in the United States. The following *directional hypothesis* summarizes her argument:

H_1: Enrolling children in SCHIP and Medicaid will decrease the percent of uninsured children.

The basic premise of her model is that variables (independent) such as the percentage of children who: graduate from high school, live below the poverty level, live in a certain region of the country, etc. have an effect on the percentage of uninsured children. Each of the variables used in the model are in rates or percentages with the exception of region. Region in this model is a dichotomous dummy variable. The model is:

$$Y=b0+b1x1+b2x2+b3x3+b4x4+b5x5+b6x6+b7x7+e$$

where:

Y = Percentage of Uninsured Children

Demographic Variables (annual)

x1 = Poverty Rate
x2 = High School Graduation Rate,
x3 = Unemployment Rate,
x4 = Percent of Population that is Caucasian,
x5 = Geographical Region (South and Southwest=0, Other States=1),

Public Health Variables (annual)

x6 = Children Medicaid Enrollee Rate, and
x7 = Children SCHIP Enrollee Rate.

What does the model reveal? Table 6.2 shows that each of the independent variables has some effect on the dependent variable. The most important item for Mrs. Smith is to show that the Medicaid and SCHIP program variables are significant. The coefficients for each of these variables are significant at the 0.01 level of analysis and in the correct direction (−0.0236 and −0.591 respectively). That is, as the percentage of Medicaid and SCHIP enrollees increase the percentage of uninsured children decreases. The negative sign next to the coefficient indicates a decrease. A positive coefficient would indicate an increase in the coefficient. For example, the model shows that the percentage of uninsured children increases as the poverty rate increases.

Other things that are useful in this table are the F score and Adjusted R^2. The R^2 coefficient ranges from 0–100. The coefficient basically defines the level of predictability for the model. In this example, the adjusted R^2 is 0.969. So, that would mean that all of the independent variables explain 96.9% of the variance in uninsured rates.

Table 6.2. OLS Children's Health Care Regression Model (Pooled Data)			
Demographic Variables		Economic Variables	
High School Graduates	−0.192 (.023)***	Unemployment Rate: −0.423 (.138)**	
Children in Poverty	0.175 (.028)***		
		Medicaid and SCHIP Variables	
White Population	−0.076 (.006)***	Medicaid Enrollees: −0.236 (.038)***	
Region	16520 (9507.7)*	SCHIP Enrollees: −0.591 (−.591)***	
Total Population	0.203 (.012)***	Intercept: −14019 (7539.7)	
F = 771.23***	R^2 = 0.970	Adjusted R^2 = 0.969 N = 301	
***Significant at the 0.01 level **Significant at the 0.05 level. *Significant at the 0.10 level.			

Source: Created by the Author.

CONCLUSION

As mentioned at the beginning of the chapter, there are a number of techniques that are useful to budget analysts and politicians in understanding how to forecast the amount of revenues needed for the budget. In addition, there are tools that allow analysts the ability to determine if policy decisions, upon implementation, are good or bad. While there are no hard and fast rules in estimating revenues, the chapter does show that there are some basic principles that should be adhered to regardless to the size of the government. Basically, good projections come from analysts who stick to the basic principles while paying close attention to population shifts, economic fluctuations, industry movement, etc. Sophisticated models are only as good as the analysts using them. These as well as other tools are quite useful and can save governments thousands or millions of dollars over multiple fiscal years.

IMPORTANT TERMS AND PHRASES

Annual Benefit
Annual Depreciation
Annual Savings
Annual Value
Average Investment
Brainstorming Model
Breakeven Analysis
Congressional Budget Office
Cost-Benefit Analysis
Cost-Effectiveness Analysis
Delphi Model
Directional Hypothesis
Discounting/Discount Rates
Dummy Variables
Econometric Model
Expected Asset Life
Extrapolation Model
First Year Value
Fixed Cost
Forecasting
Free Rider
Future Value

Hypothesis
Interest Rate
Initial Investment
Input-Output Models
Judgmental Model
Last Year Value
Marginal Cost
Micro Simulation Model
Multiple Regression Model
Net Present Value
Net Annual Cash Flow Saving
Office of Management and Budget
One Time Benefit
Operating Cost
Payback Method
Present Value
Productivity
Rate of Return
Recurring Cost
Remaining Life
Status Quo Model
Time-Series Model

CHAPTER 6 HOMEWORK EXERCISES

Directions: Complete question 1 and 2 in a word processing program and questions (3) through (8) in Excel. Do not round any numbers until the final step. Paste the Excel answers into a word processing program. Please turn in your Excel worksheets and the word file with the pasted Excel worksheets to your instructor.

(1) The mayor for Jefferson City has requested a cost-benefit analysis. In short, she wants to know if the city can save money by using outside security vendors for public events held at the city's convention center. The city manager has appointed you, the budget analyst, to conduct the analysis. Your analysis should provide three alternatives. The first alternative should provide the data for the cities' police department and the latter two alternatives should be estimates from two private companies (Security One and First Line Security). Since private companies are considered in this example, the budget should be primarily limited to personnel and operating costs. Below is a list of information that you should use when conducting your analysis. When you complete your analysis, make a recommendation to Mayor McClain. You are free to write your analysis in any form that you choose as long as you consider the information that is provided below. Last, in addition to what the city spent, you must create a budget for the remaining vendors.

- The city spent $1,250,000 in salary and benefits last year (police department) for security at the convention center for thirty-five events.
- The events averaged 25,000 people.
- A total of fifty-five officers were used, on average, for each event.
- The convention center has a main security office that requires three persons to be on duty at all times.
- There are eight points of entry that require an armed security guard.
- The events averaged five hours in length.
- Security One has contracted with the city in the past (four years) with fairly good evaluation scores on customer service. They have forty security officers who are trained in CPR and paramedic skills, with an average tenure of six years. Thirty-five of the officers are registered to carry weapons. They have four staff members with at least one person on duty at all times. Their main office is not in the downtown area.
- First Line Security is a new company that was started by the previous police chief. They have fifty security officers with an average tenure of ten years of experience and five staff members. They have an office downtown near the areas where events tend to occur (open

twenty-four hours per day). They have managed two large events thus far with few problems. They received high evaluation scores on both events. In addition, their fees tend to be slightly less than the competition for the same services.

Items to Consider: The "Benefits" section of your analysis could include: educational levels of security officers, certifications (diversity training, CPR, etc.), length of experience, permits (handgun, etc.), age; age of company, clientele list, work history of company, number and type of security vehicles; and expected length of the security contract. Also, note that the contractors are completely responsible and liable for their employees and any incidents that may occur (i.e., employee insurance; contractor must be bonded, etc.). In addition to the above items, you should consider speaking with a security or police department to see what additional items should be included in your proposal. It is not necessary to include every possible detail in your cost, but try to be holistic in your categories so as to keep your budget succinct.

(2) As a result of the population growth at the north end of Jefferson City over the last five years (5,000 people and 2,000 new homes), Mayor Mc-Clain has asked you to create a cost-effectiveness analysis plan (CEA) to manage the provision of postal services to residents in that area. In short, the residents want a new post office in their neighborhood. However, the mayor is not completely sold on the idea, but she has to make a recommendation to the Post Master General. Hence, she wants you to examine the proposals so that she can provide the council with multiple options to consider, including building a new post office at the north end of town. When you are finished considering the three options, make a recommendation to the mayor along with a narrative explaining the recommendation. That is, which option should produce the desired results with the least amount of spending? Your options should include at least three variables (cost, users, space, vehicles needed, equipment, etc.). In addition, include at least four important questions (budget, traffic patterns, location, equity, etc.) that could impact the council's decision.

(3) Jefferson City has decided to build a downtown parking garage to house the city's employee vehicles. Since the city has to demolish several buildings on the site, the project will take five years to complete. The city expects to save $35,000 a year in parking vouchers once the project is completed. Using a 5 percent discount rate, determine the present value (PV) of the $35,000 savings at the end of the five-year period (see appendix 6A).

(4) The Jefferson City Council is contemplating selling a building that is currently leased to Dr. Tarria Whitley, a local veterinarian, for $95,000. Whitley leases the building for $900 per month and is currently on a six year annually renewed lease with the option to buy the property at the close of the lease for $45,000. Using the present value formula and a 6% discount rate, calculate the total benefit of the leasing option and compare it with the option to sell the property. Should the city sell the building or continue to lease it?

(5) In this question, you will evaluate a net present value proposal.

 (a) Chief Candace Miller of the Jefferson City police department has submitted a proposal to the city's budget director requesting the purchase of ten new police cars. She estimates the department will save $20,000 a year by having the new cars. The cars will cost the city $200,000. Unfortunately, the life span of a police car is only four years at best. Using a 7% discount rate, calculate the net present value of the proposal. Explain the results.

 (b) Using the above example, calculate the NPV using the following data: Discount Rate = 5 percent, Cost of Cars = $185,000, Annual Savings = $90,000, Life span of car = five years. Explain the results (see appendix 6B).

(6) Using the data in Question 5(a) and 5(b), calculate annual depreciation, average investment, and the rate of return for the police department's proposal. Explain the results in each problem (see appendix 6C).

(7) The Parks and Recreation department has suggested renovating the municipal golf course at a cost of $1.1 million with an annual operating cost of $255,000 and an annual savings of $295,000. The expected life of the golf course is seven years before the city will have to make a major investment in improving the course. Calculate the payback period, remaining asset life, and the actual savings. Explain the results.

(8) Jefferson City has decided to invite an orchestra to play in the city's museum. Your job is to calculate the cost of an individual ticket in order for the city to breakeven on sales. The city estimates that their total fixed costs are $300,000. The variable cost is $20 per ticket.

 (a) If the city sets the price of the ticket at $75, how many tickets does the city need to sell in order to breakeven?

 (b) If the city set the price of the tickets at $50, how many tickets does the city need to sell in order to breakeven?

(9) Optional In-class Exercise: Defending Cost Effectiveness Analysis Plans (30–35 minute exercise)

Step 1: Arrange the class in groups of four or five.

Step 2: Have the groups discuss their CEA plans for question 2. That is, each group should come up with a consensus group cost-effectiveness plan based on their individual plans. The plan should include eight to ten questions to go along with a minimum of three options (20 minutes).

Step 3: Have one person from each group present the plan to the entire class (15 minutes).

NOTE

1. Review Thomas D. Lynch, Jinping Sun, and Robert W. Smith (2017), *Public Budgeting in America*, 6th ed. (Irvine, CA: Melvin & Leigh); Robert D. Lee, Jr., Ronald W. Johnson, and Philip G. Joyce (2013), *Public Budgeting Systems*, 9th ed. (Burlington, MA: Jones & Bartlett Learning); Gerasimos A. Gianakis and Clifford P. McCue (1999), *Local Government Budgeting: A Managerial Approach* (West Port, CT: Praeger); and Jonathan Gruber (2005), *Public Finance and Public Policy* (New York: Worth Publishers), for a discussion on cost-benefit and cost-effectiveness analysis.

Appendix 6A

Present Value Calculation

Present Value (PV) Calculation Worksheet			
Present Value			
Short Answer $PV = FV / (1R + 1)^5$			
PV =	(PV = 35000/1.05 to the fifth power)		
Long Answer			
Year	Savings	D.R.	PV
1. $35,000	1 + .05		
2.			
3.			
4.			
5.			
PV =			

Appendix 6B

New Present Value

Net Present Value (NPV) Calculation Worksheet			
Data from Homework Assignment 5(a).			
Discount Rate =	7%		
Cost of Cars =	$200,000		
Annual Savings =	$20,000		
Life Span =	4 years		
NPV = Annual Savings / (1+r) =			
Year	Savings	NPV	7% D.R.
1. $20,000			
2. $20,000			
3. $20,000			
4. $20,000			
$80,000	$0		
Amount Invested =	$200,000		
Total Present Value of Savings =	$80,000		
Total Present Value of Annual Savings =	$0		
Net Present Value (NPV) =			
Explanation:			

Appendix 6B

Data from Homework Assignment 5(b).			
Discount Rate =	5%		
Cost of Cars =	$185,000		
Annual Savings =	$90,000		
Life Span =	5 years		
NPV = Annual Savings / (1+r) =			
Year	Savings	NPV	5% D.R.
1. $90,000			
2. $90,000			
3. $90,000			
4. $90,000			
5. $90,000			
Total $450,000			
Amount Invested =	$185,000		
Total Present Value of Savings =	$450,000		
Total Present Value of Annual Savings =			
Net Present Value (NPV) =			
Explanation:			

Appendix 6C
Annual Calculations

Payback, Remaining Life, and Actual Savings Calculation Worksheet	
Data from Homework Assignment Questions 5(a) and 5(b).	
Renovations =	$1,100,000
Annual operating cost: =	$255,000
Annual savings:	$295,000
Life span =	7 years
NSAV =	
Payback Period =	
Remaining Life =	
Actual Savings =	
Explanation:	

Chapter 7

Financial Management

OVERVIEW

Although the main focus of this book is not on financial management, the subject matter is crucial to politicians as well as bureaucrats given the stream of time that we live in. The chapter begins by discussing financial solvency and then moves on to six specific topics. These topics include: cash management, risk management, procurement, cutback management, economic development, and debt management. These and similar topics have become increasingly more important due to things such as: poor cash management, insufficient tax bases, an increase in the use of technology, an increase in the number of retirees, population growth and depletion and slow industrial and economic activity. The overall objective of this chapter is to introduce students to basic concepts and techniques that can be used to effectively manage governments during economic prosperity as well as periods of economic downturns.

FINANCIAL CONDITION

Under the right set of circumstances, it may be necessary for a local government to use financial practices that it may not commonly employ. With that in mind two important practices are discussed in this section. First, financial practices that may compromise the financial position of a local government are examined. Second, practices that can sustain an operating deficit are discussed.

Financially Solvent or Not?

Financial solvency or *financial condition* can be defined as the ability of a local government to finance its services on continuous basis. Specifically, "financial condition refers to a government's ability to (1) maintain existing service levels, (2) withstand local and regional economic disruptions, and (3) meet the demands of natural growth, decline, and change" (Nollenberger, Groves, and Valente 2003, 2).

Maintaining existing services includes maintaining current services funded by existing revenue, funding programs that are funded by outside sources, maintaining capital facilities, and providing for future liabilities that may be currently unfunded (pensions, debt, lease purchase agreements, or postemployment benefits).

Economic disruption can occur in a number of different ways. This includes, but is not limited to: recessions, periods of high unemployment, tax delinquencies, and lower investments as a result of lower interest rates. Good planning can lessen the impact of these factors.

Growth and decline in a municipality is fairly common. However, stability can also create financial pressure. Population shifts and changes in the population can destabilize a budget. For example, the population of an area could maintain numerical stability, but not economical stability. For example, what would happen if 20% of a city's middle income population was replaced with a low income population? Would that shift affect social services and compromise the government's financial health? More than likely it would affect the entire system. However, existing tax payers may be less inclined to support these new programs. As a result, decision makers have to decide if the current tax and revenue structure can sustain expanding the new or current program. Can reserve funds or other mechanisms pay for the service? If a government cannot meet this sort of challenge it is not financially sound.

Measuring financial condition is not necessarily an easy process and there are a number of factors that hinder the process. According to Karl Nollenberger, Sanford M. Groves, and Maureen Godsey Valente (2003), "the nature of a public entity, the state of municipal financial analysis, and the character of municipal accounting practices" may hinder measuring financial condition (see also Wang, Dennis, and Tu 2007).

First, let's examine the nature of a public entity. Success is measured in the private sector in dollars. However, success in the public sector is not concerned with making a profit, but with efficiency and effectiveness of programs and services. This includes issues of health and welfare, political satisfactions and other subjective measures. As a result of subjective measures, determining financial solvency is more difficult.

Second, municipal financial analysis focuses on cash and budgetary solvency with less attention to long run and service level solvency with few exceptions. The one exception to this is with regards to investments. Hence, more attention to long run and service solvency has to improve in order to overcome this obstacle. Another issue with respect to financial analysis is the lack of normative standards. For example, what is an acceptable level of debt? What is a healthy reserve fund balance? Benchmarks established by credit rating agencies should be used in conjunction with subjective factors such as the diversity of a municipality's tax base when addressing these sort of questions.

Accounting practices is the final component that should be examined when considering financial solvency. As mentioned in chapter 1, governments often use fund accounting. Fund accounting stresses legal compliance and balancing the flow of money rather than examining program cost accounting and the measurement of long term financial health. Budgets do not tend to show the detailed cost of services provided, postponed costs, the unfunded pension liabilities, or employee benefit liabilities. Nor do they show "the reductions in purchasing power caused by inflation or the decreasing flexibility in the use of funds that result from increasing state and federal mandates. Financial statements and budgets do not show the erosion of streets, buildings, and other fixed assets. Finally, these reports are prepared for a one-year period and do not show in a multiyear perspective the emergence of favorable or unfavorable conditions" (Nollenberger et al. 2003, 3).

Nollenberger et al. (2003) developed a *Financial Trend Monitoring System* (FTMS) paradigm with eleven financial conditions factors that should affect management practices and legislative policies related to financial solvency. The paradigm is split into two dimensions: financial factors and environmental factors. Table 7.1 shows the two dimensions along with the defining organizational setting of each. This is not an exhaustive list of organizational settings (see also Rivenbark, Roenigk, and Allison 2010).

Table 7.1. Factors Affecting Financial Condition
Financial Factors
(a) Revenues: growth, flexibility, elasticity, dependability, diversity, and administration.
(b) Expenditures: growth, priorities, mandated costs, productivity, and effectiveness.
(c) Operating Position: operating results, fund balances, reserves, and liquidity.
(d) Debt Structure: short term debt, long term debt, debt schedules, and overlapping debt.
(e) Unfunded Liabilities: pension obligations, pension assets, and postemployment benefits.
(f) Condition of Capital Plant: maintenance effort and capital outlay.
Environmental Factors
(a) Community Needs and Resources: population, density, age, income, property value and distribution, home ownership, vacancy rates, business activity, crime and employment rates.
(b) Intergovernmental Constraints: intergovernmental mandates and restrictions on revenue.
(c) Disaster Risk: potential for natural disasters and local preparedness.
(d) Political Culture: attitudes toward taxes, services, and political processes.
(e) External Economic Conditions: national and regional inflation, employment and market conditions.

Source: Karl Nollenberger, Sanford M. Groves, and Maureen Godsey Valente (2003), *Evaluating Financial Condition: A Handbook for Local Government*, 4th ed. (Washington, DC: ICMA).

In order to use the system, analysts simply have to address the issues as they are laid out. Nollenberger et al. (2003) lays out three basic evaluation questions for each area: Financial, Environmental, and Organizational Setting.

Financial Factors: Does your government currently pay the full cost of operating, or is it postponing costs to a future period when revenues may not be available to pay these costs?

Environmental Factors: Do environmental factors provide enough resources to pay for the demands they make?

Organizational Setting: Does your management practices and legislative policies enable your government to respond appropriately to changes in the environment?

Essentially, the analyst examines each of the aforementioned characteristics using directional arrows. For example, population and density are found in the community needs and resources list of environmental factors. So, if you are assessing a municipality, determine if the population is increasing (↑), decreasing (↓), or remaining level (-) as indicated with the appropriate symbol. The same procedure is used for density, income movement and the other characteristics. Notice that the system does not require the user to insert an amount. You are simply concerned with the direction of the characteristic at this juncture. The direction of the symbol will determine whether further investigation is needed. In some cases, more analysis may be needed regardless to the direction of the arrow.[1] If additional analysis is needed, the user should use graph, tables, and other visual tools to show the trends.[2]

After which, the results should be evaluated. As mentioned before, trend analysis is the primary tool that the system uses. Trend analysis allows the user to: identify unfavorable trends, determine when the unfavorable trend began, consider mitigating circumstances, identify the causes underlying the unfavorable trend, compare the indicator trends to one another, compare the economic condition of the local government to national or regional trends, determine whether further analysis should be done, compare the trends to the benchmarks used by crediting firms, take other factors into consideration, and add his/her professional judgment. Last, policy statements should be developed to plan a strategy to manage the areas of concern (Nollenberger et al. 2003).

Exhibit 7.1 provides a partial example of a financial solvency statement for Jefferson City. The exhibit has several pertinent items. First, it shows the major financial indicators for the city over the last three fiscal years along with estimates for the latter two years. In the revenue section, we can see the direction of each revenue stream over time. However, note that it is necessary to explain why user fees decreased over time despite the fact the growth is still positive. Also, it is not necessary to create a chart for every single revenue source. Elected officials tend to be more concerned with major sources of revenues. However, you can use your discretion when using tables and graphs. In addition to revenues and expenditures, you should also create a table and chart for the other financial categories in your budget. These should include items such as operating expenditures, debt structure and the capital plant.

Exhibit 7.1. Financial Solvency Model for Jefferson City						
A. Revenue	*FY 17*	*FY 18*	*FY 19*	*FY 20 (est.)*	*FY 21 (est.)*	*Dir.*
Property Taxes	$5,890,423	$6,234,129	$6,398,490	$6,589,123	$6,657,239	↑
Sales Taxes	1,239,459	1,298,098	1,359,128	1,459,872	1,590,213	↑
Franchise Fees	239,125	$245,908	251,908	275,234	289,990	↑
User Fees	245,129	254,890	278,568	278,578	279,001	↑
TOTAL	$7,624,136	$8,033,025	$8,288,094	$8,602,807	$8,816,443	
B. Expenditures*	*FY 17*	*FY 18*	*FY 19*	*FY 20 (est.)*	*FY 21 (est.)*	*Dir.*
Personnel	$5,336,895	$5,703,448	$5,967,428	$6,021,965	$6,171,510	↑
Utilities	152,483	160,661	165,762	172,056	176,329	↑
Supplies	304,965	321,321	331,524	344,112	352,658	↑
Equipment	686,172	642,642	580,167	774,253	793,480	↑
Capital Fund	1,143,620	1,204,954	1,243,214	1,290,421	1,322,466	↑
TOTAL	$7,624,135	$8,033,026	$8,288,095	$8,602,807	$8,816,443	

*Figures are rounded to the nearest dollar amount.
Revenue Explanations: Each revenue source has increased incrementally overtime. However, user fees have clearly leveled off as a result of more residents using internal roads rather than the toll roads. This is more than likely the direct result of widening Stateline Road to three lanes.
Expenditure Explanations: Expenditures for the city are consistent with revenue allocations over time. The data in the table shows growth in each subcategory. Hence, expenditures are stable with little volatility.

Source: Created by the Author.

Detecting an Operating Deficit

Generally speaking, a deficit in one year may or may not cause much consternation. The government may use reserves to cover the deficit. However, frequent short falls should raise a red flag. If a city ignores the causes of the deficit or continues to maintain the same level of services and expenditures at the current pace without a commensurate increase in revenues, more serious issues will have to be addressed. The following paragraphs briefly discuss several items that suggest that a government may have an operating deficit.

In some instances, governments may have a *budget surplus*. This allows them the flexibility to put money into a *budget reserve* to be used when *budget shortfalls* occur. Reserves are also useful because they can reduce the need to increase taxes. However, if the budget reserve continues to drop over several years, it could be an indicator that expenditures are exceeding revenues (Nollenberger et al. 2003; Stewart, Hamman, and Pink-Harper 2018).

Short-term borrowing can be another indicator of operating deficits. *Short-term borrowing* is debt that is incurred and expected to be paid within a single fiscal year and is usually done for cash flow purposes, particularly if the government's major funding source is property taxes (Stewart 2011). Property taxes are usually paid every six months. As a result, a government might need to borrow to pay bills. If revenues or fund balances are not high enough, *tax anticipation notes* (TAN) can be issued to cover operating needs. The debt service will be paid when the next property tax collection takes place. In some cases, a city can pay off the debt and then re-borrow the funds or pay only the interest on the loan. This is called *rolling over* short-term debt. Unfortunately, this is a clear indicator that a problem exists and can lead to debt obligations, perhaps causing higher interest rates on future borrowing, negatively affect the city's credit rating, or force the city to reduce service and raise revenues (see Lauth 1997).

City administrators can also borrow from other funds. Internal borrowing occurs when one fund borrows from another fund rather than from external sources. Not all internal *transfers* are loans. Some funds have lower expenditures and consistently operate with surpluses. As a result, internal transfers may be made as a matter of policy. For example, states that operate liquor stores will transfer excess "profits" to the general fund. The term "borrow" clearly suggests the intent to return funds to the original source within a designated period of time. Frequent borrowing can create a liability that the city cannot manage and subsequently impact services.

A city can also sell assets to bring in *one-time revenues*. If one-time revenues are used to fund current operating expenditures, rather than for one-time expenditures, the city is sustaining a deficit. *Saleable assets* include items such as buildings, land, as well as equipment. Selling city assets may affect services, in that services may have to be reduced the following year unless more revenue can be generated. Furthermore, if the assets that are sold are not excess, the city may incur additional costs to procure replacements in the future.

Accounting gimmicks can also be used to balance a budget. For example, if the last day in a pay period falls on the last day of the fiscal year, the staff may wait the extra day to record that expense. As a result, expenses for the current year appear smaller. Typically, three accounting gimmicks are used to manipulate the budget: (1) postponing current cost to future periods, (2) accruing revenues from a future fiscal year to the current fiscal year, and (3) extending the length of the current fiscal year. An example would include: extending the period from twelve to thirteen months, so that revenues collected in the thirteenth month can be counted in the current fiscal year (Nollenberger et al. 2003).

Deferment of a payment is the last practice that is indicative of an operating deficit. This occurs when a city receives invoices in the current fiscal year, but delays the payment until the next fiscal year. For example, a city only pays invoices when it has the cash available to make the payment. Deferment of payment of the city's obligation to the pension fund is a major indicator of financial stress.[3]

Another indicator of financial stress is deferment of maintenance expenditures for things like streets, public buildings, equipment, and bridges. If these items are not maintained, it has a negative domino effect on everything else. Service is likely to diminish, efficiency will drop, and replacement costs are likely to increase (Mikesell 2018; Nollenberger et al. 2003).

The techniques and gimmicks that have been discussed are used to try to solve budget deficiencies. However, they are detected when the government undergoes the audit at the end of the year. A major reason for auditing a government is to disclose such practices. For example, delaying payment of the payroll may address the budget problem, but the expenditure will be recorded on the financial statements prepared in accordance with Generally Accepted Accounting Principles (GAAP). The same is true for the pension obligation— it will be recorded as an expenditure and a fund liability. Paying pensions on a pay-as-you-go basis on the budget basis will not resolve a shortfall on the GAAP basis since the true pension liability will be reported on the GAAP statements. The same is true for accruing future revenues in the current fiscal year—GAAP reporting will reveal this practice. This is why it is important for state and local governments to have their financial statements audited.

The above items essentially reinforce the point that agency heads and directors should pay close attention to activities within their agency, revenue and expenditure trends, and other conditions that could impact their budget and cause a deficit.

EXTERNAL CASH MANAGEMENT PRACTICES

Determining how much money is needed at one particular point in time can be an arduous task for a local government. Basically, expenditures must equal/balance revenues collected by the end of the fiscal year. Two problems can arise when revenues are collected and expenditures are made. First, there could be a *cash flow problem*. A cash flow problem occurs when the amount of revenue available is not sufficient to cover immediate expenditures. Barring any unforeseen occurrences, cities do not tend to have cash flow problems because they know when tax collections are due. Hence, they can time their expenditures with revenue receipts. At the other end of the spectrum, a city may have an *idle cash problem*. This problem occurs when a city has more money on hand than its immediate financial obligations and does not take any measures to invest the surplus funds. Good c*ash management* occurs when a city meets all of its financial obligations and invests the balance.

The concept of cash management is another concept that is not as simple as it may appear. In order to engage in cash management, a government needs to know how much money is available at any given time and how much is needed to pay obligations. Further, estimates of future revenues may also be needed. This may require daily, weekly, or monthly forecasts. This information can be used to construct a *cash budget.* There are four steps to calculating a monthly cash budget: (1) Estimate cash receipts for the month, (2) Estimate cash disbursements that will take place during the month, (3) Subtract cash receipts from cash disbursements to determine excess or deficit (*net cash flow*), and (4) Add this month's balance to the prior month's balance to find the projected total cash balance.[4]

Aman Khan (1997) and M. Corrine Larson (2004) discusses six ways to achieve effective cash management: managing liquidity, accelerating collections, maximizing investment earnings, reduce borrowing, managing disbursements efficiently and providing accurate and timely reporting, and depositing checks in a timely fashion (see also Clark and Hughes 1997).

- *Managing Liquidity*: There should always be enough funds on hand to meet obligations.
- *Accelerating Collections*: Monies owed should be collected in the most efficient and effective manner available.
- *Maximizing Investment Earnings*: Available cash should be invested until they are needed. However, the government should minimize exposure to risk.
- *Reduce Borrowing*: Careful cash management can help prevent the need for internal borrowing from other funds or issuing tax anticipation notes to cover budget shortfalls.
- *Manage Disbursements Efficiently*: Determine the most effective manner to disburse funds by reducing guess-work and reducing the opportunity of fraud. Determine if a centralized or decentralized disbursement system works best.
- *Depositing Checks*: Checks should be deposited as soon as possible. This can reduce the amount of time that is needed to collect the payment and clear the banking system (*float*).

Once the government has determined that funds are available for investment, analyst can use the *Economic Ordering Quantity Formula* (EOQ) to determine the cash position of the government (Khan 1996; Larson 2004; Lynch, Sun, and Smith 2017; Thai 2004). "In this approach, an analyst weighs carrying cost, which foregone earned interest represents, against the total cost of the transaction. This model recognizes that the government incurs an opportunity cost for holding rather than investing idle cash. And each bank transaction (for example, transferring from securities to cash) involves an administrative cost to the government. If the government is to save idle cash and earn more than its administrative cost for investing, then it must recognize that more transactions drive up the cost of investing. To make money on investments, more transactions require a higher cash amount to invest" (Lynch et al. 2017, 255–56; see also Khan 1996). Smaller governments tend to hold a certain number of days' expenditures as cash rather than use sophisticated methods. Exhibit 7.2 provides a formula to calculate optimal transfer size, number of transfers, average cash balance, and initial cash balance.

Exhibit 7.2. Economic Ordering Quantity Formula

$P = b\,(T/c) + vT + i\,(c/2)$

P = Total cost of cash management
b = Fixed cost per transaction of transferring funds from marketable securities to cash or vice versa
T = Total amount of cash payments or expenditures over the period
c = Size of the transfer, which is the maximum amount of cash
v = Variable cost per dollar of funds transferred
i = Interest rate on marketable securities

The formula used to solve for the *optimal transfer size and initial cash balance* is:

$c = \sqrt{2bT/i}$

The *average cash balance* is:

$c = \sqrt{2bT/i}\ /\ 2$

The *total number of transfers* is computed by dividing the cash payments (T) by C.

Transfers = T/c

Let's look at an example. Jefferson City has total cash payments of $8 million (T) for a 6-month period. The payment over this period is steady. The cost per transaction is $75 (b), the interest rate is 4% for the period (i), and the cost per dollar of funds transferred is .06% (v). Therefore:

$c = \sqrt{2bT/i} = \sqrt{2(75)(8,000,000)/.04} = \$173,205.08$

So, the optimal initial cash balance and transfer size is $173,205.08, and the average cash balance is $86,602.54 ($173,205.08 / 2). If you divide $8,000,000 by $173,205.08 you will find that the total number of transfers equals 46 (46.19). The total cost of cash management for the 6-month period:

= $75 ($8,000,000 / $173,205.08) + .0006 ($8,000,000 / 1) + .04 ($173,205.08 / 2)

= $3,464.10 + $4,8000 + $3,464.10
= $11,728.20

^ Note that the interest rate (i) and the cost per dollar of funds transferred (v) is converted in the formula (4% = .04 and .06% = .0006).

MANAGING CASH INTERNALLY

Regardless of the size of a government agency, day-to-day functions require funds to be spent by cash or check. As a result, it is important for managers to manage cash internally by instituting controls on spending and records in order to limit mismanagement of funds, fraud, and abuse. Managing cash internally improves bookkeeping, improves internal controls, and auditing. Even though it is impossible to completely eliminate problems, these pointers will improve the process.[5]

- Use checks as much as possible to pay for services. Checks should always be associated with an invoice or voucher. Cash is harder to trace and invites theft and fraud. In addition, this not only prevents fraud, but overpayment, double payment, and no payment. Petty cash is the only exception to this rule.
- Never write checks payable to cash. This impedes the auditing process. Again, a voucher or invoice should be included with all transactions.
- The person writing the checks should not be used to reconcile the accounts. It is more difficult to cover up a potential crime when a second person is involved in the process.
- Checks should be used in numerical order and signed only by authorized staff. Checks should never be pre-signed for later use. These three things make it easier to track checks and allow minimum time for checks to be negotiated.
- Maintain firm control over blank and voided checks.
- Use separate bank accounts for each fund in order to maintain merging of funds. This also facilitates the auditing process.
- Sporadically audit petty cash. This should not be an elaborate and costly procedure.
- Make sure that the correct check number is placed on vouchers and invoices.
- Cash and checks should be deposited at least once a day. It should be done more often if a large sum of money is involved. This lessens the likelihood of theft, robbery, and allows the investment of idle cash.
- Use computer technology to facilitate fund transfers as well as any other financial transactions. This includes accepting credit card payments.
- Negotiate with banks for better rates as well as services.
- Take advantages of discounts for prompt payment.

RISK MANAGEMENT

Risk is a very active term that is used formally or informally in government at all levels. Like most things, there is a cost associated with risk, *cost of risk* (cost of loss and cost of uncertainty). As a result, it is necessary for city officials to be proactive in managing risk. This might entail using a small army of staff, who may have additional responsibilities, to perform risk related functions. More often than not, risk managers tend to be found in or work very closely with the finance office. What are the responsibilities of risk managers? Given the continued complexity and dynamic nature of government it is difficult to construct an exhaustive list of responsibilities under the label risk manager. Nonetheless, the following list highlights some of these functions (Lee, Johnson, and Joyce 2013; Lynch et al. 2017; Keown, Martin, Petty, and Scott 2005; Miller and Hildreth 1996; Young and Reiss 2004).

• Risk Financing (including the purchase of insurance)
• Management of insurable risks
• Maintain records of losses, loss costs, premiums, and related costs
• Occupational health and safety programs
• Workers' compensation management
• Compliance with regulatory and legal requirements
• Catastrophe planning
• Contract review
• Security
• Coordinate all activities involving risk
• Public policy research
• Some involvement in employee benefits
• Some involvement in the management of financial risk and accidental losses

From a budgetary perspective there are two important issues related to risk: purchase insurance to cover the risk or self-fund the risk. If you opt to purchase insurance, then you have fewer problems. The amount of the insurance is a known amount, but you also have to cover any deductibles that might be needed. If you self-fund the risk (self-insurance is an oxymoron—by definition, insurance means you transferred the risk to someone else), there may be all kinds of problems. Many governments self-fund health care for employees and liability. However, several questions are raised. How will the government finance it? Will they use an internal charge for each funding source? Will they use general fund money? Will they fund it on a pay-as-you-go basis? These are the kinds of issues that are involved in self-financing.

FRAMING RISK MANAGEMENT

According to Peter C. Young and Claire Lee Reiss (2004), risk management incorporates five fundamental elements: (1) Mission Identification, (2) Risk and Uncertainty Assessment, (3) Risk Control, (4) Risk Financing, and (5)

Program Administration. Exhibit 7.3 provides a framework that describes the major components of risk management (See appendix 7A for an example of a risk management assessment plan).

(1) *Mission Identification*: Mission identification provides the goals and objectives associated with risk management as they relate to the overall purpose of the bureaucratic and political structure. It is very important in this step that analysts ensure that the plan advances the goals of the organization and those of political leaders.

(2) *Risk and Uncertainty Assessment*: This is a three-pronged process that includes *risk and uncertainty identification, risk analysis*, and *risk measurement*. Identification of risk and uncertainty is "a systematic process of discovering an organization's risks and exposures to risk" (Young and Reiss 2004, 481). Given the dynamic nature of government, identifying risk is an ongoing process. There are two basic types of risks: *asset exposure* and *liability exposure*.

Physical structures, funds (stocks, bonds, money, etc.), personnel, or intangible assets (community reputation, bond rating, credit score, etc.) fall into the asset exposure category. Liability exposure focuses on legal liability, moral, and ethical responsibilities. There are numerous forms of liability exposure. This includes things such as premise liability (injuries on government property), contractor liability (work performed by entities employed by the government), employee liability, product or service liability (firefighting services), environmental liability (leaks in land-fills or water treatment facilities), employment practices liability (sexual harassment and discrimination), and police and law enforcement liability (wrongful arrest, excessive force).

There are many other types of exposures that may relate to specific types of government agencies and departments. Although legal exposure may be easier to identify than moral liability, they are equally important. For example, placing a water treatment facility in a poor neighborhood because the residents are the least likely to resist the move rather than choosing the best location based on other well-grounded factors could lead to exposure (Young and Reiss 2004).

Risk analysis helps analysts to determine how dangerous conditions lead to actual losses. Large governments may have a number of sophisticated techniques and devices at their disposal to determine risk, but smaller governments with fewer resources are more often than not left to use other less costly means. This includes things such as: examining the causes of previous loss, soliciting feedback from similar cities about their losses, seeking advice from risk control staff about common vulnerabilities, conducting informational sessions with staff at every level, consulting the government's

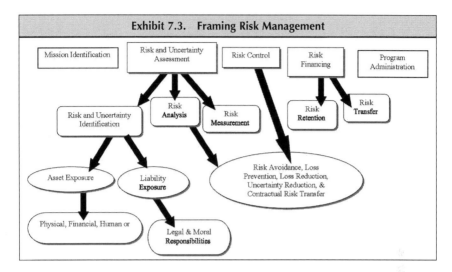

Exhibit 7.3. Framing Risk Management

risk manager or insurance broker, identifying and examine incidents that could have been disastrous (Young and Reiss 2004).

Risk measurement focuses on the impact of risk on the cities resources and on its capacity to maintain services. Since some ventures are more risky than others, it is wise to focus on or prioritize activities that may have the greatest impact on the organization as a whole. Measurement can vary based on the size of the government. Larger governments, with greater resources, may "conduct a quantitative analysis of their loss history to determine the frequency, severity, and financial or operational impact of different types of losses. Smaller local governments may have to rely on intuitive estimates of the effects of what they believe to be their greatest exposures. In such cases, measurement may be limited to categorizing risks according to frequency (how often losses occur) and severity (the financial and other impact of losses when they do occur)" (Young and Reiss 2004, 484; see also Miller and Hildreth 1996).

(3) *Risk Control*: Risk Control emphasizes "avoiding, preventing, reducing, transferring, or neutralizing risks and uncertainties" (Young and Reiss 2004, 484). This can include items such as wearing safety goggles to complex evacuation plans. Risk avoidance, loss prevention, loss reduction, uncertainty reduction, and contractual risk transfer are the major categories in risk control.

Risk avoidance is simply avoiding some activity that can cause a risk of loss. This is difficult to carry out since the government must provide services even during difficult circumstances. For example, a government may close one lane of a highway because of bridge construction in order to avoid possible liability issues (Miller and Hildreth 1996).

Loss prevention controls are intended to prevent losses from occurring such as work place safety techniques and procedures that limit the opportunities to commit fraudulent acts and theft. *Loss reduction* controls limit the amount and magnitude of losses that do occur from accidents. This would include things such as the wearing of protective gear inside hazardous waste areas or having an adequate number of fire extinguishers in the right places.

Uncertainty reduction procedures are designed to direct attention to the areas where risks are most likely to occur. Examining an agencies loss history to see where resources should be concentrated can expedite this process. Another option is to contract the risk producing activity to an outside entity. This is called *contractual risk transfer*. The third party entity would assume any responsible for losses resulting from loss. "Responsibility is generally assumed through a combination of contractual indemnification, hold-harmless agreements, and insurance requirements" (Young and Reiss 2004, 484). For example, a city may contract with an outside vendor to collect waste.

Whether to choose one method or another depends solely upon the government. There are a number of possible risk methods. In some cases, the government must employ risk control techniques while others are optional. When risk control methods are optional, cities should fully research their functions and use limited resources in the most productive manner.

(4) *Risk Financing*: Risk financing has two components: securing reimbursement for losses that occur and, providing resources to programs that decrease uncertainty and risk or improve positive outcomes. Examples include: "qualifying with the state as a self-insured entity, buying insurance, establishing a letter of credit, and participating in a public risk pool" (Young and Reiss 2004, 484). Another example is establishing a safety program for an agency.

There are two categories of risk financing, risk retention and risk transfer. *Risk retention* occurs when a government assumes all or part of the risk or loss. *Risk transfer* occurs when another organization, like an insurance company, assumes the risk and pays for the loss when it occurs for a premium. Governments can use an amalgamation of risk financing techniques (Miller and Hildreth 1996; Young and Reiss 2004).

(5) *Program Administration*: Program administration is concerned with a variety of technical and general management actions, such as purchasing insurance, creating hedging arrangements, administering claims, and implementing loss control programs and safety instruction. In order to be the most effective, staff should have technical as well as management capabilities (Miller and Hildreth 1996; Young and Reiss 2004).

PROCUREMENT

Similar to the private sector, governments must spend revenues to purchase (*procurement*) equipment in order to maintain the infrastructure as well as provide services in the most efficient and effective manner (Lee et al. 2013). Khi V. Thai (2004) defines procurement as "buying, purchasing, renting, leasing, or otherwise acquiring any supplies, services or construction, and it also encompasses the development of requirement and specifications, the selection of vendors, the solicitation of sources, the preparation and award of contracts, and all phases of contract administration" (421).

Why is it important to discuss procurement? First, the government must provide services in an efficient and effective manner. Second, the government must secure equipment at the most reasonable price available. Third, the government must ensure that the procurement process is free of fraud and abuse. Lastly, given the size of government, procurement also helps the government to achieve some of its broader economic goals.

The remainder of this section discusses the procurement of equipment at the most reasonable price using a life-cycle cost technique. There are two things that are important in the procurement process when a life-cycle cost application is used: cost and quality. Cost entails the bid price of the item, the life-time maintenance cost of the asset, the energy cost, and the final disposal cost or repurchase price of the item (Ammons 2002). Quality refers to the degree to which the government needs are met with the purchase. Responsible bidders should be required to submit documents indicating the expected energy consumption, anticipated life span of the equipment, and expected use over a one-year period (Gianakis and McCue 1999: Nollenberger et al. 2003). All of this information is vital in order for this process to be effective.

The basic formula for a life-cycle cost model is:

Life-Cycle Cost = Acquisition Cost + Lifetime Maintenance Cost +
Lifetime Energy Cost – Trade in Allowance – Expected Resale Value

The example in exhibit 7.4 shows the results of applying the life-cycle cost model to the purchase of two trucks with similar horsepower and amenities. If you focus your decision to purchase on the price of the trucks in this example, you would buy the truck from the second bidder because it is six thousand dollars cheaper than the other truck. However, when you look at the other items, particularly energy cost and diesel mileage along with maintenance cost, you note that the disparities between the two trucks changes dramatically.[6]

Exhibit 7.4. Life-Cycle Costing		
Life-Cycle Cost	Truck Bid 1	Truck Bid 2
Bid Cost	$45,000	$39,000
Expected Use	100,000 miles	100,000 miles
Life Expectancy	6 years	6 years
Efficiency Rating	85%	75%
Energy Cost	$17,936.03	$26,900*
($2.69 per gallon)	(15 mpg)	(10 mpg)
Maintenance Cost	$8,814 / 6yrs	$21,000 / 6yrs^
Life-Cycle Cost	$71,750.03	$86,900

Life-Cycle Cost Difference $15,149.97 ($86,900 − $71,750.03 = $15,149.97)
*(100,000 miles / 15 mpg) x $2.69 = $17,933.33; and 100,000 miles / 10 mpg x $2.69 = $26,900

^ $1,469.00 per year for Bid 1 and $3,500.00 per year for Bid 2.

Source: Roderick C. Lee (1996), "Life-Cycle Costing," in *Budgeting: Formulation and Execution*, ed. Jack Rabin, W. Bartley Hildreth, and Gerald J. Miller (Athens, GA: Carl Vinson Institute of Government, University of Georgia), 420–23.

In fact, the cost difference of the two trucks over a six-year period is almost $15,150. So, which truck should the government purchase? It is pretty clear that the truck from the first bidder should be accepted. However, the government should ensure that the information that is used in the model is accurate and based on tried and tested measures from responsible bidders. Further, the government should be certain that it will likely keep the truck for a six-year period. If any of these values change, the difference between the two bids will change as well (Nollenberger et al. 2003). Also, note that if there are multiple bids, you must subtract the two lowest bids from each other.[7] There are a number of other items that can be used in a life-cycle cost model such as trade in value of an existing piece of equipment, acquisition cost, failure cost, labor cost, and expected resale value. For obvious reasons, more information allows decision makers to make more informed decisions.

CUTBACK MANAGEMENT

Without question, cities are more likely to see fewer resources than surpluses in their budgets. As a result, it is necessary to engage in what is called *cutback management*. In simple terms, this is implementing cost cutting reductions in resources while attempting to maintain services at their current level. Under the worst conditions, cutback management can lead to the demise of programs as well as a reduction in services. Quite naturally, this process can and does have an adverse impact on all sectors of the economy.

Causes of Cutbacks

According to Charles H. Levine (1996) cutbacks result primarily from five things: problem depletion, erosion of the economic base, inflation, taxpayer revolt, and limits to growth. *Problem depletion* occurs when a public sector problem is solved, eliminated, controlled or the pressure to solve the problem subsides. This can be long or short-term problems/crises such as program consolidation, program termination or a school closing (Levine 2004). For example, the city of Memphis, Tennessee closed several schools due to low enrollment rates, and as a result they consolidated the students into one school. On the one hand, this caused many political headaches despite the fact that it saved the city money. On the other hand, it created more busing expenditures (Kiel 2011).

A second cause of cutbacks is *erosions in the tax base*. There is an array of items that can cause the tax base to erode in a city. This includes things such as: the relocation of citizens to suburbs, an aging population, the movement of industry to other locations, aging or deterioration of the housing stocks resulting in lower valuations, and the growth of dependent populations (Raymond and Menifield 2011). Levine (1996) offers further explanation of this phenomenon in his discussion of *environmental atrophy*. He points out that those who cannot afford to move to the suburbs are left to make up for the loss in the tax base and as a result are worse off. The third cause is *inflation*. Inflation is an increase in the amount of money and credit relative to available goods resulting in a substantial and continuing rise in the price level. The funds needed to operate a government efficiently and effectively has continued to rise dramatically over time. Some suggests that it has doubled in the last ten years (2005–2015). Unless the government raises taxes or other revenue generating tools, they are forced to cut back services (Gorina, Maher, and Joffe 2017).

Taxpayer revolt is the fourth reason that Levine (1996) argues causes cutbacks. "These explanations usually include reference to the difficulty of tracing the well-being of individual taxpayers to specific government services, the desire of voters to alleviate the impact of inflation on their personal disposable incomes, the backlash of taxpayers against the salary increases of unionized public workers and the services offered to the poor and minorities, and the cumbersomeness of financing local services through the mechanism of the property tax" (131). The last cause of cutbacks is limits to growth. The Midwest saw many of their cities become "rustbelts" because of the out migration of businesses to the west and south. Many cities in this region are landlocked and lack the ability to attract new residents or businesses. There is also a severe imbalance between imports and exports in the United States. This is particularly true when we look at depletable resources and energy sources such as fossil fuels. There is currently no end in sight for this problem. Generally speaking, history suggests that economic growth will slow down in the foreseeable future.

Cutbacks in government are particularly difficult because it will inevitably impact all aspects of service. Levine (1996) argues that change in services is most palatable when those affected have something to gain. Unfortunately, the impact of cutbacks consistently means that the outcome will have a negative impact on the consumer and as a result cooperation will be at a minimum. There are also a plethora of traditions, procedures and agreements in place that will constrain the ability of the government to make the cuts. This includes things such as affirmative action and collective bargaining agreements, veteran's preferences and civil service procedures. Cutbacks also affect the morale of public servants. They are not inclined to work harder during these periods to make up for a decrease in staff or revenue. Last, cutbacks affect the overall behavior of administrators and staff because everyone is forced to deal with having fewer resources (Levine 1996).

Cutback Strategies

There are five general strategies that can be used to cutback resources. The first strategy is to resist or *smooth* the cuts. Generally speaking, budget managers engage in what is called *budget maximizing*. That is, they attempt to get as much revenue as possible in their budget. Hence, budget maximizing. As a result, they will almost instinctively resist the cuts. In some cases, managers will cut the most pertinent services first to show policy makers that they need their entire budget allotment. When this and other strategies do not work, managers will reluctantly try to limit the impact of the cuts without reducing services, selling assets, instituting layoffs and defaulting on contractual obligations.

The second option is to make a one-time drastic cut with the hope of recuperating later or institute small cuts over several fiscal years in order to minimize the impact. The problem with making a large cut is that the funds may never return to their current levels. The problem with small cuts is that the agency may function at the same level suggesting that the cuts were warranted. As a result, the funds are less likely to return at the same level in the near future. Public outcry over either one of these options is also likely to impact decisions. In fact, some agency heads may use this tactic in order to advertise their resistance. Like most tactics, it can come with political repercussions because politicians are not ignorant of the behavior.

One commonly used technique is to make across the board cuts. While this may help to improve morale among the employees, it is not a good management strategy because all agencies are not equivalent and do not contribute equally to the goals and objectives of government. In some cases, agencies and programs may be cut after they are prioritized based on the goals of the government. However, these debates essentially facilitate things such as the *budget maximizing strategy* and political turf battles (Arapis and Bowling 2019).

The fourth strategy looks at the *efficiency* versus *equity* question. Efficiency is "meant to mean the sorting, sifting, and assignment of cuts to those people and units in the organization so that for a given budget decrement, cuts are allocated to minimize the long-term loss in total benefits to the organization as a whole, irrespective of their distribution" (Levine 2004, 514). Equity "is meant to mean the distribution of cuts across the organization with an equal probability of hurting all units and employees irrespective of impacts on the long-term capacity of the organization" (Levine 2004, 514). This quandary results from the cost of providing services to the various groups and the makeup of personnel. The poor, elderly and minorities are the most dependent upon the government and tend to be the most costly to serve. Hence, blind cost cutting based on restricted productivity measures can be very damaging to them. This quandary is further exasperated due to the recent rise in minority employment and the prevalence of laying-off the last one hired first. Nonetheless, history suggests that the politically weak are disproportionately adversely impacted by budget cuts (Levine 1996; 2004).

The fifth and final cutback mechanism is *attrition*. That is, employees leave the public work force and create a void. Administrators can and often do leave the position open for a period of time in order to save resources. In some cases, it may be possible to shift those responsibilities to other employees or outsource the tasks at a cheaper rate. However, the implications of shifting the responsibilities to other employees can be financially detrimental to the agency in the long run. If an organization can run smoothly without the position it would clearly suggest that the position was not needed and thus should be removed from the organization chart. This is probably the most commonly used method. It is very hard for a government to lay off employees. There are both civil service laws as well as collective bargaining agreements that have to be followed. By the time you try to go through this process, one or more years may pass. Thus, it is easier to just use attrition to cutback resources.

Marvin J. Druker and Betty D. Robinson (1993) point out several additional strategies that have been employed at the state and local levels. These include: freezing vacancies, implementing an early retirement plan, offering voluntary leave, implementing mandatory furloughs and layoffs, reducing hours, job sharing, increasing the workweek, deferring pay increases, reducing the cost of benefits, shutting down operations, implementing user fees, cutting salaries, lagging payrolls, and reorganizing the work force (see also Lauth 1997). Herbert A. Marlowe Jr. and Ronald C. Nyhan (1997) made these additional suggestions based on work examining the Palm Beach County Government: reduce travel and office equipment, privatize functions, reassign costs, defer capital spending, implement franchise fees, defer library projects, reduce the level of service, and defer replacing equipment.

CREATING A PRO-BUSINESSES ENVIRONMENT IN YOUR CITY

In order to create a pro-business environment in a city, policy makers often use tax incentives, as a part of their economic development policies. However, one has to think beyond tax incentives in today's markets. Large, wealthy corporations such as Amazon and Apple often want more. More specifically, they are also interested in things like equity, quality of life, and how cities plan to create a sustainable future for their residents. This section of the chapter discusses the financial packages that cities often create for businesses, but also quality of life information that would be useful in creating an inviting environment for businesses.

FINANCIAL INCENTIVES

One of the most commonly used mechanisms to lure cities into an area are tax breaks and tax incentives. Tax breaks and subsidies come in many forms, short and long term in nature. The aim of a tax incentive is to attract more businesses to an area by making it less expensive for a business to operate in the area. However, it is important to remember that tax incentives come at a cost and residents normally bear that burden. Hence, these incentives should have clear ties to the economic development plan of the city. In addition, the goals of the incentives should be measurable with impact assessments (Buss 2001; Propheter 2017; Rubin 2020).

There are three critical questions to ask when creating and offering a tax incentive program. First, will the tax incentive change the businesses behavior? That is, does it encourage job creation or increase investments by the business? Second, will the tax incentive create a net economic benefit and is it equitable? The targeted business often affects other business in the area, so the indirect benefit must be considered as well. Conversely, one has to also consider the negative impact of tax incentives directed towards a particularly entity. Last, does the tax incentive provide an effective approach to achieving its objectives compared to other policies?

Below are some examples of typical financial incentives:

(1) *Tax Exemptions*: These exemptions fully excuse corporations from paying certain liabilities.
(2) *Tax Refunds and Rebates*: Refunds and rebates allow a firm to recoup taxes already paid to a state or municipality.
(3) *Tax Credits*: Tax credits allow a city more flexibility to offset a portion of its tax obligation, and they can often be carried forward to subsequent tax years or be sold in the secondary market.
(4) *Tax Reductions or Abatements*: These reductions partially offset the amount of taxes that a firm is obligated to pay (for example, property tax abatement).

Some very specific examples include: corporate tax exemptions, personal income tax exemptions, excise tax exemptions, land and capital improvement tax exemptions, equipment and machinery tax exemptions, goods in transport tax exemptions, manufacturer's inventories tax exemptions, raw materials for manufacturing tax exemptions, job creation tax incentive exemptions, industrial investment tax incentives, tax stabilizing agreements, accelerated depreciation, and research and development tax exemptions (Buss 2001).

When considering a financial incentive, a city should carefully consider their end goal. For example, a city may want to entice business to serve as feeders for a large corporation, create new jobs, create private investment or research and development. Therefore, the tax incentive package could include the following qualifications. The business must:

(1) Belong to a certain industry that is desired in an area
(2) Provide a minimum level of funding on a particular project
(3) Create a minimum number of jobs
(4) Reach of minimum payroll threshold

In addition to tax incentives, cities often expend resources for infrastructure improvements in order to lure new businesses. This includes things like new roads, bridges, airport expansions, and additional bus and light rail lines.

When determining whether a tax goal was reached, there are essentially two things to consider: cost and benefits (see chapter 6). That is, were the cost of the incentives less than the benefits received?

QUALITY OF LIFE INCENTIVES

When all other things are equal, quality of life will often be the determining factor for a business to locate to your city. Many corporations want and need information about the quality of life in a city. For example, they may want detailed information about: primary, secondary, and higher education institutions in the region; economic development plans for the area; infrastructure upgrades and plans; access to waterways and highways; airport, train and busing access; housing information; parks and churches; existing office space; employment and diversity data; hotels; and crime data.

Let's flesh out education in order to thoroughly understand the level of detail that may be needed. Education can be split into several parts. For example, cities commonly have public and private primary and secondary schools as well as colleges and universities. A prospective business may want to know the answers to the following questions regarding primary and secondary education.

Primary and Secondary Schools

(1) How many primary and secondary schools are in the city?
(2) What is the student to teacher ratio?
(3) Are foreign language courses available beginning in the primary grades?
(4) What is level of diversity in the schools (teachers and students)?
(5) Are schools located in residential neighborhoods, or close to parks, and churches?
(6) Are any of the schools recognized as outstanding elementary, middle or high schools?
(7) What percentage of high school graduate on time and pursue higher education?
(8) Do the high schools offer AP or any college credit courses?
(9) What is the average SAT score for your high schools?
(10) Are there alternative schools that focus on the arts or science fields?

As you can see, there is an unlimited amount of data that can be provided to the prospective business. Hence, it is critically important that you are prepared to provide as much up front data as possible and foresee any questions that may come up along the way and plan accordingly. You should be prepared to address questions such as these as well as have responses for everything that was mentioned in the preceding paragraph. Again, you have to think about what is important to the company and its employees.

Let's consider an example of a company that manufactures vehicles. What might they want to know about quality of life? They might be very interested in knowing whether engineering courses are offered in the high schools or if the local university offers degrees, certificates or courses that would produce employees for the corporation. Also, they may be interested in knowing if the city has an incubator program to promote engineering creativity. Again, there is no limit to the type and quantity of information that can be collected for quality of life. In short, your goal is to paint a picture that casts your city in the best light. Hence, you should highlight your assets and create a plan that addresses your deficiencies. There is nothing wrong with pointing out negative information as long as you have a plan to ameliorate the issue.

DEBT MANAGEMENT AND INVESTMENT

Why do governments incur debt? States and local governments can incur *debt* when "(1) covering deficits (annual expenditures greater than annual revenues),[8] (2) financing capital-project construction, and (3) covering short periods within a fiscal year in which bills exceed cash on hand" (Mikesell 2018, 543). As shown in exhibit 7.5, the amount of local debt over time has been relatively stable since the 1930s. However, there have been slight increases since the 1970s.

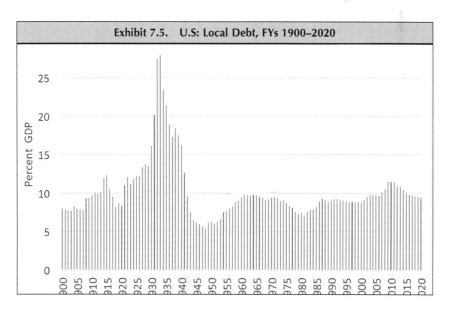

Although not included here, the amount of full faith and credit bonds more than doubled and long-term debt for education nearly tripled during the late 1990s and early 2000s.[9] Hence, it is apparent that governments are moving towards greater debt rather than less debt. As a result, it is important that governments have a debt management policy to facilitate debt.

Debt Management Policy

The Government Finance Officers Association (GFOA) lists a debt management policy as a "recommended practice." Specifically, they recommend that state and municipal governments adopt a comprehensive written debt management policy. Further, they recommend that these policies be reviewed and revised annually to reflect changes in debt policy (http://www.gfoa.org).

A debt management policy provides benefits to citizens and bureaucrats. First, it assures bondholders that debt burdens and operational debt expenditures will be maintained at controllable levels with a plan to meet capital infrastructure needs. Second, it provides staff with a framework to work from and assures the legislative body that any proposals brought forward by staff meets the policy mandates set out by the legislative body. Third, it assures continuity in financial operations whether there is a change in the legislative body or management personnel.

Last, Moody's Investor Services points out that a strong debt management policy is a practice that a city can use to strengthen its credit position. Since debt has a potential long-term impact on future budgets it is important that it is issued with great care. If something goes awry in the process, the ramification for tax-paying citizens can be a source of great consternation. The basic rule of debt policy is to never issue debt for a project that has a life span shorter than the debt payback period (see chapter 6). Hence, knowing when to issue debt is an important question and this is particularly true for long term debt.

However, long-term debt could very well be appropriate for long-life capital structures such as public buildings. Economic development by definition often requires financing large scale expenditures prior to an expansion in revenue. If future revenue will cover the cost of the project, an argument can be made to fund the project using long-term debt.

However, some governments with large fund balances and a growing general fund opt to use the pay-as-you-go method to funding capital projects out of the operating budget. As discussed earlier, there are several advantages to using this method. However, there are inefficiency and inequity issues that could arise. John L. Mikesell (2018) points out four factors. First, given population shifts, individuals paying for the project may not be present to receive benefits when the project is completed. Second, the high cost of the project in a single year may discourage construction even if it is reasonable. Third, it might cause instability in the tax rate. It might be artificially high during the construction phase and artificially low when the project comes to fruition. Last, it "produces annual debt service charges that are fixed by contract (see also Mikesell 2018, 674). Therefore, when the areas tax base grows, the tax rate required for debt service for a project will decline over time" (555).

Appendix 7D and 7E contains the Debt Management and Fiscal Policy (General Policy) and the Debt Management Policy for the city of Lawrence, Kansas. As shown, the policy contains some additional items not discussed in the earlier paragraphs. This includes: the structure of debt financing (possible source of funding); debt administration and financing; refunding of debt; conduit financing; arbitrage liability management; and credit ratings. It is important that governments consider all of these items when creating a debt management policy.

ADDITIONAL BUDGET OPTIONS

Cutback and debt management has also caused governments to look more closely at utilizing zero-based budgeting and performance budgeting techniques. *Zero-based budgeting* (ZBB) is a future oriented budgeting strategy that requires analysis of current and future expenditures, "allows for tradeoffs between programs and units below their present funding levels, allows a ranking of decision packages by political bargaining and negotiation so that attention is concentrated on those packages or activities most likely to be affects by cuts. As a result, ZBB allows both analysis and politics to enter into cutback decision making and therefore can incorporate an expression of the *intensity of need* for resources by participating managers and clients while also accommodating estimates how cuts will affect the activity levels of their units" (Levine 2004, 515–16).

With that said, ZBB is not without faults, analysis and political disagreements can come at a high price. While elements of ZBB are currently utilized, it is not widely used today.

Performance based budgeting (PBB) concentrates on agency-activity objectives and outcomes rather than the purchase of resources. In simple terms, the budget is tied to accomplishing objectives (see chapter 1). As a result, agencies that fail to reach their stated outcomes can be targeted for cuts. Again, if the budget maximizing strategy is at work, this would suggest that agency heads are requesting the maximum amount of funds that they can get and only use performance measures that they know they can accomplish (Mikesell 2018).

CONCLUSION

While there are many other tools that can be used to assist city administrators and analysts in improving the financial position of the city, the chapter provides a sample of several administrative and management techniques that can be useful when applied at the right moment. Other important topics not covered would include bond management. It is important that administrators realize that economies do not tend to turn around overnight. This is particularly true in situations where management practices are in disarray. However, the chapter shows that minor changes can have a major impact on budget decisions and the morale of staff and supervisors.

IMPORTANT TERMS AND PHRASES

Asset Exposure
Attrition
Average Cash Balance
Average Final Compensation
Budget Maximizing Strategy
Budget Reserve
Budget Shortfall
Budget Surplus
Cash Budget
Cash Flow Problem
Cash Management
Contractual Risk Transfer
Cost of Risk
Cutback Management
Debt Capacity
Debt Instrument
Debt Management
Deferment of Payments
Disability
Dividends
Economic Ordering Quantity
   Formula (EOQ)
Efficiency
Environmental Atrophy
Erosion in the Tax Base
Equity
Equity Securities
Idle Cash Problem
Inflation
Initial Cash Balance
Interest Rates
Internal Transfers
Investing
Liability Exposure

Life-Cycle Cost
Long Term Borrowing
Loss Prevention
Loss Reduction
Net Cash Flow
Operating Deficit
One Time Revenues
Optimal Cash Balance
Optimal Transfer Size
Performance Based Budgeting
Portability
Procurement
Problem Depletion
Risk Analysis
Risk Avoidance
Risk Control
Risk Financing
Risk Management
Risk Measurement
Risk Retention
Risk Transfer
Rolling Over
Saleable Assets
Smoothing
Short-term Borrowing
Stocks
Tax Anticipation Notes (TAN)
Tax Payer Revolt
Transfer
Transfer Size
Uncertainty Reduction
Variable Cost
Vesting
Zero-Based Budgeting

CHAPTER 7 HOMEWORK EXERCISES

Directions: Please read all of the questions as well as the accompanying materials prior to answering the questions. Answer question 1,4–6 in a word processing program and questions 2 and 3 in Microsoft Excel. Please turn in your Excel worksheets and the word file (inclusive of the pasted Excel worksheets to your instructor).

(1) Jefferson City has a severe budget crisis and the Mayor has asked you to help the budget director in preparing a report outlining a 5 percent cut to the city's budget. Jefferson City has 200,000 permanent residents and an additional 25,000 people come to the city for work each day. They have a budget of $200 million dollars and all of the expected departments (administration, communications, budget, public safety, economic and housing development, engineering, public works, recreation, water & sewer utilities, city clerk, municipal court, etc.). The city also has a museum, a large public theater and provides subsidies for a minor league baseball team as well as a golf course. The city currently has $30 million dollars in its rainy day fund, but the Mayor has advised you not to consider it as an option. You cannot raise funds, only trim the budget.

   (a) Based on what you have learned and what you know about city functions, which part of the budget would you examine first? Why?
   (b) Which items would you cut? Why? Provide your alternatives to the mayor.

(2) The budget manager for Jefferson City, has requested that you assist her with the management of the city's funds. Specifically, she wants you to calculate the two scenarios listed below based on the following information. See appendix 7A.

   (a) The city has total cash payments of $20 million (T) for a 6-month period. Assume that the payment over this period is steady. The cost per transaction is $60 (b), the interest rate is 3 percent for the period (i), and the cost per dollar of funds transferred is .05% (v).

   Calculate the optimal initial cash balance and transfer size
   Average cash balance
   The number of transfers
   The total cost of cash management

   (b) The city has total cash payments of $13 million (T) for a 6-month period. Assume that the payment over this period is steady. The cost per transaction is $45 (b), the interest rate is 5 percent for the period (i), and the cost per dollar of funds transferred is .04 percent (v).

Calculate the optimal initial cash balance and transfer size
Average cash balance
The number of transfers
The total cost of cash management

(3) Prepare a life-cycle cost analysis for the procurement of a front end loader for Jefferson City based on data from three companies. Also, the city is trading in the old front-end loader. Note that the Trade in and Re-sale Value should be subtracted from the amount of the life-cycle cost. All calculations should be rounded to the nearest dollar amount. Solve for the energy cost prior to calculating the life-cycle cost. When you finish your calculations, indicate which bid should be accepted. Briefly explain your response. See appendix 7B for a copy of the spreadsheet.

(4) Using the sample risk assessment form that is located in appendix 7C, conduct a risk assessment of a public service project that is occurring, will occur, or has recently taken place in your city or at your university. You are completing this question from the perspective of a city employee. You are free to modify this assessment to fit your circumstances. In addition, you should include the risk assessment policy that the city or university that you choose operates under when you turn in your assignment if it is available. You should come to class prepared to discuss your risk assessment plan. If needed, consult with public officials when completing this assignment. Lastly, explain the overall results of your assessment. Is the project worth the risks?

Suggestions: Construction projects, road construction, large renovation projects, clear cutting land, household waste or hazard waste disposal issues, providing security at a public facility, investment of public funds, or any changes in the infrastructure are suitable topics for this question. Other items can be more thematic or policy in nature. For example, what are the risks involved in raising property taxes when 95% of the property owners are in the low middle-income bracket and operate small businesses? Will this result in an increase in the number of delinquent property tax payments and thus reduce the amount of revenue to the city as well as potential loss of property and bankruptcy? Other broad categories could include any type of service that the city provides.

(5) Using one set of the factors (environmental or financial) used to determine financial solvency as discussed in the chapter, analyze the financial

condition of a municipality or county in your local area (identify the factors that you are using as well as the city). Your analysis should focus on the condition of the city, not an agency within the city. Your trend analysis must use at least 5 years of data. Hence, you will need budget data for at least five years for the city or county that you have chosen and be familiar with financial or environmental trends in the area. It is not possible to examine each characteristic, so limit your table/graph, etc. construction to four key financial or economic factors. First, create a table with each factor indicating the direction of the trend. Second, create four graphs, tables, etc. examining the factors that require more analysis. Third, write a brief evaluation of the factors and develop a policy statement based on your findings. If you are not familiar with table or graph construction, review chapter 8 in this text prior to completing this question. Use the example in the chapter as a template.

(6) In no more than two pages, create a "Quality of Life Plan" to lure the business cited below to your city. The plan should focus on *one* of the elements cited in the chapter (excluding education). Your plan should include at least five questions and responses that are related to the element. The goal of this exercise is to get you into the mindset of preparing this type of report, so think carefully about the non-tax incentives needed to lure a corporation to your city.

Lachezar's Clothing Manufacturer
Employees: 1,000
Income Level of Employees: 15 percent Low income; 25 percent Low Middle Income; 25 percent Middle Income; 25 percent Upper Middle Income; 10 percent Upper Income

(7) Optional In-Class Assignment: Risk Assessment Evaluation (30–35 minutes total)

Step 1: Split the class into groups of four or five and have each group member present (4 minutes) their risk assessment in their assigned group. For the purpose of this assignment, we are going to consider the group an appointed (by mayor) evaluation team. The objective of the team is to evaluate each risk assessment and report the results to the mayor. That is: do the benefits of the project out way the risks? For the purpose of this assignment, we will assume that the project has not been vetted and approved. In addition, the person who makes the presentation is not an advocate for the project. They are simply presenting the assessment to the team.

Step 2: After each assessment has been presented, the team should rank the projects in terms of least risky (1) to most risky (5).

Step 3: One person from the team should briefly present the results to the entire class.

Note: Each student should bring hard copies of their tables and graphs for distribution within their assigned group.

NOTES

1. The following items require further analysis if the arrow is in the downward slope indicating a decrease in the item: population density, personal income per capita, property value, home ownership, number of jobs in the community, % elastic revenues, tax revenues, % user charges, enterprise operating position, % fund balances, % liquidity, % pensions assets, maintenance effort and capital outlay. The remaining items would require further analysis if the arrow indicates an increase. The only exception is the population and revenues per capita factor.

2. Chapter 8 of this volume provides details on displaying data.

3. Review Robert L. Bland and Irene S. Rubin (1997), *Budgeting: A Guide for Local Governments* (Washington, DC: ICMA); John L. Mikesell (2018), *Fiscal Administration: Analysis and Applications for the Public Sector*, 10th ed. (Belmont, CA: Wadsworth Cengage Publishers); Karl Nollenberger, Sanford M. Groves, and Maureen Godsey Valente (2003), *Evaluating Financial Condition: A Handbook for Local Government*, 4th ed. (Washington, DC: ICMA); and Irene S. Rubin (2006), *The Politics of Public Budgeting: Getting and Spending, Borrowing and Balancing*, 5th ed. (Washington, DC: C Q Press), for a discussion of pensions and the pay-as-you-go method.

4. See Aman Khan (1997), "Learning from Experience: Cash Management Practices of a Local Government," in *Case Studies in Public Budgeting and Financial Management*, ed. Aman Khan and W. Bartley Hildreth, 553–68 (Dubuque, IA: Kendall Hunt Publishing); Robert D. Lee, Jr., Ronald W. Johnson, and Philip G. Joyce (2013), *Public Budgeting Systems*, 9th ed., (Burlington, MA: Jones & Bartlett Learning); Thomas D. Lynch, Jinping Sun, and Robert W. Smith (2017), *Public Budgeting in America*. 6th ed. (Irvine, CA: Melvin & Leigh); and Arthur J. Keown, John D. Martin, J. William Petty, and David F. Scott Jr. (2005), *Financial Management: Principles and Applications*, 10th ed. (Upper Saddle River, NJ: Pearson Prentice Hall), for a review of cash management.

5. See Lee et al. (2003), *Public Budgeting Systems*; M. Corrine Larson (2004), "Cash and Investment Management," in *Management Policies in Local Government Finance*, 4th ed., ed. J. Richard Aronson and Eli Schwartz (Washington, DC: ICMA), 451–77; and Lynch et al. (2017), *Public Budgeting in America*, for additional information on internal cash management.

6. Note that the life expected use of the truck in bid 1 is not exactly 100,000 miles in the final analysis. The data was forced to reflect whole numbers rather than cents. This is an acceptable practice given the amount of miles expected over the life of the vehicles.

7. Laws have to be in place in order for this to occur.

8. Laws have to be in place in order for this to occur.

9. See chapter 4 of this volume for a discussion of financing debt.

Appendix 7A
Risk Management Assessment Plan

Economic Ordering Quality Formula	
(1) Calculate the Optimal Initial Cash Balance and Transfer Size	
Average Cash Balance	
Total Number of Transfers	
Calculate the Total Cost of Cash Management	
(2) Calculate the Optimal Initial Cash Balance and Transfer Size	
Average Cash Balance	
Total Number of Transfers	
Calculate the Total Cost of Cash Management	

Appendix 7B

Life-Cycle Cost

Jefferson City Life-Cycle Cost Problem			
Element	*Anderson's Heavy Equipment*	*Wechsler's International Company*	*McClain's Front End*
Bid Price	$77,180	$78,500	$82,000
Trade-in Value	$3,300	$2,900	$3,500
Expected Use	85,000 miles	85,000 miles	85,000 miles
Life Expectancy	5 years	5 years	5 years
Efficiency Rating	82%	80%	89%
Energy Cost	? (12 mpg)	? (11 mpg)	? (14 mpg)
Resale Value	$6,000	$5,200	$6,500
Maintenance Cost	$24,000	$22,000	$20,000
Life-Cycle Cost	?	?	?
Life-Cycle Cost Difference:	$	Currently, diesel costs $3.94 per gallon.	

Source: Created by the Author.

Appendix 7C
Risk Assessment and Questionnaire

Risk Assessment Questionnaire						
Project Title						
Project Location						
Project Supervisor						
Brief Description of the Work or Policy:						
Each of the questions used in this assessment are scored using a risk factor rubric from 0–5. A zero indicates no risk and a five indicates high risk. Your description of risk should detail how the organization is managing the risk. Limit your description of the risk to no more than half of a page. Use as much space as you need to describe the risk. Read the notes at the bottom of this assessment prior to addressing the question.						
(1) Human Resource Risk						
(a) Description of Risk:						
(b) Overall Risk Factor	0	1	2	3	4	5
(2) Environmental Risk						
(a) Description of Risk						
(b) Overall Risk Factor	0	1	2	3	4	5
(3) Information and Technology Risk						
(a) Description of Risk						
(b) Overall Risk Factor	0	1	2	3	4	5
(4) Regulatory Risk						
(a) Description of Risk						
(b) Overall Risk Factor	0	1	2	3	4	5
(5) Internal Control Environmental Risk						
(a) Description of Risk						
(b) Overall Risk Factor	0	1	2	3	4	5
(6) Asset/Revenue Management Risk:						
(a) Description of Risk						
(b) Overall Risk Factor	0	1	2	3	4	5
(7) Consumer Impact:						
(a) Description of Risk						
(b) Overall Risk Factor	0	1	2	3	4	5
(8) Equipment Risk:						
(a) Description of Risk						
(b) Overall Risk Factor	0	1	2	3	4	5

Risk Assessment Questionnaire						
(9) General Field Work Hazards						
(a) Description of Risk						
(b) Overall Risk Factor	0	1	2	3	4	5
RISK SUMMARY						
(a) Average Risk Score	0	1	2	3	4	5
(b) Total Risk Score						
Description of Substantive Points and Methods to Managing the Risk:						
Risk Questionnaire Notes						

The questions that are listed below offer you a snap shot of the sort of issues that will come up during your query. Feel free to add any additional information that you find.

(1) *Human Resource Risk*: Do employees work? Do employees work near water? Do employees work in an isolated area? Have all employees been properly trained (safety)? What is the possibility of employee fatigue, accidents, or allergic reactions occurring? Are there any non-city/university employees working? If yes, are they insured by their company?

(2) *Environmental Risk*: Will weather conditions impact completion of the project? Will terrain or field boundaries affect the project? Is animal or plant life affected by the project? Is hazardous waste a byproduct of the construction? Is there a chance that the environment may be polluted with hazardous waste? Will the ground water, lakes, or nearby streams be impacted by the project? Is there a procedure to facilitate hazardous waste cleanup or disposal?

(3) *Information and Technology Risk*: Generally speaking, this section examines computers, computer technology and information. Are computer systems needed to complete the project? Are new computer programs or hardware needed to complete the project? Is there a potential for loss of software, data, or computer hardware? Is there a contingency plan to ensure the integrity of data and computer systems?

(4) *Regulatory Risk*: What is the level of regulation (local, state or federal)? Are regulatory staff needed on site (Fire Marshall, FEMA, OSHA, etc.)? Have the rules, statutes, and law regulating the sector been examined? Are external contractors used? If yes, are they bonded? Are liability plans in place?

(5) *Internal Control Environment Risk*: Is there any potential for fraud? Have there been problems in the past? If so, how many and what were the outcomes? What procedures were added to ensure that the potential for fraud was reduced/eliminated?

(6) *Asset/Revenue Management Risk*: If a service is rendered, what sort of accounting system will be used when the project is completed? How are funds dispersed and collected? Does the potential for cost overruns exist?

(7) *Consumer Impact*: Who is the client base? How will clients or the public be affected by the project? That is, how will they be affected by the construction of the project as well as the services provided by the project?

(8) *Equipment Risk*: What sort of equipment is needed? Is new equipment needed? Will the new equipment be used for other projects?

(9) *Other Hazards or Issue*: Is there anything else that is not covered in the categories listed above?

Appendix 7D

City of Lawrence: Debt Management and Fiscal General Policy

The Debt Management Policy Statement sets forth comprehensive guide-lines for the financing of capital expenditures. It is the objective of the policies that (1) the City obtain financing only when desirable, (2) the process for identifying the timing and amount of debt financing be as efficient as possible and (3) the most favorable interest rate and other related costs be obtained. Debt financing, to include general obligation bonds, special assessment bonds, revenue bonds, temporary notes, lease/purchase agreements, and other City obligations permitted to be issued or incurred under Kansas law, shall only be used to purchase capital assets that will not be acquired from current resources.

The useful life of the asset or project shall exceed the payout schedule of any debt the City assumes. This allows for a closer match between those who benefit from the asset and those that pay for it. To enhance creditworthiness and prudent financial management, the City is committed to systematic capital planning, intergovernmental cooperation and coordination, and long-term financial planning. Evidence of this commitment to capital planning will be demonstrated through adoption and periodic adjustment of the City's Capital Improvement Plan and the annual adoption of a multi-year Capital Improvement Budget.

RESPONSIBILITY FOR DEBT MANAGEMENT

The primary responsibility for making debt-financing recommendations rests with the Director of Finance. In developing such recommendations, the Finance Director shall be assisted by other City staff. The responsibilities of City staff shall be to: Consider the need for financing and assess progress on the current Capital Improvement Budget and any other program/improvement deemed necessary by the City Manager; Test adherence to this policy statement and to review applicable debt ratios listed in the Debt Issuance Guidelines.

- Review changes in federal and state legislation that affect the City's ability to issue debt and report such findings to the City Manager as appropriate;
- Review annually the provisions of ordinances authorizing issuance of general obligation bonds of the City;
- Review the opportunities for refinancing current debt; and recommend services by a financial advisor, bond trustees, bond counsel, paying agents and other debt financing service providers when appropriate. In developing financing recommendations, the City staff shall consider:
- Options for interim financing including short term and inter-fund borrowing, taking into consideration federal and state reimbursements;
- Effects of proposed actions on the tax rate and user charges;
- Trends in bond markets structures;
- Trends in interest rates; and,
- Other factors as deemed appropriate.

USE OF DEBT FINANCING

Debt financing will not be considered appropriate for any recurring purpose such as current operating and maintenance expenditures. The City will use debt financing only for one-time capital improvement projects and unusual equipment purchases under the following circumstances: The project is included in the City's capital improvement budget and is in conformance with the City's general plan; The project is the result of growth-related activities within the community that require unanticipated and unplanned infrastructure or capital improvements by the City; The project's useful life, or the projected service life of the equipment, will be equal to or exceed the term of the financing; There are revenues sufficient to service the debt, whether from future property taxes, user fees, or other specified and reserved resources, debt supported by user fees, special assessments or special charges shall be preferred, The debt shall be primarily used to finance capital projects with a relatively long life, typically ten years or longer.

The equipment is an item that is purchased infrequently, has an expected useful life of at least five years, and costs in excess of $100,000.

STRUCTURE AND TERM OF DEBT FINANCING

Debt will be structured to match projected cash flows, minimize the impact on future property tax levies, and maintain a relatively rapid payment of principal. As a benchmark, the City shall strive to repay at least 50 percent of the initial principal amount within ten years.

General Obligation Bonds

The City shall use an objective analytical approach to determine whether it desires to issue new general obligation bonds. Generally, this process will compare ratios of key economic data. The goal will be for the City to maintain or enhance its existing credit rating. These ratios shall include, at a minimum, debt per capita, debt as a percent of statutory debt limit, debt as a percent of appraised valuation, debt service payments as a percent of governmental expenditures, and the level of overlapping net debt of all local taxing jurisdictions. A set of ratios shall be adopted and itemized in the City's Debt Issuance Guidelines. The decision on whether or not to issue new general obligation bonds shall, in part, be based on (a) costs and benefits, (b) the current conditions of the municipal bond market, and (c) the City's ability to issue new general obligation bonds as determined by the aforementioned benchmarks.

Revenue Bonds

For the City to issue new revenue bonds, projected annual revenues as defined by the ordinance authorizing such issuance, shall be a minimum of 125 percent of the issue's average annual revenue bond service or at a higher amount if required by the bond indentures. If necessary, annual adjustments to the City's rate structures will be considered in order to maintain the required coverage factor. Revenue bonds will be the preferred financing option for enterprise funds.

Special Assessment Bonds

The City shall maintain a watchful attitude over the issuance of special assessment bonds for benefit district improvements. The City's share of any benefit district project may not exceed more than 95 percent of any proposed costs related to a benefit district. The developer shall be required to deposit 25 percent of the costs allocated to the benefit district prior to authorization. In most cases, the debt will have a maximum term of ten years, however, a longer term may be allowed provided it does not exceed the life of the improvements included in the benefit district. The benefit district will be assigned costs such as administration, engineering, financing and legal associated with the formation of the district and issuance of any debt.

Debt Issuance With Intergovernmental Agencies

The City will typically not use of its debt capacity for projects by entities or other special purpose units of government that have the ability to issue tax exempt debt. The City's issuance of debt will be made only (1) after the prior commitment of the full assets and resources of the authority to debt service; (2) if project revenues, or development authority revenues pledged to debt service, are at least 115 percent of debt service; (3) if debt service reserves provided by the authority's own resources are equal to at least six months debt service; and (4) if all other viable means financing have been examined. The City will also enter into arrangements with other governmental entities where a portion of the project costs will be reimbursed by the other government. An agreement as to how the project costs will be allocated and reimbursements made must be approved by the governing bodies.

Structure of Debt Obligations

The City normally shall issue bonds with an average life of ten years or less for general obligation and special assessment bonds and ten to twenty years for revenue bonds. The typical structure of general obligation bonds will result in even principal and interest payments over the term of the debt. There shall be no "balloon" bond repayment schedules, which consist of low annual payments and one large payment of the balance due at the end of the term. There shall always be at least interest paid in the first fiscal year after a bond sale. In cases where related revenues may not occur for several years, it may be desirable to capitalize the interest by increasing the size of the issue and deferring the principal payments so that only interest is paid on the debt for the first few years.

Call Provisions

Call provisions for bond issues will be evaluated based upon current market conditions. All bonds shall be callable only at par.

Variable Rate Long-Term Obligations

The City may choose to issue bonds that pay a rate of interest that varies according to pre-determined formula or results from a periodic remarketing of the securities, consistent with state law and covenants of pre-existing bonds, and depending on market conditions.

DEBT ADMINISTRATION AND FINANCING

Capital Improvement Budget

A Capital Improvement Budget shall be prepared and submitted to the City Commission annually. The budget shall provide a list of projects and the means of financing. The budget should cover a five-year period of time.

The projects included in the budget should be part of the City's Capital Improvement Plan. Projects must be in either the Capital Improvement Budget or Plan to be authorized.

Bond Fund

Generally, payment of general obligation bonds and special assessment bonds shall be from the City's Bond and Interest Fund. However, in situations where General Obligation bonds are to be paid from user fees or sales taxes, bond payments should be made from the fund that receives the revenue. The minimum fund balance in the Bond and Interest Fund will be maintained at a level equal to or greater than 50 percent of the total principal and interest payable from that Fund for the upcoming year.

Reserve Funds

Adequate operating reserves are important to insure the functions of the City during economic downturns. The City shall budget a contingency reserve in the General Fund of no less than $150,000. The City will maintain working capital in an enterprise fund sufficient to finance 120 days of operations, if the fund supports debt payments. In addition, all reserves specified by bond indentures must be maintained. The Equipment Reserve Fund will be funded sufficiently to ensure that adequate funds are available to purchase replacement equipment on a timely basis.

Finance Department

It shall be the responsibility of the Finance Department to prepare the Preliminary and final Official Statements. The City Clerk is responsible for collecting and maintaining all supporting documentation such as minutes of the City Commission meetings and relevant resolutions and ordinances. In the case of general obligation bonds, an estimate of the mill levy required to pay off the debt should be provided to the City Commission. The department will also be responsible following applicable secondary disclosure requirements.

Investments

The bond proceeds will be invested in accordance with the City's investment policy. Adherence to the guidelines on arbitrage shall be followed, which at times, may require that the investment yield be restricted. In most cases, the investment will be selected to maximize interest with the assumption that the City will meet the IRS spend down requirement that allows for an exemption from arbitrage calculations.

Bond Counsel

The City will utilize external bond counsel for all debt issues. All debt issued by the City will include a written opinion by Bond Counsel affirming that the City is authorized to issue the debt, stating that the City has met all Federal and State constitutional and statutory requirements necessary for issuance, and determining the debt's federal income tax status. The City's Bond Counsel will be selected on a competitive basis.

Underwriter's Counsel

City payments for Underwriters Counsel will be authorized for negotiated sales by the Department of Finance on a case-by-case basis depending on the nature and complexity of the transaction and the needs expressed by the underwriters.

Financial Advisor

The City may utilize an external financial advisor. The utilization of the financial advisor for debt issuance will be at the discretion of the Director of Finance on a case-by-case basis. For each City bond sale, the financial advisor will provide the City with information on structure, pricing and underwriting fees for comparable sales by other issuers. The Financial Advisor will be selected on a competitive basis for a period not to exceed five years.

Temporary Notes

Use of short-term borrowing, such as temporary notes, will be undertaken until the final cost of the project is known or can be accurately projected. In some cases, projects might be funded with internal funds that will be reimbursed with bond funds at a future date.

Credit Enhancements

Credit enhancement (letters of credit, bond insurance, etc.) may be used if the costs of such enhancements will reduce the debt service payments on the bonds or if such an enhancement is necessary to market the bonds.

Competitive Sale of Debt

The City, as a matter of policy, shall seek to issue its temporary notes, general and revenue bond obligations through a competitive sale. In such instances where the City, through a competitive bidding for its bonds, deems the bids received as unsatisfactory or does not receive bids, it may, at the election of the City Commission, enter into negotiation for sale of the bonds. In cases where the circumstances of the bond issuance are complex or out of the ordinary, a negotiated sale may be recommended if allowed by State statute.

REFUNDING OF DEBT

Periodic reviews of all outstanding debt will be undertaken to determine refunding opportunities. Refunding will be considered (within federal tax law constraints) if and when there is a net economic benefit from the refunding or the refunding is needed in order to modernize covenants essential to operations and management or to restructure the payment of existing debt. City staff and the financial advisor shall monitor the municipal bond market for opportunities to obtain interest savings by refunding outstanding debt. As a general rule, the present value savings of a particular refunding will exceed 3 percent. Refunding issues that produce a net present value savings of less than 3 percent will be considered on a case-by-case basis. Refunding issues with negative savings will not be considered unless there is a compelling public policy objective.

CONDUIT FINANCINGS

The City may sponsor conduit financings in the form of Industrial Revenue Bonds for those activities (i.e., economic development, housing, health facilities, etc.) that have a general public purpose and are consistent with the City's overall service and policy objectives as determined by the City Commission. All conduit financings must insulate the City completely from any credit risk or exposure and must first be approved by the City Manager before being submitted to the City Commission for consideration. The City should review the selection of the underwriter and bond counsel, require compliance with disclosure and arbitrage requirements, and establish minimum credit ratings acceptable for the conduit debt. Credit enhancement, such as insurance, may be required for certain issues.

ARBITRAGE LIABILITY MANAGEMENT

Federal arbitrage legislation is intended to discourage entities from issuing tax-exempt obligations unnecessarily. In compliance with the spirit of this legislation, the City will not issue obligations except for identifiable projects with good prospects of timely initiation. Temporary notes and subsequent general obligation bonds will be issued timely so that debt proceeds will be spent quickly. Because of the complexity of arbitrage rebate regulations and the severity of non-compliance penalties, the City will be engage outside consultants to calculate potential arbitrage liability.

CREDIT RATINGS

Rating Agency Relationships

The Director of Finance shall be responsible for maintaining relationships with the rating agencies that assign ratings to the City's debt. This effort shall include providing periodic updates on the City's general financial condition along with coordinating meetings and presentations in conjunction with a new debt issuance.

Use of Rating Agencies

The City will obtain a rating from Moody's Investors Service. The Finance Director will recommend whether or not an additional rating shall be requested on a particular financing and which of the major rating agencies shall be asked to provide such a rating.

Rating Agency Presentations

Full disclosure of operations and open lines of communication shall be made to rating agencies used by the City. The Finance Director, with assistance of City staff, shall prepare the necessary materials and presentation to the rating agencies.

Financial Disclosure

The City is committed to full and complete financial disclosure, and to cooperating fully with rating agencies, institutional and individual investors, City departments and agencies, other levels of government, and the general public to share clear, comprehensible, and accurate financial information. The City is committed to meeting secondary disclosure requirements on a timely and comprehensive basis. Official statements accompanying debt issues, Comprehensive Annual Financial Reports, and continuous disclosure statements will meet (at a minimum), the standards articulated by the Government Accounting Standards Board (GASB), the National Federation of Municipal Analysts, and Generally Accepted Accounting Principles (GAAP). The Finance Director shall be responsible for ongoing disclosure to established national information repositories and for maintaining compliance with disclosure standards promulgated by state and national regulatory bodies.

Appendix 7E
City of Lawrence: Debt Management Policy

TERMINOLOGY

Arbitrage. Arbitrage refers to the rebate amount due to the Internal Revenue Service where funds received from the issuance of tax-exempt debt have been invested and excess interest earnings have occurred.

General Obligation Bonds. Bonds backed by the full faith and credit of the City. The taxing power may be an unlimited ad valorem tax or a limited tax, usually on real estate and personal property. A special tax rate levied for the Bond & Interest Fund annually to pay for general obligation LTO service. Because it is secured by an unlimited tax levy, this structure has strong marketability and lower interest costs.

Revenue Bonds. Bonds secured by revenues generated by the facility from dedicated user fees. Planning for such issues generally are more complex because future costs and revenues directly affect each other. Credit enhancements (e.g., insurance or letter of credit) may be needed because of the limited source of LTO service payments that may be available in outlying years.

Special Assessment Bonds. Bonds issued to develop facilities and basic infrastructure for the benefit of properties within the assessment district. Assessments are levied on properties benefited by the project. The issuer's recourse for non- payment is foreclosure and the remaining LTO becomes the City's direct obligation.

Temporary Notes. Notes are issued to provide temporary financing, to be repaid by long-term financing. This type of bridge financing has a maximum maturity of four years under Kansas law.

Source: http://www.lawrenceks.org/policies/debtmanagementpolicy.pdf

Chapter 8

Effectively Communicating Data

OVERVIEW

In addition to having quality information at the right time, the second most important function of a budget office is to effectively and efficiently represent the data in presentations. This need is exacerbated by the limited amount of time that policy makers spend reviewing budgets and accompanying paper work. The main purpose of this chapter is to show you how to effectively display budgets and related data. The chapter begins with a discussion of data quality, sources of data, and data appropriateness. Then, commonly used methods to displaying data as well as the advantages and disadvantages of each tool are described. Each of these methods employs the use of spread-sheet and/or data processing programs as well as Microsoft PowerPoint.

DATA QUALITY, SOURCES AND APPROPRIATENESS

Finding data is not necessarily a difficult task for someone in a budget office. Data can generally be found in the budget director's office, at the various agencies, and from the chief executive. However, finding reliable comparative data for a different city or state could be a problem. There are two basic types of data: primary and secondary. For the purposes of this chapter, we focus on primary data. Primary data can be collected first hand out of department data-bases or via surveys or interviews (telephone, mail, in person, or the internet). There are several advantages and disadvantages to using this method when you consider the specific ways to collect primary data. The chief advantage of using this method lies in the fact that you can get the data that you want in the form that you want it, in order to best address your needs. That is, you can design the charts, graphs, and address budget or finance questions exactly the way that you want them. Hence, it is imperative that you use the best data available to address the issue at hand. However, this does not suggest that secondary data sets cannot address your needs in a similar fashion.[1]

DISPLAYING DATA

A general rule of thumb for tables and graphs is that they should be understandable to the decision-makers. Hence, it is important that the title of the figures and labels used to describe the data are effective, appropriate, and timely. The data/figure should essentially be self-explanatory. That is, the user should not have to read a paragraph of text to understand the contents of the table. Charts, tables, and graphs that originate from an outside source should include the source of the data as well as any explanatory notes and include an appropriate title or label.

TABLES

Tables are the most common way to visually describe data. Therefore, it is very important that the analyst use the space that they have effectively and efficiently. Basically, a table should be completely self-explanatory. Thus, the analysts should pay close attention to not only the data in the table, but the labels, titles, or subtitles as well.

For example, table 8.1 provides fund revenue balances for Jefferson City for 2020 and 2021. This is *raw* or unprocessed data. Users of the table can look at the table and discern at a glance that the general fund receives 69 percent of the revenue and that this is a 2 percent increase from 2020. Also, note how the analyst used a title that clearly describes the data in the table and provided the reader with labels that accurately portray the data in as few words as possible. If the table or anything in it is not self-explanatory, the analyst should make sure that a description of all the data and symbols used are included in a note at the bottom of the table. For example, note the asterisk located next to the phrase, "2020 (est.) Amount." This signifies that the reader should read the information below where it indicates that the data is in millions.

Table 8.2 provides the reader with the revenue sources by percentage for the general fund in Jefferson City. As you can see, the majority of the funds listed in the table come from property taxes (59 percent) followed by sales taxes (18 percent) and federal & state revenues (15 percent). Although, it is not included in this study, a budget presentation for Jefferson City would also include a table with revenue sources for the remaining funds in table 8.1.

Table 8.3 is a *trend analysis*. Trend analysis is essentially a table that shows the change in a variable over time. It is one of the easiest forecasting methods to use when describing revenues and expenditures that are stable over time. In

Table 8.1. Jefferson City All Fund Revenues 2021 Estimates (in millions)

	2020 (act) Amount	2020 Percent	2021 (est) Amount	2021 Percent
General Fund	$38,967	67%	$39,412	69%
Utility	7,977	14%	7,865	13%
Athletic Club	3,556	6%	3,721	6%
Great Hall	169	0%	162	0%
Sanitation	3,973	7%	3,648	6%
Special Revenue	2,400	4%	2,309	4%
Storm Water Mgmt.	1,012	2%	1,152	2%
TOTAL REVENUES	$58,054	100%	$58,269	100%

Source: Created by the Author.

Table 8.2. Jefferson City General Fund Revenues 2020–2021 (in millions)

	2020 (act) Amount	2020 Percent	2021 (est) Amount	2021 Percent
Property Taxes	$22,301	59%	$23,092	59%
Sales Taxes	7,075	18%	7,132	18%
Federal & States Rev.	5,606	14%	5,062	13%
License, Fees & Other	3,478	9%	3,439	9%
Investment Income	57	0%	235	1%
TOTAL	$38,517	100%	$38,960	100%

Source: Created by the Author.

Table 8.3. Operating Revenue Collection for Jefferson City, FYs 2018–2021

	2018 (act)	2019 (act)	2020 (est)	2021 (est)	Dir
Metered Water Sales	$3,970,827	$4,904,500	$4,600,000	$4,625,000	—
Sewer Service Fees	$2,444,113	$2,720,000	$2,700,000	$2,725,000	↑
Other Revenue	$234,362	$209,930	$180,000	$180,000	—
TOTAL	$6,649,302	$7,834,430	$7,480,000	$7,530,000	

Source: Created by the Author

short, a trend analysis assumes that future revenue and expenditures will be comparable to those in the past. The more data included in a trend analysis will yield a more reliable forecast.

For example, the data in table 8.3 provides the reader with operating revenue collections for Jefferson City for FYs 2018–2021. In addition, a column is included to show the general direction of revenue collection over time. The dash indicates that the revenue source is relatively stable over time while the upward facing arrow indicates that the revenue source is increasing. Depending on the purpose of the data, it may be useful to include narratives explaining exceptional cases in the data (i.e., revenue spiked or decreased dramatically due to some phenomenon) as well as the general direction of the trend. These exceptions may require the analyst to conduct some additional research.

While the data in table 8.3 is useful, it is somewhat limited. For example, it may be more useful for a policy maker or a budget analyst to know the percentage change in the variable for each year rather than the numerical amount. For example, the data in table 8.4 shows the percent change in the revenue amounts listed in table 8.3 from one fiscal year to the next (formula needed to calculate the change is: [(2019 actual 2018 actual) / 2018 actual = Percent Change]). For example, the data show that the revenue collected for metered water sales increased 23.5 percent ([\$4,904,500–\$3,970,827]/\$3,970,827 = 23.5%) from FY 2018 to FY 2019 while other revenue decreased 10.4 percent ([\$209,930–\$234,362]/\$234,362= −10.4%) during the same period. Again, this sort of data can give the user a sense of the trend over time. Similar to the raw data examined above, any gross variations in the data should be explained in a footnote or in a narrative.

Table 8.4. Percent Changes in Revenue Collections for Jefferson City, FYs 2019–2021			
Revenues	FY 2019	FY 2020	FY 2021 (est.)
Metered Water Sales	23.5%	−6.2%	0.5%
Sewer Service Fees	11.3%	−0.7%	0.9%
Other Revenue	−10.4%	−14.3%	0.0%
AVERAGE	8.1%	−7.1%	0.5%

Source: Created by the Author.

As with most things, there are usually rules of engagement. Trend analysis is not immune to this process. Karl Nollenberger, Sanford M. Groves, and Maureen Godsey Valente (2003) provides several steps that one can use when conducting a trend analysis. Please see the steps below.

NOLLENBERGER ET AL.'S STEPS TO
CONSTRUCTING A TREND ANALYSIS

(1) After analyzing the revenue structure, split the structure into categories. Then, consider using two sub categories: most stable and least stable revenues.

(2) After analyzing the expenditure structure, split it into two categories, salary and non-salary. Then, break non-salary into its component parts. Lastly, analyze the profile of debt separately.

(3) Create a historical picture of both revenues and expenditures over the period used with plots, tables and graphs. Make sure that the consumer is knowledgeable of any changes made in the data as a result of policy changes. For example, if political leaders lowered property tax assessments on commercial property, it is likely to affect property tax revenues.

(4) Predict how each revenue and expenditure will change based on available data and information. Three possible scenarios should be considered: (a) The item will not change. (b) The item will change by the same average amount as it did in past years. (c) The item will maintain the same rate of change as it did in past years (Nollenberger et al. 2003).

As with most forecasting methods, there are always some drawbacks. The main drawback to trend analysis is that it cannot predict how major events or the economy will affect revenue or expenditure streams. The model assumes that nothing has changed in the model. Further, trend analysis cannot answer the "what if" questions. For example, what would happen if the shoe company down the street that employs three hundred residents moved south to Mexico? Despite this weakness, trend analysis remains a very useful tool for local governments with stable resources and expenditures (Nollenberger et al. 2003).

CHARTS AND FIGURES

There are several different ways to display data using charts. Charts are used quite frequently in budgeting and finance and other disciplines to visually show the relationship between variables. The main advantage of a chart is that the reader can look at the data and determine the relationship in seconds. Hence, it is important that the chart clearly convey the message that the analyst is trying to distinguish right away. That is, the chart must be completely self-contained. The reader should be able to look at the chart and understand the labels and data with minimum explanations from written text or verbal communication. One other item to note is that the statistical packages that create charts do not use exact numbers in the labels or legend unless the user requests the exact number. In most cases, data presented in the legend are rounded to the nearest hundredth or thousandth.

There are several different types of charts and each of them provide the analyst with options depending on what they are attempting to convey to the consumer. These include: scattergrams, line graphs, pie charts, bar graphs, and column graphs.

SCATTERGRAMS

Scattergrams are frequently used to show a pattern or relationship between two variables. They are easy to construct in a spreadsheet program and are very easy to understand. For example, the data in exhibit 8.1 shows that personal income is more likely to increase as years of college education increases. Note that the independent variable is on the horizontal axis and the dependent variable is on the vertical axis. This format is always used when creating charts with two variables. However, scattergrams may not be the best option for all data. It works best with ratio and interval data, but it is also possible to use scattergrams with nominal and ordinal data.

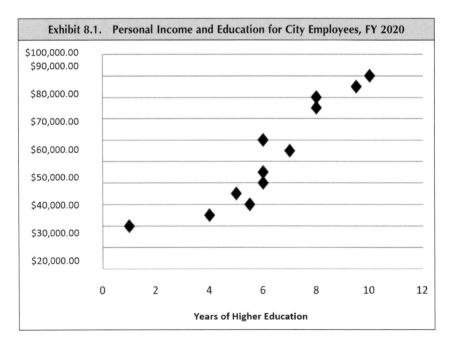

Exhibit 8.1. Personal Income and Education for City Employees, FY 2020

LINE GRAPHS

Line graphs are very useful for showing patterns over time or simply displaying data. The only real difference between a line graph and a scattergram is the addition of a line that plots the data rather than the individual data points.

Exhibit 8.2 is an example of a line graph showing unemployment rates in Jefferson City from 2012 to 2021. The direction of the line shows that the rate has vacillated over time, but it is generally in a positive direction. That is, the unemployment rate has risen over the period.

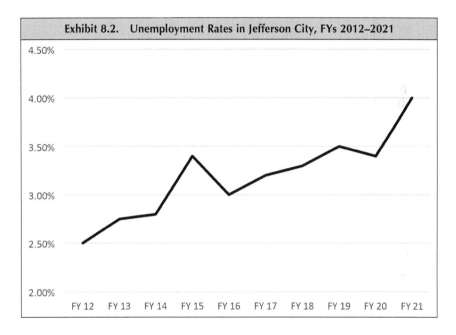

Exhibit 8.2.   Unemployment Rates in Jefferson City, FYs 2012–2021

Exhibit 8.3 is also a line graph. It shows actual revenue collections for the license fees in Jefferson City for fiscal years 2014–2019 and estimates for fiscal years 2020–2021. Line graphs are a very good way to provide a quick glimpse of the budget trend. This is particularly true when decision makers want an overall picture of the budget.

Exhibit 8.4 is also a line graph that plots the percentage change in property tax and user fees over a six-year period. This and similar graphs are very useful when comparing multiple revenue streams. Note that the amount of the revenue collection is not the key factor in the graph. As shown, the change in both revenue streams is fairly consistent over time.[2]

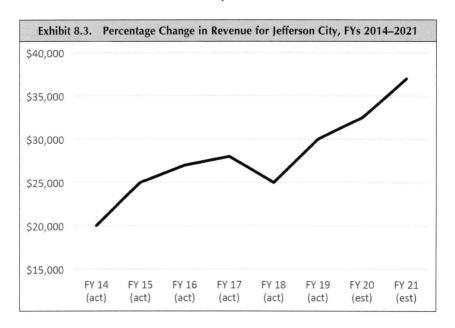

Exhibit 8.3. Percentage Change in Revenue for Jefferson City, FYs 2014–2021

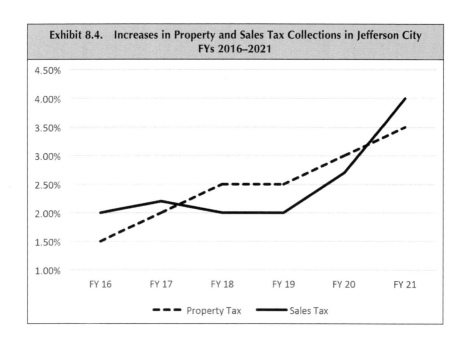

Exhibit 8.4. Increases in Property and Sales Tax Collections in Jefferson City FYs 2016–2021

PIE CHARTS

A pie chart shows the contribution of values to a whole. They are useful when the data is represented in percentages. It is more difficult to use raw data in a pie chart and bar graph, particularly when there are disparate differences in the data. Pie charts are not useful in describing data that has negative changes.

In exhibit 8.5, the revenue collections for Jefferson City are shown for fiscal year 2021 in an exploded three dimension chart. As shown, the city received 60 percent of its revenue from property tax collections, 25 percent from sales taxes, 9 percent from franchise fees, and 6 percent from business licenses. The consumer can see at a glance that the majority of the revenue for the city came from property taxes and sales taxes and that franchise fees and business licenses make up a smaller portion of the budget in FY 2021. This format is useful when there are several revenue categories that are small.

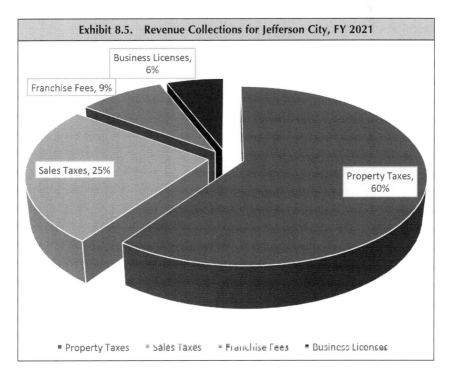

Exhibit 8.5.   Revenue Collections for Jefferson City, FY 2021

The pie chart in exhibit 8.6 is a one dimensional exploded pie chart that shows the contributions of each revenue source to the overall budget for Jefferson City in FY 2021. This format is also useful when there are several revenue categories that are small.

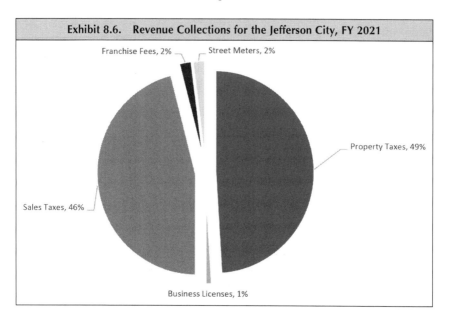

Exhibit 8.6.   Revenue Collections for the Jefferson City, FY 2021

Franchise Fees, 2%   Street Meters, 2%

Property Taxes, 49%

Sales Taxes, 46%

Business Licenses, 1%

BAR / COLUMN CHARTS

Bar and column charts are very similar to pie charts in that they are not very useful for negative numbers. However, unlike a pie chart, it is possible to show negative growth using a bar chart. It is however necessary to alert the user that the chart shows the change in the revenue stream versus the actual contributions of each revenue source. For example, look at the example in exhibit 8.7a. The chart shows, even at a glance, the percentage contribution from each revenue source. As you can see, the size of the bar increase as the contribution increases.

However, exhibit 8.7b shows the change in revenue collections from FY 2020 to FY 2021. Notice that the city had increases in every revenue source except for street meters where the revenue decreased 4 percent from the amount collected in FY 2020. It is necessary that users realize that the figure only shows the percentage growth in the revenue sources. Thus, it is very important that the label on the figure indicate exactly what the data represents.

The disadvantage of this chart, as well as the pie charts above, is the lack of a dollar amount. The user does not know how much revenue is included in each of these categories. So, they may be duped into thinking that there may be a problem where none exists.

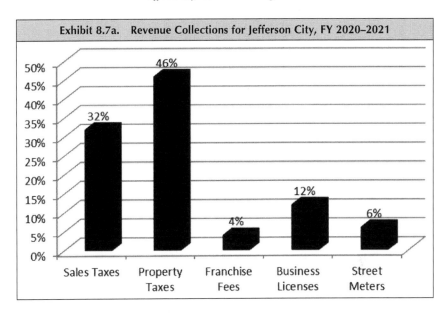

Exhibit 8.7a. Revenue Collections for Jefferson City, FY 2020–2021

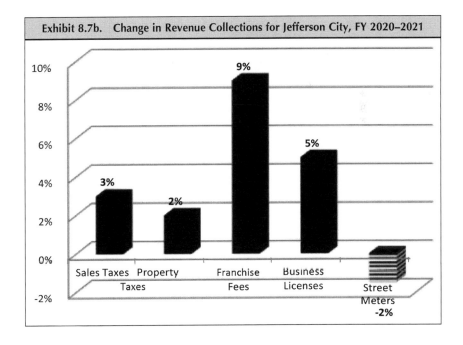

Exhibit 8.7b. Change in Revenue Collections for Jefferson City, FY 2020–2021

MICROSOFT POWERPOINT PRESENTATIONS

Handouts and paper presentations are remnants of the past when it comes to professional presentations.[3] Paper copies can still be used, but their roles are somewhat cursory in formal presentations. Therefore, it is important that you become proficient in constructing PowerPoint presentations or a similar program.

When you open the PowerPoint software for example, you will notice that it very user friendly. The program has quite a few preset templates (slide design, formats, etc.) that you can use when constructing your presentation. You should examine the basic rules listed below when constructing presentations.

Basic Rules For Constructing PowerPoint Presentations

Step 1: Determine the substantive contents of the presentation. Do not go overboard with tables and figures. If possible, determine what is expected in the presentation prior to beginning the presentation.

Step 2: Determine your design template. This step is more important than you might think. You do not want to use a gaudy design that is inappropriate and takes away from your presentation. I would strongly caution you not to use a lot of cartons in your presentations, a dark background or light colored words.

Step 3: Determine the format of your text and tables. Most PowerPoint presentations do not have text written in long sentences and paragraphs. You should include a brief introductory page, with a stated purpose, an outline of your tables, charts, etc., and a conclusion with bullets, but not much text in the middle of the presentation. It is your job as the presenter to have notes to fill in the blanks for explanation. Hence, use the tables and graphs and offer verbal explanations of the data. Make sure that each figure is appropriately labeled.

Step 4: Decide if you want your presentation to be interactive and linked to a web site, videos, or another program. That is, do you want to leave your presentation and visit a website or some other location that may have additional information? If so, ensure that those links are vital and working prior to the presentation. This function can be quite useful in situations where the audience may want or need more information on the spot. However, you should remember that presentations come with time constraints. Hence, do not waste time waiting for a web page to load or searching for a website.

CONCLUSION

As mentioned at the beginning of the chapter, there are a number of techniques that are useful in assisting budget analysts and policy makers in understanding how to present data. The more time that you spend creating charts and learning new programs, the more proficient you will become in using them. Remember, you want to get the most from any opportunity that you have to get your points across as well as address the questions that have been posed to you. When policy makers and administrations meet, time and clarity is the essence to success.

IMPORTANT TERMS AND PHRASES

Bar Graph	Raw Data
Chart	Revenue Collections
Line Graph	Revenue Estimates
Pie Chart	Scattergram
PowerPoint Presentation	Secondary Data
Primary Data	Trend Analysis

CHAPTER 8 HOMEWORK EXERCISES

Directions: Complete questions 1–5 in Microsoft Excel and paste the answers into a word processing program. The data for questions 1–5 are located in the appendix 8A to chapter 8. Question six should be printed out in Microsoft PowerPoint. Make sure that you check to ensure that your charts and figures correspond with the actual data. All of your responses should be submitted to your instructor along with the Excel file and accompanying worksheets.

Background Information: Governor Rebecca Davis, of the state of Alexander, is preparing her state of the state address and wants to focus on poverty and infant mortality issues. As a result, she has contacted you, the state vital statistics director, to provide data on poverty and infant mortality in the state's fifty counties. More specifically, she wants you to determine if there is a link between poverty and income and between health care spending and infant mortality in the different regions of the state. Using the county level data in the Excel spreadsheet, complete the following tasks.

(1a) Create a three dimensional pie chart showing the percentage (round to whole number) of the counties that represent each region (Central, East, North, South, and West) in the data. Label the chart Regions A (see exhibit 8.5).

(1b) Using the county data in the Excel spreadsheet, create a bar graph showing the number of counties that represent each region in the state. Label the chart Regions B (see exhibit 8.7).

(1c) Which one of these techniques best describes/visually represent the data?

(2a) Using the template on the worksheet for question 2, create a table with the average infant mortality rate and poverty rate by region for the 50 counties in the state of Alexander. Label the table Alexander Statistics.

(2b) Create pie charts that answer this question: What percentage of HCS and PCI dollars go to each region of the state? Using the same data, create two column graphs showing the percentage distribution of HCS and PCI for each region of the state. Label each of the charts (HCS Pie Chart, HCS Column Chart, PCI Pie Chart, and PCI Column Chart). Which one of the charts best describes the data? Explain.

(2c) Create a pie chart and a bar chart using the average poverty rate variable by region data. Label the charts Poverty Pie Chart and Poverty Bar Chart respectively. Which one of the charts best describes the data?

(3a) Create a scattergram that examines the following hypothesis: Per capita income has an impact on poverty rates. Format the horizontal axis to a minimum of $25,000. Label the scattergram, "Income and Poverty Rates". What is your assessment of the direction of the relationship?

(3b) Create a scattergram that examines the following hypothesis: Health care spending has an impact on infant mortality rates. Format the vertical axis to a minimum of 4%. Label the scattergram, "HC and Infant Mortality". Describe the results.

(3c) Create a line graph of average health care spending and average per capita income by region. Note: you should have two lines in your graph.

(4a) Using the data from question 1, create a line graph with markers that shows both the infant mortality rate averages and poverty rate averages for each region. Label the graph "IM and Poverty" graph respectively (see exhibit 8.4).

(4b) Create a column and a bar graph for the average infant mortality rate and poverty rate variables by region. Label the column graph IM and Poverty Column Graph and the bar graph "IM and Poverty Bar Graph" (see exhibit 8.7).

(4c) Which of these three graphs best describes the data?

(5) Explain health care spending in each region of the state.

(5a) Using the data listed below (in millions), calculate the percentage change for average HCS spending in each region from year to year. Describe the findings using only percentages (round the percentages to one digit to the right of the decimal) in your table.

Health Care Spending in Alexander, FYs 2017–2021				
Region	*2017 (act)*	*2018 (act)*	*2019 (act)*	*2020 (est)*	*2021 (est)*
Central	$3,890	$4,090	$4,862	$5,300	$6,000
East	2,890	3,498	3,723	4,400	5,500
North	4,798	4,990	5,074	5,600	6,200
South	13,000	18,987	17,903	15,300	14,000
West	5,790	5,981	5,611	6,450	7,500
TOTAL	$30,368	$37,546	$37,173	$37,050	$39,200

(5b) Using the HCS percentage change data that you calculated in 5a, create line graphs describing the growth or decline in spending by region. Note: The various regions should appear in the legend, not the year. All of these graphs should be completed in one step.

(5c) Using the original raw data for the Health Care Spending (HCS) allocations described above, create line graphs describing the growth or decline in spending by region. All of the regional line graphs should be completed in one step (one graph with five lines). Also, format the data labels so that the dollar amount for each year and region appears on the graph. Note: The various regions should appear in the legend, not the year.

(6) The last step in your report is to create a PowerPoint presentation for Governor Davis. Your presentation should include the following slides in the order that they are listed. When you finish creating the slides, copy and paste the slides into your word processing file. Place four slides on each printed page. Each slide should have a label based on the information listed below:

- Slide 1: Title of presentation as well as your name and title.
- Slide 2: Write a general overview/introduction of the regions over the period (text only).
- Slide 3: Prepare a short bullet outline of each chart/diagram/table used in the PowerPoint presentation.
- Slide 4: Using the data in Question 1b, present the number of counties included in each region. Label the table Regions.
- Slide 5: Present the average infant mortality and poverty table data by region for 2020 (question 2a). Labels (IM and Poverty).
- Slide 6: Present the line graph from question 4a.
- Slide 7: Present the HCS and PCI table data (question 2b).
- Slide 8: Present the scattergram in question 3a (Income and Poverty).
- Slide 9: Present the scattergram in question 3b (HCS and Infant Mortality).
- Slide 10. Present the line graph from question 5c.
- Slide 11: Write a brief conclusion to your findings.
- Print out your presentation (four PowerPoint slides per sheet of paper). Save an electronic copy of the presentation and bring it to class.

NOTES

1. Secondary data are existing data sets collected for another purpose by someone else. There are a number of factors such as timeliness of the data, aggregating data, searching for data, purchasing data, as well as the source of secondary data that will affect your decision to use the data. Secondary data is particularly useful when conducting comparative or longitudinal studies. This data can be found in libraries, reference books,

databases, government agencies, internet, etc. However, all data is not equal. That is, data is only as good as the entity that collected it. For example, there are a number of entities that collect statistics on various federal agencies. However, the U.S. Census Bureau is one of the most respected institutions responsible for collecting data on the U.S. population on a variety of different subjects from agriculture issues to vital statistics that are used across the world. Therefore, you want to stick to the official source, rather than using data from a less credible source.

2. When using Microsoft Excel, make sure that you understand how to use the "series" button to move and add variables to the graph.

3. See appendix 8B for an outline describing the contents of a research proposal and a research paper.

Appendix 8A

Counties in the State of Alexander

Counties in the State of Alexander						
County	*Year*	*Region*	*HCS*	*IM*	*PCI*	*POV*
Bedford	2020	Central	$5,089.60	9.9%	$32,517	19%
Bledsoe	2020	Central	$6,393.70	6.9%	$35,427	14%
Carter	2020	Central	$9,640.10	8.0%	$35,242	14%
Cocke	2020	Central	$3,992.00	9.1%	$35,840	22%
Coffee	2020	Central	$2,752.50	7.9%	$37,624	11%
Decatur	2020	Central	$6,934.20	8.0%	$46,764	8%
Fayette	2020	Central	$6,857.70	7.5%	$35,479	13%
Giles	2020	Central	$540.50	8.5%	$30,220	23%
Hamilton	2020	Central	$3,867.90	8.3%	$31,684	18%
Haywood	2020	Central	$3,634.50	7.8%	$35,983	13%
Lake	2020	Central	$7,943.30	7.9%	$42,189	11%
Lewis	2020	Central	$700.50	7.3%	$45,236	15%
Benton	2020	East	$4,080.30	7.7%	$31,339	18%
Cannon	2020	East	$1,367.80	7.5%	$39,827	10%
Clay	2020	East	$6,124.50	7.6%	$33,654	12%
Crockett	2020	East	$6,082.30	7.3%	$31,155	17%
Dyer	2020	East	$7,594.30	8.9%	$41,652	10%
Franklin	2020	East	$931.70	8.1%	$33,644	14%
Hancock	2020	East	$1,757.00	8.7%	$39,874	14%
Houston	2020	East	$655.20	9.2%	$36,932	13%
Humphreys	2020	East	$7,602.40	8.3%	$34,159	16%
Knox	2020	East	$1,035.00	10.5%	$37,849	21%
Chester	2020	North	$1,395.70	6.8%	$32,570	12%
Cumberland	2020	North	$5,557.90	9.2%	$35,729	19%
Dekalb	2020	North	$2,413.30	7.3%	$34,947	12%
Dickson	2020	North	$9,994.00	7.9%	$34,381	14%
Fentress	2020	North	$4,709.90	10.0%	$29,580	21%
Grainger	2020	North	$1,909.90	8.9%	$37,902	11%
Greene	2020	North	$1,266.50	7.3%	$43,014	7%

(continued)

Counties in the State of Alexander (*Continued*)						
County	*Year*	*Region*	*HCS*	*IM*	*PCI*	*POV*
Hardin	2020	North	$15,997.00	7.7%	$35,117	13%
Henry	2020	North	$1,913.10	7.4%	$40,381	12%
Hickman	2020	North	$6,834.70	8.6%	$31,981	15%
Jefferson	2020	North	$2,753.60	11.0%	$32,440	10%
Lauderdale	2020	North	$6,139.60	7.1%	$36,782	11%
Blount	2020	South	$26,254.60	6.2%	$43,216	12%
Bradley	2020	South	$3,701.70	7.6%	$42,725	12%
Carroll	2020	South	$18,694.80	7.0%	$39,226	12%
Claiborne	2020	South	$13,000.10	6.7%	$41,927	10%
Grundy	2020	South	$12,244.90	7.9%	$50,240	4%
Hardeman	2020	South	$29,914.90	5.6%	$47,474	5%
Henderson	2020	South	$17,090.50	7.6%	$38,897	12%
Jackson	2020	South	$22,325.20	6.3%	$37,061	16%
Anderson	2020	West	$1,192.20	9.1%	$31,126	17%
Campbell	2020	West	$5,262.00	8.9%	$45,903	5%
Cheatam	2020	West	$2,108.10	8.9%	$39,948	8%
Davidson	2020	West	$10,811.10	6.5%	$50,037	5%
Gibson	2020	West	$10,444.80	8.5%	$34,747	14%
Hawkins	2020	West	$4,228.70	8.5%	$34,320	16%
Johnson	2020	West	$8,353.60	7.8%	$43,227	10%
Lawrence	2020	West	$2,486.00	7.5%	$29,515	17%

Source: Created by the Author.

Appendix 8B
Writing a Research Proposal

(1) *Research Question/Hypothesis*: The first thing that you need to do is to articulate the subject of the paper in the form of a research question or hypothesis.

(2) *Cursory Review of Literature*: Conduct a cursory review of the literature (3–4 articles, book, etc.) to determine what other scholars have found relative to your subject. Pay close attention to the issues and the variables used to test their hypothesis/research questions. You can use this literature to justify the need or to verify that there is a gap in the literature that you intend to fill. You can also use this review to extend research that has been conducted. What is true today may not be true tomorrow.

(3) *Data and Methods*: Find the secondary data that you need for the paper or determine or decide that you are going to collect primary data yourself via surveys, etc. Be specific as to the location of the data, i.e., websites, etc. Then, decide what sort of research design that you will use. For example, cross sectional, time series, or meta analysis. Last, what are you going to do with the data? That is, what sort of statistical analysis will you run on the data [univariate, bivariate (crosstabs), regression, etc.] that will allow you to answer your hypothesis/research questions.

Note: The proposal should be no more than two pages.

WRITING A RESEARCH PAPER

(1) *Title/Title Page*: The title of your paper should fit the main theme of the paper. It should be centered in bold print (16 to 18-point font) and should not be more than ten words. Place your name one or two line spaces directly under the title in a smaller font size. The date of submission and the class in which the assignment was made should also be included.

If you are presenting the paper at a conference, put your mailing address as well your phone number and email address under your name. Lastly, put the name, date and location of the conference under your demographic information.

Side note: You might want to construct a rough outline of the main headings in the paper highlighting the main point or items that you want to cover as you move along. This becomes more relevant as the length of the paper increases (for example, not necessary for a five-page paper, but important for papers over ten pages in length).

(2) *Abstract*: This is a one or two paragraph synopsis of your paper. First and foremost, the abstract should identify your hypothesis/research question in the first or second line. Then, detail the procedure/application that you used to test your hypothesis/research question (survey data, archival study, regression analysis, content analysis, etc.). This sentence[s] should also identify your main data sources (i.e., Survey data, Census data, etc.). Lastly, the abstract should provide the reader with your main research findings if you have completed the research. Frequently, proposals for research are just that. If you have completed the research, provide the major findings in one or two sentences. If you have not completed the research, then leave this part out of your proposal. When you finish the research you can go back and rewrite this section with the exact findings. This step is critical because you should be able to polish and refine your statement at this point. An abstract should not be longer than 130 words or ¾ of a page.

(3) *Introduction*: The introduction to the paper provides the main point of departure for your subject matter. The main objective is not only to clearly convey your hypothesis/research question, but also to validate your study relative to other studies. However, you do not want to delve too deep into the research of other scholars in this section. The literature review section contains this information. Do not force the reader to read more than one paragraph to find your hypothesis/research question. The purpose of your study should be crystal clear to the reader. Researchers frequently begin the introduction with several cursory sentences providing some interesting points or data concerning the subject matter. The introduction can range from half a page to two pages depending on how much background information you include. Ensure that you stay focused when writing this section.

Main Points Summarized:

- Present relevant background or contextual material
- Define terms or concepts when necessary
- Explain the focus of the paper and your specific purpose
- Validate your thesis or purpose statement by showing why it is important
- Reveal your plan of organization for the paper

(4) *Literature Review/Previous Literature*: In short, this is a summation of the works of other scholars who have conducted research on your dependent variable/main subject. The bulk of your literature review should be based on scholarly refereed research. Generally speaking, web based only articles are still only moderately acceptable in research. This does not include refereed journals that are available online. I am specifically referring to articles that were written and did not go through the process of having other professional researches read it and provide some sort of stamp of approval (commonly called non refereed research). Literature can be ranked in terms of level of acceptance (most acceptable to least acceptable): (1) university press books and refereed articles, (2) non university press books and text books, (3) articles from research institutes, government agencies, or think tanks such as the Urban Institute, Brookings, Congressional Budget Office, and OMB, (4) web sites, news magazines (*Newsweek, U.S. News and World Report*, etc.), and newspaper articles. There is also some disparity among web sites, newspapers, and news magazines, so be careful when citing them.

A literature review is normally written by date or subject matter. In some instances, there may be two areas of research that cover your subject, so it would be wise to split them into two sections with an appropriate heading for each and then discuss them by date. The most recent material should appear first. This is not necessarily true if there is a classic pioneering article or book in the field. If everyone else is citing the piece, then you should as well. Your goal is not to summarize the research, but to cite the research design and the findings as it applies to your work. If multiple authors have the same findings, then cite them together in one sentence. The literature review can range from two to four pages depending on how much work has been conducted in your area. Carefully cite the research you are building from, synthesizing the information as much as possible rather than just describing each individual research piece. Academic reviewers often go to this section first to see what basis the research is basing their theoretical/research design upon since this section demonstrates the writer's knowledge and understanding of the state of the current research in the area.

Main Points Summarized:

- Use your outline and prospectus as flexible guides
- Build your paper around points you want to make (i.e., don't let your sources organize your paper)
- Integrate your sources into your discussion
- Summarize, analyze, explain, and evaluate published work rather than merely reporting it
- Move up and down the "ladder of abstraction" from generalization to varying levels of detail back to generalization

(5) *Data and Methods*: The main objective of this section is to inform the reader of your data sources, research application and model. It is not necessary to list the exact location of your data sources. For example, if you use data from the U.S. Census Bureau's web site, you should simply list the main web site. The reader simply needs to have enough information to find the location of the data if they look for it. You should also indicate the time frame covered in the research.

It is easier to describe secondary data than primary data. When using primary data, you must detail the exact collection method as well as any other nuances that you employed when collecting the data. This is particularly true with content analysis studies and primary survey data. Review the article by Charles E. Menifield, Geigen Shin, and Logan Strother (2019), "Do White Law Enforcement Officers Target Minority Suspects?" *Public Administration Review* 79(1): 56–68, for an example of writing the data and methods section for a project requiring data collection. Review the article by Charles E. Menifield, Winfield H. Rose, John Homa, and Anita Brewer Cunningham (2001), "The Media's Portrayal of Urban and Rural School Violence: A Preliminary Analysis," *Deviant Behavior* 22(5): 447–64, for an example of content analysis. The article that is listed on our website with this handout also uses secondary data analysis. Methodology refers to the statistical application that you use in your study. This includes chi square analysis, regression analysis, correlations, factors analysis, etc.

Lastly, you should put your model in this section. This includes items such as illustrations describing your model or regression models. Each of the terms that you use to describe your illustration or variables in your model must be described in detail. For example, you may have an education variable in your model. It is necessary to inform the reader how you measure education: in years, grades, or degrees completed. Depending on how many variables that you have in your paper, it may be necessary to include an appendix or footnotes/endnotes with the full description of the variable along with any coding that you used.

Main Points Summarized:

• Provide the location of data sources
• Describe the variables used in your paper (in the paper or in the appendix)
• Describe the methodology used and it limitations (regression, survey or content analysis, archival studies, etc.)
• Present your model/paradigm/etc.

(6) *Findings/Results*: This section provides the reader with the results of your analysis. No conclusions are drawn in this section. So, if you test three hypotheses, you might simply list them one by one and provide the results for each. If you have tables and charts describing your findings, place them in this section. Your tables should stand alone. That is, the reader should be able to discern what is in the table or illustration without reading the text. However, the text should clearly explain what is in the table[s]. You should not refer extensively to the literature review in the findings. The tables and charts must be carefully constructed so that the reader can readily understand labels, headings, sources or data, etc.

Main Points Summarized:

• Repeat research question/hypothesis followed by the findings
• Present tables, charts and graphs
• Do not draw any conclusions based on previous research

(7) *Conclusions*: The first thing that you want to do in your conclusion is remind the reader of your hypotheses/research questions. Then, confirm or reject those propositions as well as compare them to the findings of other scholars. It is okay to indicate that you did not find what you expected to find. Scholars frequently indicate how their research was limited and what they would do or recommend to future researchers. It is not necessary to reinvent the wheel in this section. It is a summary, not a regurgitation of the findings. Depending on the number of hypothesis tested, your conclusion can range from a paragraph to a couple of pages in length.

After you have drafted your conclusion section, go back to the introduction and make sure that the two are still linked! Did you do what you said you were going to do? Is the paper organized the way you said it would be? Does your concluding paragraph(s) clearly address the purpose of the paper?

Main Points Summarized:

- If the argument or point of your paper is complex, you may need to summarize the argument for your reader.
- If prior to your conclusion you have not yet explained the significance of your findings or if you are proceeding inductively, use the end of your paper to add your points up, to explain their significance.
- Move from a detailed to a general level of consideration that returns the topic to the context provided by the introduction.
- Perhaps suggest what about this topic needs further research

(8) *References/Bibliography*: Please consult a style manual for proper citation methods. There are three main techniques (APA, MLA, and Chicago Manual of Style), and they do change over time. So, you should consult the most recent version of the technique that you are using.

(9) *Endnotes/Footnotes*: These are short explanatory sentences that are conservatively used throughout your paper. For the most part, they are used to offer additional explanation, definitions or other pieces of information that may be useful to the reader. Do not put things in the notes that can be included in the paper. If you are using quantitative analysis in your paper it may be better if you use an appendix along with notes. Use notes sparingly.

(10) *Appendices/Footnotes/Endnotes*: The appendix contains information that is not needed directly in the text. This would include items such as the coding scheme for your models, definitions of terms, and additional information about your data. There is no set amount or type of information that should be included in your appendix.

Notes: The items that are included in this summary should be included in a basic run of the mill research paper. There is no exact model to follow when writing a research paper. Different journals use different models and professors often want different things. The more you read scholarly research and write research papers the more adept you will become in your writing skills.

You may also include other items such as a background section discussing a policy or a definition that your paper focuses on. However, it is recommended that you do not go overboard in this process.

The information contained in this summary is not applicable and should not be mistaken for "research papers" that are really literature reviews. It is possible to conduct a content analysis or an archival study on the work of other scholars. However, to simply go to the library and find articles and books on a subject and write a paper is not a research paper, but a literature review disguised as a research paper. The term research suggests that you have gone beyond what other writers have done and conducted some sort of analysis that presumably has not been done before.

Research papers frequently use a Times Roman 12-point font and are double spaced. Unless indicated otherwise, there is no real page limit. However, research papers do not tend to extend beyond 40 pages. The following websites offers additional information on writing using the APA style http://webster.commnet.edu/apa/ or http://www.apastyle.org.

AIDS TO WRITING RESEARCH PAPERS

Guidelines for Writing a Research Report.
Harbrace College Handbook.
Making Sense: A Student's Guide to Research and Writing Social Sciences.
MLA Handbook for Writers of Research Papers.
Model Research Papers from Across the Disciplines.
Put it in Writing: Learn how to Write Clearly, Quickly and Persuasively.
Research and Report Writing [video recording].
Research Paper Smart: Where to Find it, how to Write it, how to Cite it.
Understanding Style: Practical Ways to Improve your Writing.
Webster's New World Student Writing Handbook.
Writing Handbook.
Writing Research Papers: A Norton Guide.

References

Afonso, Whitney. 2018. "Time to Adoption of Local Option Sales Taxes: An Examination of Texas Municipalities." *Public Finance Review* 46(4): 558–82.

Ammons, David N. 2002. *Tools for Decision Makers: A Practical Guide for Local Government*. Washington, DC: C Q Press.

Analytical Perspectives: Budget of the United States Government. 2004. Washington, DC: GOP.

Andrews, Matt. 2011. "The (Il)logics of Federal Budgeting, and Why Crisis Must Come." *Public Administration Review* 71(3): 345–48.

Arapis, Theodore, and Cynthia Bowling. 2019. "From Maximizing to Minimizing: A National Study of State Bureaucrats and Their Budge Preferences." *Journal of Public Administration Research and Theory* 30(1): 144–60.

Aronson, J. Richard, and Eli Schwartz. 2004. "Cost-Benefit Analysis and the Capital Budget." In *Management Policies in Local Government Finance*, 5th ed., edited by J. Richard Aronson and Eli Schwartz, 133–53 Washington, DC: ICMA.

Axelrod, Donald. 1995. *Budgeting for Modern Government*. 2nd ed. New York: St. Martin's Press.

Bahl, Roy W., Jr. 2004. "Local Government Expenditures and Revenues." In *Management Policies in Local Government Finance*, 5th ed., edited by J. Richard Aronson and Eli Schwartz, 79–99. Washington, DC: ICMA.

Ball, Ian. 2012. New Development: Transparency in the Public Sector. *Public Money & Management* 32(1): 35–40.

Bartle, John R., Kenneth A. Kriz, and Boris Morozov. 2011. "Local Government Revenue structure: Trends and Challenges." *Journal of Public Budgeting, Accounting & Financial Management* 23(2): 268–87.

Bierhanzl, Edward J., and Paul B. Downing. 2004. "User Charges and Special Districts." In *Management Policies in Local Government Finance*, 5th ed., edited by J. Richard Aronson and Eli Schwartz, 315–51. Washington, DC: ICMA.

Difulco, Robert, Beverly Bunch, William Duncombe, Mark Robbins, and William Simonsen. 2012. "Debt and Deception: How States Avoid Making Hard Fiscal Decisions." *Public Administration Review* 72(5): 668–77.

Bland, Robert L. 2005. *A Revenue Guide for Local Government*. 2nd ed. Washington, DC: ICMA.

Bland, Robert L., and Wes Clarke. 1999. "Budgeting for Capital Improvements." In *Handbook of Government Budgeting*, edited by Roy T. Meyers, 653–77. San Francisco: Jossey Bass.

Bland, Robert L., and Irene S. Rubin. 1997. *Budgeting: A Guide for Local Governments*. Washington, DC: ICMA.

Block, Sandra. 2019. "9 States with No Income Tax." *Kiplinger*. October 1. https://www.kiplinger.com/slideshow/taxes/T054-S001-states-without-income-tax/index.html (accessed January 31, 2020).

Bretschneider, Stuart, and Wilpen L. Gorr. 1999. "Practical Methods for Projecting Revenues." In *Handbook of Government Budgeting*, edited by Roy T. Meyers, 308–29. San Francisco: Jossey Bass.

Bryson, John M. 2010. "The Future of Public and Nonprofit Strategic Planning in the United States." *Public Administration Review* 70(1): 255–67.

Buss, Terry F. 2001. "The Effect of State Tax Incentives on Economic Growth and Firm Location Decisions: An Overview of the Literature." *Economic Development Quarterly* 15(1): 90–105.

Carney, James D., and Stanley Schoenfeld. 1996. "How to Read a Budget." In *Budgeting: Formulation and Execution*, edited by Jack Rabin, W. Bartley Hildreth, and Gerald J. Miller, 140–53. Athens, GA: Carl Vinson Institute of Government, University of Georgia.

Carroll, Deborah. A. 2009. "Diversifying Municipal Government Revenue Structures: Fiscal Illusion or Instability?" *Public Budgeting & Finance* 29(1): 27–48.

Chantrill, Christopher. 2020. "Recent US Local Government Debt," *usgovernmentspending.com*, https://www.usgovernmentspending.com/local_debt_chart (accessed January 9, 2020).

Chapman, Ronald. 1996. "Capital Financing: A New Look at an Old Idea." In *Budgeting: Formulation and Execution*, edited by Jack Rabin, W. Bartley Hildreth, and Gerald J. Miller, 292–96. Athens, GA: Carl Vinson Institute of Government, University of Georgia.

Chen, Greg. G., Lynne A. Weikart, and Daniel W. Williams. 2015. *Budget Tools: Financial Methods in the Public Sector*. 2nd ed. Los Angeles: Sage.

City of Alexandria Virginia. 2018. "Proposed Operating Budget, Fiscal Year 2018." https://www.alexandriava.gov/uploadedFiles/budget/info/budget2018/FY%202018%20Proposed%20Operating%20Budget.pdf (accessed January 4, 2020).

Clark, Anna Fountain and Evgenia Gorina. 2017. "Emergency Financial Management in Small Michigan Cities: Short-Term Fix or Long-Term Sustainability?" *Public Administration Quarterly* (41)3: 532–68.

Clynch, Edward J., Douglas G. Feig, and James B. Kaatz. 2001. "Local Government Casino Gaming Tax Receipts in Mississippi: An Impact Appraisal." Paper presented at the Southeastern Conference for Public Administration Conference, Baton Rouge, Louisiana.

Colorado. Department of Public Safety. 2018. *Impact of Marijuana Legalization in Colorado: A Report Pursuant to Senate Bill 13-283*. Prepared by Jack K. Reed. October 2018. https://cdpsdocs.state.co.us/ors/docs/reports/2018-SB13-283_Rpt.pdf (accessed January 5, 2020).

Dabbicco, Giovanna. 2019. "The Potential Role of Public Sector Accounting Frameworks Towards Financial Sustainability Reporting." In *Financial Sustainability of*

Public Sector Entities: The Relevance of Accounting Frameworks, edited by Josette Caruana, Isabel Brusca, Eugenio Caperchione, Sandra Cohen, and Francesca Manes Rossi, 19–40. Basingstoke, UK: Palgrave Macmillan.

Decker, J. Winn, and Bruce D. McDonald III. 2019. "Consensus Forecasting." In *The Palgrave Handbook of Government Budget Forecasting*, edited by Daniel Williams and Thad Calabrese, 397–412. Cham, Switzerland: Palgrave Macmillan.

Doss, C. Bradley, Jr. 1993. "Capital Budgeting Practices." In *Handbook of Comparative Public Budgeting and Financial Management*, edited by Thomas D. Lynch and Lawrence L. Martin, 265–88. New York: Marcel Dekker.

Downing, Paul. B. 1983. "User Charges and Service Fees." In *Budget Management: A Reader in Local Government Financial Management*, edited by Jack Rabin, W. Bartley Hildreth, and Gerald J. Miller, 73–82. Athens, GA: Carl Vinson Institute of Government, University of Georgia.

Druker, Marvin J., and Betty D. Robinson. 1993. "State's Responses to Budget Shortfalls: Cutback Management Techniques." In *Handbook of Comparative Public Budgeting and Financial Management*, edited by Thomas D. Lynch and Lawrence L. Martin, 189–206. New York: Marcel Dekker.

Fleeter, Howard, and L. Lee Walker. 1997. "Revenue Forecasting." In *Case Studies in Public Budgeting and Financial Management*, edited by Aman Khan and W. Bartley Hildreth, 209–25. Dubuque, IA: Kendall Hunt Publishing.

Franklin, Emily, Carolyn Bourdeaux, and Alex Hathaway. 2019. "State Revenue Forecasting Practices: Accuracy, Transparency, and Political Participation." In *The Palgrave Handbook of Government Budget Forecasting*, edited by Daniel Williams and Thad Calabrese, 155–76. Cham, Switzerland: Palgrave Macmillan.

Friedman, Marvin. 1983. "Calculating Compensation Costs." In *Budget Management: A Reader in Local Government Financial Management*, edited by Jack Rabin, W. Bartley Hildreth, and Gerald J. Miller, 116–27. Athens, GA: Carl Vinson Institute of Government, University of Georgia.

Government Accounting Standards Series. 1999. "Statement 34 of the Government Accounting Standards Board: Basic Financial Statements-and Management's Discussion and Analysis-for State and Local Governments." Governmental Accounting Standards Board, No 171-A.

Gianakis, Gerasimos A., and Clifford P. McCue. 1999. *Local Government Budgeting: A Managerial Approach.* West Port, CT: Praeger.

Gleason, Patrick. 2017. "Amid Budget Shortfalls, State Attorneys General Waste Scarce Taxpayer Dollars on Partisan Witch Hunt." *Forbes.* January 16. https://www.forbes.com/sites/patrickgleason/2017/01/16/amid-budget-shortfalls-state-attorneys-general-waste-scarce-taxpayer-dollars-on-partisan-witch-hunt/#4c7b15765375 (accessed June 9, 2017).

Gorina, Evgenia, Craig Maher, and Marc Joffe. 2017. "Local Fiscal Distress." *Public Budgeting & Finance* (38)1: 72–94.

Governing. The Future of States and Localities. 2019. "State Marijuana Laws in 2019 Map." *Governing.* https://www.governing.com/gov-data/safety-justice/state-marijuana-laws-map-medical-recreational.html (accessed January 5, 2020).

Government Finance Officers Association. http://www.gfoa.org.

Gruber, Jonathan. 2005. *Public Finance and Public Policy.* New York: Worth Publishers.

Han, Seung Hun, Michael S. Pagano, and Yoon S. Shin. 2019. "The Evolving Nature of Japanese Corporate Governance: Guaranteed Bonds vs. Rated Bonds." *Journal of International Financial Markets, Institutions and Money* 58(C): 162–83.

Hildreth, W. Bartley, and Laurie W. Adams. 1997. "The Politics of Pension Investment Returns." In *Case Studies in Public Budgeting and Financial Management,* edited by Aman Khan and W. Bartley Hildreth, 463–81. Dubuque, IA: Kendall Hunt Publishing.

Hildreth, W. Bartley, and Gerald J. Miller. 1996. "Pension Policy, Management, and Analysis." In *Budgeting: Formulation and Execution,* edited by Jack Rabin, W. Bartley Hildreth, and Gerald J. Miller, 431–37. Athens, GA: Carl Vinson Institute of Government, University of Georgia.

Holder, William W. 2004. "Financial Accounting, Reporting, and Auditing." In *Management Policies in Local Government Finance,* 5th ed., edited by J. Richard Aronson and Eli Schwartz, 207–23. Washington, DC: ICMA.

Howard, S. Kenneth. 2002. "Planning and Budgeting: Who's on First." In *Government Budgeting: Theory, Process, and Politics,* 3rd ed., edited by Albert C. Hyde, 349–57. Toronto and London: Wadsworth.

Hughes, Jesse. W. 1997. "Comparative Analysis of Key Governmental Financial Indicators." In *Case Studies in Public Budgeting and Financial Management,* edited by Aman Khan and W. Bartley Hildreth, 493–504. Dubuque, IA: Kendall Hunt Publishing.

Johnson, Craig L., and Kenneth A. Kriz. 2019. "A Review of State Tax Increment Financing Laws." In *Tax Increment Financing and Economic Development: Uses, Structures, and Impact,* 2nd ed., edited by Craig L. Johnson and Kenneth A. Kriz, 31–56. Albany, NY: SUNY Press.

Joyce, Philip G. 2011. "The Obama Administration and PBB: Building on the Legacy of Federal Performance-Informed Budgeting?" *Public Administration Review* 71(3): 356–67.

Kelly, Janet M., and William C. Rivenbark. 2015. *Performance Budgeting for State and Local Government.* Armonk, NY: M. E. Sharpe.

Keown, Arthur. J., John D. Martin, J. William Petty, and David F. Scott Jr. 2005. *Financial Management: Principles and Applications.* 10th ed. Upper Saddle River, NJ: Pearson Prentice Hall.

Khan, Aman. 1996. "Cash Management: Basic Principles and Guidelines." In *Budgeting: Formulation and Execution,* edited by Jack Rabin, W. Bartley Hildreth, and Gerald J. Miller, 313–21. Athens, GA: Carl Vinson Institute of Government, University of Georgia.

———. 1997. "Learning from Experience: Cash Management Practices of a Local Government." In *Case Studies in Public Budgeting and Financial Management,* edited by Aman Khan and W. Bartley Hildreth, 553–68. Dubuque, IA: Kendall Hunt Publishing.

Kiel, Daniel. 2011. "A Memphis Dilemma: A Half-Century of Public Education Reform in Memphis and Shelby County from Desegregation to Consolidation." *University of Memphis Law Review* (41): 787–815.

Kioko, Sharon. N. 2011. "Structure of State-Level Tax and Expenditure Limits." *Public Budgeting & Finance* 31(2): 43–78.

Kittredge, William P., and Sarah M. Ouart. 2005. *Budget Manual for Georgia Local Government*. Athens, GA: Vinson Institute, University of Georgia.

Krueger, Skip, and Robert W. Walker. 2010. "Management Practices and State Bond Ratings." *Public Budgeting & Finance* 30(4): 47–70.

Lande, Evelyne, and Sébastien Rocher. 2011. "Prerequisites for Applying Accrual Accounting in the Public Sector." *Public Money & Finance* 31(3): 219–22.

Larson, M. Corrine. 2004. "Cash and Investment Management." In *Management Policies in Local Government Finance*, 4th ed., edited by J. Richard Aronson and Eli Schwartz, 451–77. Washington, DC: ICMA.

Laughlin, Richard. 2012. "Debate: Accrual Accounting: Information for Accountability or Decision Usefulness?" *Public Money & Management* 32(1): 45–46.

Lauth, Thomas P. 1997. "Reductions in the FY 1992 Georgia Budget: Responses to a Revenue Shortfall." In *Case Studies in Public Budgeting and Financial Management*, edited by Aman Khan and W. Bartley Hildreth, 221–48. Dubuque, IA: Kendall Hunt Publishing.

Lee, Robert D., Jr., Ronald W. Johnson, and Philip G. Joyce. 2013. *Public Budgeting Systems*. 9th ed. Burlington, MA: Jones & Bartlett Learning.

Lee, Roderick C. 1996. "Life-Cycle Costing." In *Budgeting: Formulation and Execution*, edited by Jack Rabin, W. Bartley Hildreth, and Gerald J. Miller, 420–23. Athens, GA: Carl Vinson Institute of Government, University of Georgia.

LeLoup, Lance T. 1977. *Budgetary Politics: Dollars, Deficits, Decisions*. Brunswick, OH: King's Court.

Levine, Charles H. 1996. "Cutback Management in an Era of Scarcity: Hard Questions for Hard Times." In *Budgeting: Formulation and Execution*, edited by Jack Rabin, W. Bartley Hildreth, and Gerald J. Miller, 130–33. Athens, GA: Carl Vinson Institute of Government, University of Georgia.

———. 2004. "Organizational Decline and Cutback Management." In *Government Budgeting: Theory, Process, Politics*. 3rd ed., edited by Albert C. Hyde, 514–16. Toronto: Wadsworth.

Liner, Charles D. 1983. "Projecting Local Government Revenue." In *Budget Management: A Reader in Local Government Financial Management*, edited by Jack Rabin, W. Bartley Hildreth, and Gerald J. Miller, 83–90. Athens, GA: Carl Vinson Institute of Government, University of Georgia.

Lynch, Thomas D., Jinping Sun, and Robert W. Smith. 2017. *Public Budgeting in America*. 6th ed. Irvine, CA: Melvin & Leigh.

Makowsky, Michael D. and Wagner, Richard E. 2009. "From Scholarly Idea to Budgetary Institution: The Immergence of Cost-Benefit Analysis." *Constitutional Political Economy* 20(1): 57–70.

Marlowe, Herbert A., Jr., and Ronald C. Nyhan. 1997. "Innovations in Public Budgeting: Applying Organizational Development Processes to Downsizing." In *Case*

Studies in Public Budgeting and Financial Management, edited by Aman Khan and W. Bartley Hildreth, 365–76. Dubuque, IA: Kendall Hunt Publishing.

McLean, Mary. 2018. *Understanding Your Economy: Using Analysis to Guide Local Strategic Planning*. New York: Routledge.

Mendonsa, Arthur A. 1983. "Revenue Sources." In *Budget Management: A Reader in Local Government Financial Management*, edited by Jack Rabin, W. Bartley Hildreth, and Gerald J. Miller, 63–71. Athens, GA: Carl Vinson Institute of Government, University of Georgia.

Menifield, Charles E., Winfield H. Rose, John Homa, and Anita Brewer Cunningham. 2001. "The Media's Portrayal of Urban and Rural School Violence: A Preliminary Analysis." *Deviant Behavior* 22(5): 447–64.

Menifield, Charles E., Geigen Shin, and Logan Strother. 2019. "Do White Law Enforcement Officers Target Minority Suspects?" *Public Administration Review* 79(1): 56–68.

Meyers, Roy T. 1999. "Strategies for Spending Advocates." In *Handbook of Government Budgeting*, edited by Roy T. Meyers, 548–67. San Francisco: Jossey Bass.

Mikesell, John L. 2004. "General Sales, Income, and Other Nonproperty Taxes." In *Management Policies in Local Government Finance*, 5th ed., edited by J. Richard Aronson and Eli Schwartz, 289–314. Washington, DC: ICMA.

———. 2018. *Fiscal Administration: Analysis and Applications for the Public Sector*. 10th ed. Belmont, CA: Wadsworth Cengage Learning.

Miller, Gerald J. 1996. "Cost-Benefit Analysis." In *Budgeting: Formulation and Execution*, edited by Jack Rabin, W. Bartley Hildreth, and Gerald J. Miller, 211–30. Athens, GA: Carl Vinson Institute of Government, University of Georgia.

Miller, Gerald J., and W. Bartley Hildreth. 1996. "Advantages of a Risk Management Program." In *Budgeting: Formulation and Execution*, edited by Jack Rabin, W. Bartley Hildreth, and Gerald J. Miller, 424–30. Athens, GA: Carl Vinson Institute of Government, University of Georgia.

Mou, Haizhen. 2019. *Measuring Policy Content and Outcomes: A Quantitative Study of Balanced Budget Laws*. London: Sage.

Musell, R. Mark. 2009. *Understanding Government Budget: A Practical Guide*. New York: Routledge.

Musgrave, Richard A. 1959. *The Theory of Public Finance: A Study in Public Economy*. New York: McGraw-Hill.

National Association of State Budget Officers (NASBO). 2018. *The Fiscal Survey of States: An Update of State Fiscal Conditions*. Washington, DC.

Nice, David. 2002. *Public Budgeting*. Stamford, CT: Wadsworth/Thompson Learning.

Nollenberger, Karl, Sanford M. Groves, and Maureen Godsey Valente. 2003. *Evaluating Financial Condition: A Handbook for Local Government*. 4th ed. Washington, DC: ICMA.

Norris, Donald E., and M. Jae Moon. 2005. "Advancing E-Government at the Grassroots: Tortoise or Hare?" *Public Administration Review* 65(1): 64–75.

Novick, David. 2002. "What Program Budgeting Is and Is Not." In *Government Budgeting: Theory, Process, and Politics*, 3rd ed., edited by Albert C. Hyde, 52–68. Toronto and London: Wadsworth.

Oregon. 2004. "State Budget Update: November 2004." National Conference of State Legislatures. Denver, CO. https://www.ncsl.org/print/fiscal/sbu2005-0411.pdf.

Pariser, David B., and Richard C. Brooks. 1997. "A Comparative Study of State, County and City Government Audit Recommendation Follow-Up Systems." *Journal of Business and Public Affairs* 23(2): 25–30.

Petersen, John E. 2004. "Public Employee Pension Funds." In *Management Policies in Local Government Finance*, 5th ed., edited by J. Richard Aronson and Eli Schwartz, 501–32, Washington, DC: ICMA.

Poister, Theodore H. 2010. "The Future of Strategic Planning in the Public Sector: Linking Strategic Management and Performance." *Public Administration Review* 70(1): S246–54.

Propheter, Geoffrey. 2017. "Towards Enhancing Tax Abatement Transparency: Reviewing the Promises and Limitations of GASB 77." *Journal of Public Budgeting, Accounting and Financial Management* (29)4: 439–63.

Rabin, Jack, W. Bartley Hildreth, and Gerald J. Miller, eds. 1996. *Budgeting: Formulation and Execution*. Athens, GA: Carl Vinson Institute of Government, University of Georgia.

Raphaelson, Arnold H. 2004. "The Property Tax." In *Management Policies in Local Government Finance*, 5th ed., edited by J. Richard Aronson and Eli Schwartz, 257–88. Washington, DC: ICMA.

Raymond, Eric S., and Charles E. Menifield. 2011. "A Tale of Two Cities: An Exploratory Study of Consolidation and Annexation Policies in the Cities of Memphis and Nashville." *Public Administration Quarterly* 35(3): 404–41.

Riley, Susan L., and Peter W. Colby. 1991. *Practical Government Budgeting: A Workbook for Public Managers*. Albany: State University of New York Press.

Rivenbark, William C., Dale J. Roenigk, and Gregory S. Allison. 2010. "Conceptualizing Financial Condition in Local Government." *Journal of Public Budgeting, Accounting and Financial Management* 22(2): 149–77.

Rogers, Jacqueline H., and Marita B. Brown. 1999. "Preparing Agency Budgets." In *Handbook of Government Budgeting*, edited by Roy T. Meyers, 441–501. San Francisco: Jossey Bass.

Rose, Shanna. 2010. "Institutions and Fiscal Sustainability." *National Tax Journal* 63(4): 807–37.

Rubin, Irene S. 2020. *The Politics of Public Budgeting: Getting and Spending, Borrowing and Balancing.* 9th ed. Washington, DC: C Q Press.

Rubin, Marilyn Marks, and Katherine G. Willoughby. 2011. "Measuring Government Performance: The Intersection of Strategic Planning and Performance Budgeting." Transatlantic Dialogue Conference: Dialogue on Strategic Management of Public Organizations, Newark, New Jersey.

Schick, Allen. 1966. "The Road to PPB: The Stages of Budget Reform." *Public Administration Review* 26(4): 245–59.

Seckler-Hudson, Catheryn. 2002. "Performance Budgeting in Government." In *Government Budgeting: Theory, Process, and Politics*, 3rd ed., edited by Albert C. Hyde, 462–74. Toronto and London: Wadsworth.

Sigelman, Lee. 1986. "The Bureaucrat as a Budget Maximizer: An Assumption Examined." *Public Budgeting and Finance* 6(1): 50–59.

Solano, Paul L. 2004. "Budgeting." In *Management Policies in Local Government Finance*, 5th ed., edited by J. Richard Aronson and Eli Schwartz, 155–206. Washington, DC: ICMA.

Srithongrung, Arwiphawee [a.k.a. Arwi Kriz]. 2008. "The Impacts of State Capital Management Programs on State Economic Performance." *Public Budgeting & Finance* 28(3): 83–107.

———. 2010. "State Capital Improvement Programs and Institutional Arrangements for Capital Budgeting: The Case of Illinois." *Journal of Public Budgeting, Accounting & Financial Management* 22(3): 407–30.

Stalebrink, Odd. J., Kenneth. A. Kriz, and Weiyu Guo. 2010. "Prudent Public Sector Investing and Modern Portfolio Theory: An Examination of Public Sector Defined Benefit Pension Plans." *Public Budgeting & Finance* 30(4): 28–46.

Stewart, LaShonda M. 2011. "Does the Form of Government Influence Mississippi Counties' Unreserved Fund Balance during Relative Resource Abundance and Relative Resource Scarcity." *Public Budgeting & Finance* (31)4: 478–506.

Stewart, LaShonda M., John A. Hamman, and Stephanie A. Pink-Harper. 2018. "The Stabilization Effect of Local Government Savings: The Case of Illinois Counties." *Public Budgeting & Finance* (38)2: 25–39.

Swain, John W., and B. J. Reed. 2010. *Budgeting for Public Managers*. Armonk, NY: M. E. Sharpe.

Tax Policy Center. 2018. "The Tax Policy Center Briefing Book: A Citizen's Guide to the Tax System and Tax Policy." Washington, DC.

Thai, Khi V. 2004. "Procurement." In *Management Policies in Local Government Finance*, edited by J. Richard Aronson and Eli Schwartz, 421–50. Washington, DC. ICMA.

Thurmaier, Kurt M., and Katherine G. Willoughby. 2001. *Policy and Politics in State Budgeting*. Armonk, NY: M. E. Sharpe.

U.S. General Accounting Office. 1993. *Performance Budgeting: State Experiences and Implications for the Federal Government*. Washington, DC: GPO.

U.S. Social Security Administration. N.d. http://www.ssa.gov.

Vogt, A. John. 1983. "Budgeting Capital Outlays and Improvements." In *Budget Management: A Reader in Local Government Financial Management*, edited by Jack Rabin, W. Bartley Hildreth, and Gerald J. Miller, 128–41. Athens, GA: Carl Vinson Institute of Government, University of Georgia.

———. 1996. "Budgeting Capital Outlays and Improvements." In *Budgeting: Formulation and Execution*, edited by Jack Rabin, W. Bartley Hildreth, and Gerald J. Miller, 276–91. Athens, GA: Carl Vinson Institute of Government, University of Georgia.

———. 2004. *Capital Budgeting and Finance: A Guide for Governments*. Washington, DC: ICMA.

Wang, Wen, and Yilin Hou. 2009. "Pay-as-You-Go Financing and Capital Outlay Volatility: Evidence from the States Over Two Recent Economic Cycles." *Public Budgeting & Finance* 29(4): 90–107.

Wang, Wen, and Zhirong (Jerry) Zhao. 2011. "Fiscal Effects of Local Option Sales Taxes on School Facilities Funding: The Case of North Carolina." *Journal of Public Budgeting, Accounting & Financial Management* 23(4): 507–33.

Wang, XiaoHu. 2006. *Financial Management in the Public Sector: Tools, Applications, and Cases.* Armonk, NY: M. E. Sharpe.

Wang, XiaHu, Lynda Dennis, and Yuan Sen (Jeff) Tu. 2007. "Measuring Financial Condition: A Case of U.S. States." *Public Budgeting and Financial & Finance* 27(2): 1–21.

Weimer, David L., and Aidan R. Vining. 1989. *Policy Analysis: Concepts and Practice.* Englewood Cliffs, NJ: Prentice Hall.

Wildavsky, Aaron. 1979. *The Politics of the Budgetary Process.* 3rd ed. Boston: Little Brown.

Wildavsky, Aaron, and Naomi Caiden. 2004. *The New Politics of the Budgetary Process.* 5th ed. New York: Pearson/Longman.

Yan, Wenli. 2012. "The Impact of Revenue Diversification and Economic Base on State Revenue Stability." *Journal of Budgeting, Accounting & Financial Management* 24(1): 58–81.

Young, Peter C., and Claire Lee Reiss. 2004. "Risk Management." In *Management Policies in Local Government Finance*, edited by J. Richard Aronson and Eli Schwartz, 479–99. Washington, DC: ICMA.

Index

297

Colorado, Department of Public Safety, 146

compensation, 50, 144, 90n3; average final, 76, *77*, 86, 88, *97*, 235; unemployment, 52, 134; Workers' (men's), *33*, 219. *See also* benefits; expenses; salary/wage

Congressional Budget Office (CBO), 177, 198, 281

cost, 2–5; accounting, 211; allocated fixed, 147, 154, 159, *170*; allocation, 1–3, 6, 8–9, 13, 20, 61, *62*, *117*, *213*, 273; -benefit analysis (CBA), 149, 175, 178, 181–85, 196, 198–99; -effectiveness analysis (CEA), 175, 181–85, 198, 200, 202; fixed (FC), 100, 111–12, 147, 154, *170*, 193, 198, 201, 233; future, 180, 232–33, 255, 260; interest, 74, 108–10, 178, 181, 214, 235, 236–37, 247, 250–51, 255; life-cycle, 223, *224*, 235, 237, *242*; marginal, 100, 111–12, 198; operating (OC), 83, 106, 112, 191, 198–99, 201, *207*; project, 9, 17–18, 20, 60, 99, 102–4, *107*, 108–10, 112, *113*, 114, *116*, 117–20, 181, 186–87, 192–94, 231–32, 237, 247, 249–50, 252; recurring, 100, 111–12, 181, 198, 248; start–up, 60, 100; traceable fixed (TFC), 147, 154, *170*; unit (UVC), 100, 111–12, 145, 193–94; variable (VC), 112, 147, 154, 159, *170*, 193, 200–201, 235; -volume profit (CVP), 147, 154. *See also* budget; effectiveness; expenses; profit

Cunningham, Anita Brewer, 282

Dabbicco, Giovanna, 6

data, 50, 54, *170*, 190, 201, *206–8*, 261; analysis/interpretation, 122, 177–78, 180–81, 195, 199, 279, 282; calculations of, xvii, 75; communication of, xiii, 257–69, 271–74, 283; comparison of, 83,

177, 182, 213; demographic, 52, *196*, 230, 249, 280; errors, 82; and the future, 186; historical, 177–78, 238, 260, 280; internal, 178; nominal/ordinal, 195, 262; primary, 257, 270, 279, 282; processing programs, 257; quality/reliability/validity, xiii, 80, 179, 181, *246*, 257–58, 260–61, 274n1; ratio, 195, 262; raw, 260, 265, 270; secondary, 257, 270, 273n1, 279; sources, xiii, 80, 257, 261, 274n1, 282–83; survey, 280, 282. *See also* budget; charts/graphs/tables; model

debt, 13, 108, 210, 247, 249, 252–54; capacity, 227, 235; costs of, 108, 233; financing, 108, 121n8, 233, 240, 247–48, 250; funds, 14, 17–18; grants, 102; instruments, 108, 235; legal issues, 110, 121n7; management, xiii, 231–33, 235, 247–49; markets, 108; payment of, 13, 18, 108–9, 214, 232, 247, 249–52; rating, 109, 254; refunding of, 253; sale of, 252; service fund, *14*, 18, 20; structure, 213, 250; tax exemptions, 110, 249–50, 255; terms, 18, 109, *211*, 214, 232, 247; type of, 109. *See also* finance

Decker, J. Winn, 178

deficit, 1, 20, 42, 133, 175, 177, 209, 213–16, 231, 235; carry over, 1; tax, *153*

Dennis, Lynda, 210

depreciation, *123*, 229; annual, 190–91, 198, 201; remaining life (RL), 192, 198, *207*

disability, 75–77, 235

dividends, 74, 86–87, 162, 179, 235. *See also* finance; income; interest

Doss, C. Bradley, Jr., 103

Downing, Paul. B., 12, 147

Druker, Marvin J., 228

Duncombe, William, 108

About the Author

Charles E. Menifield is dean of the School of Public Affairs and Administration (SPAA) at Rutgers, the State University of New Jersey–Newark. His research interests lie primarily in the areas of budgeting and financial management, public health and welfare, and policing. Other areas include, health and education finance, and public administration education.